Praise for *The Irony of Modern Catholic History*

"This deeply learned and crisply written book reaffirms George Weigel's status as the preeminent American Catholic intellectual of our time. Weigel recasts recent history to show how we owe much of what is best and most noble in modernity to Catholicism and why, even in this season of ecclesial despair, Catholics have sound reasons to be hopeful."

—SOHRAB AHMARI, author of
From Fire, By Water: My Journey to the Catholic Faith

"Fascinating and visionary—George Weigel is deeply learned and passionately engaged—one of the important intellectual assets of the twenty-first-century Catholic Church."

—LANCE MORROW

THE IRONY OF
MODERN CATHOLIC
HISTORY

ALSO BY GEORGE WEIGEL

THE IRONY OF MODERN CATHOLIC HISTORY

How the Church
Rediscovered Itself and Challenged
the Modern World to Reform

GEORGE WEIGEL

BASIC BOOKS
New York

Basic Books
Hachette Book Group
1290 Avenue of the Americas, New York, NY 10104
www.basicbooks.com

Printed in the United States of America
First Edition: September 2019

Published by Basic Books, an imprint of Perseus Books, LLC, a subsidiary of Hachette Book Group, Inc. The Basic Books name and logo is a trademark of the Hachette Book Group.

The Hachette Speakers Bureau provides a wide range of authors for speaking events. To find out more, go to www.hachettespeakersbureau.com or call (866) 376-6591.

The publisher is not responsible for websites (or their content) that are not owned by the publisher.

Print book interior design by Jeff Williams.

Library of Congress Cataloging-in-Publication Data
Names: Weigel, George, 1951– author.
Title: The irony of modern Catholic history : how the Church rediscovered itself and challenged the modern world to reform / George Weigel.
Description: First Edition. | New York, NY : Basic Books, an imprint of Perseus Books, a subsidiary of Hachette Book Group, 2019. | Includes bibliographical references and index.
Identifiers: LCCN 2019013176 (print) | LCCN 2019019951 (ebook) | ISBN 9780465094349 (ebook) | ISBN 9780465094332 (hardcover)
Subjects: LCSH: Catholic Church—History—19th century. | Catholic Church—History—20th century. | Catholic Church—History—21st century.
Classification: LCC BX1386 (ebook) | LCC BX1386 .W45 2019 (print) | DDC 282.09/034—dc23
LC record available at https://lccn.loc.gov/2019013176

ISBNs: 978-0-465-09433-2 (hardcover), 978-0-465-09434-9 (ebook)

LSC-C

10 9 8 7 6 5 4 3 2 1

In Memoriam

DON J. BRIEL

1947–2018

Contents

Contents

Contents

Prologue

The Ironies in the Fire

Mark Twain dubbed it the "awful German language," but it does have its uses, and one of them is to teach us that "history" has two dimensions: there is *Historie* (what happened) and there is *Geschichte* (what the things that happened mean). The latter helps get the former into focus. The former grounds the latter in reality. Facts are important, but history is never just a question of "the facts," for "the facts" are always read through an interpretive framework.

Thus two historians study Ronald Reagan with the same basic biographical facts at hand: the first portrays him as a great president, the man who won the Cold War and gave America an era of prosperity and confidence; the second tells the story of an amiable lightweight who was preternaturally lucky and left office before his incapacities revealed themselves to the world. Both historians are working with the same materials; what distinguishes them is a matter of focus.

What follows here is very much a matter of focusing, or, better, refocusing. This is not in any sense a comprehensive

1

history of the Catholic Church over the past 250 years. Rather, it is the refocusing of a story written about in much greater detail by a host of other authors. Think of what follows as akin to *emblemata*: those framed mosaic arrangements, often telling a story from history or mythology, that were much favored as decorations in the homes of the ancient Roman aristocracy. Using bright pieces of stone fashioned by distinguished historians, including Hubert Jedin, J. N. D. Kelly, Owen Chadwick, Eamon Duffy, and John O'Malley, I have rearranged the stones—the actors and action within each of this drama's five acts—and placed them in a new frame. If the word "narrative" had not been pummeled into incoherence through overuse, "renarrativizing" might be the word of choice to describe the way the story of Catholicism-and-modernity is told here. But reframing or refocusing will do.

Four vignettes help set the stage for the drama to come.

Gaeta, Italy, August 2, 1849. Pope Pius IX, taking temporary refuge in the port city of Gaeta after fleeing anticlerical revolutionary forces in Rome, becomes the first pontiff to set foot on sovereign American territory by visiting USS *Constitution*, accompanied by his host and protector, King Ferdinand II of the Two Sicilies. Pius, who has serious doubts about the American idea of religious freedom embodied in the constitutional separation of Church and state, is greeted by a twenty-one-gun salute as he steps onto the main deck of the frigate known as "Old Ironsides," and receives another royal salute when he leaves, after meeting the ship's Catholic crew members and dispensing rosaries. The Pope returns to Rome; but time is running out on his control of the Papal States, which ends on September 20, 1870, when troops of the Kingdom of Italy break through Rome's Porta Pia and claim the Eternal City as the capital of a united Italian nation. Having declined an offer by American seminarians to take up arms in his defense, and after ordering papal troops to surrender after firing one volley for the sake of honor, Pius IX retires inside the

Leonine Wall, calling himself "The Prisoner of the Vatican," and never steps outside until his death in 1878. When his body is transferred to the Basilica of St. Lawrence Outside the Walls in 1881, the Roman mob attacks the procession and tries to throw the casket into the river.

Vatican City, December 7, 1965. At the conclusion of its fourth and final session, the Second Vatican Council adopts its Declaration on Religious Freedom, which is then promulgated by Pope Paul VI. *Dignitatis Humanae*, as the Declaration is known from the first words of its Latin text, has been one of the most extensively debated documents of Vatican II. Its proponents include American bishops who want the universal Church to acknowledge that the American constitutional arrangement on Church and state is something good for the Church; Western European bishops who want to get beyond the antagonisms launched by the French Revolution and other radical secularist movements; East-Central European bishops seeking another weapon with which to fight communism; and ecumenically minded bishops eager to advance the cause of Christian unity. The opposition comes primarily from bishops skeptical about political modernity, who still believe that Catholic establishment—the old alliance of altar and throne—is the ideal arrangement. The overwhelming vote in favor of *Dignitatis Humanae* (2,308 to 70) demonstrates that this opposition is a marginal force in the mid-twentieth-century Church. Catholicism is now fully committed to religious freedom as the first of civil rights—and by extension, to those political systems that guarantee religious freedom in their constitutions or their laws. Neither proponents nor opponents realize the profound impact that *Dignitatis Humanae* will have, not only on the Catholic Church, but on the course of world politics over the next twenty-five years.

Warsaw, Poland, June 2, 1979. The recently elected pope, John Paul II, returns to his native land and is greeted by his countrymen as no other Pole in history. On a triumphal drive from the Warsaw airport to the city center, which seems less a motorcade than a religious procession, he passes the Church of the Holy Cross: destroyed during the 1944 Warsaw Uprising, the reconstructed church displays the statue of Christ bearing the Cross that was recovered from beneath the rubble of the Nazi-destroyed capital—a metaphor in stone for what will unfold in Poland over the next decade. At a Mass attended by hundreds of thousands jammed into and around Warsaw's Victory Square, and with Polish Communist Party leader Edward Gierek looking on nervously from a nearby hotel window, John Paul preaches an epic homily. Drawing on themes from *Dignitatis Humanae*, he reasserts Poland's Catholic identity, defends religious freedom for all, and calls for a national renewal in which the Holy Spirit revitalizes a land battered and demoralized by five and a half wartime years of a draconian German occupation and more than thirty years of communist brutality. The vast crowd chants, "We want God! We want God!" while the political heirs of the German philosopher who dismissed religion as the opiate of the people watch from a safe distance, wondering how this could have happened and where it will lead. Where it will lead is toward a new kind of twentieth-century revolution: a revolution of conscience in which people who rediscover the truth of their cultural identity and the truth about human dignity find new forms of nonviolent political resistance. Fourteen months later, the Solidarity movement is born at the Lenin Shipyards in the Baltic port city of Gdańsk. Nine years after that, Poland, along with the other countries of the Warsaw Pact, liberates itself from what is arguably the greatest tyranny in history.

Aparecida, Brazil, May 31, 2007. Latin American Catholicism, the demographic center of the world Church at the turn of the third millennium, has been in turmoil for decades. Since Vatican II, the Church south of the Rio Grande has been badly split by controversies: over liberation theology and its challenge to authoritarian and militarist regimes; over economic development and how it should be pursued; and over the appropriate response to an explosion of evangelical and Pentecostalist Protestantism throughout Latin America. Now, over several weeks in May 2007, the bishops of the continent face the fact that the old ethnic and cultural transmission belts, and the close linkage between Church and state that often buttressed them, can no longer pass the Catholic faith to the next generation. Catholicism-by-osmosis, they admit, is finished. The Fifth General Conference of the Bishops of Latin America and the Caribbean, hosted by the Latin American Episcopal Council (Consejo Episcopal Latinoamericano, or CELAM), then ends and issues a final report that comes to be known as the Aparecida Document, from the Brazilian city where the conference was held. In that report, the bishops explain that "the Church is called to a deep and profound rethinking of its mission . . . out of a personal and community encounter with Jesus Christ that raises up disciples and missionaries." A little less than six years later, one of the principal drafters of the Aparecida Document, Cardinal Jorge Mario Bergoglio, SJ, the archbishop of Buenos Aires, is elected to the Chair of Peter, takes the regnal name Francis, and declares that he longs for a Church "permanently in mission" in which every Catholic is a "missionary disciple"—not a Church allied to political power, but a Church reenergized by the Gospel.

THIS SEQUENCE OF dramatic scenes is striking, not least because neither the protagonists nor the antagonists in the first scene—nor those standing in the wings of the stage—could have imagined the second, third, and fourth. For throughout much of the nineteenth century, both the intellectual and political leaders of secular modernity and the leaders of the Catholic Church labored under the false assumption that the relationship between the Church and the modern world was a battle to the death: a zero-sum game in which someone was going to win, decisively, and someone was going to lose, fatally.

Secular modernity's false premise was that Catholicism, intransigent in its truth claims and often allied to authoritarian power, was inimical to the modern project in its cultural, economic, social, and political forms. As Voltaire had famously cried, Catholicism was "*l'infâme*"—the horror that must be "crushed." So when Pius IX lost Rome, it seemed to those of this cast of mind, and even to milder proponents of Enlightenment thought, that the Catholic Church was finished as a consequential player in history. That turned out to be exactly wrong. For in the twenty-first century, the Catholic Church is more vital and more consequential than it was when Pius IX sought refuge on Old Ironsides.

As for the Church, its leaders' false premise was the mirror image of that held by modern secularists and was neatly captured in the last of the eighty condemned propositions in Pius IX's *Syllabus of Errors*: it was inconceivable, according to the *Syllabus*, that "the Roman Pontiff can, and ought to, reconcile himself, and come to terms with progress, liberalism, and modern civilization." And because Pius IX identified the Office of Peter with the Catholic Church in a virtual one-to-one correspondence, Proposition 80 in the *Syllabus* meant that the entire Church, not just the pope, was at war with modernity in all its forms. Why? Because, in Pius's view, and that of his chief supporters, the triumph of secular modernity would inevitably lead to the death of religious conviction. That, too, turned out to be exactly wrong. For as the third scene above demonstrated, religious conviction was a major factor in late twentieth-century world affairs. And there is little sign in the early twenty-first century that history will confirm the old secularization hypothesis in its hard form: that modernization inevitably involves the demise of religious faith, religious practice, and religious communities. Some of that is, obviously, happening. Viewed globally, however, the secularized parts of the world are the outliers.

How did these two false premises unravel during the period between Pius IX's flight to Gaeta and the Aparecida meeting of CELAM? How did it happen that, through its encounter with modernity, Catholicism became more coherent, less defensive, and more influential in shaping the course of world affairs? How did the encounter with modernity lead the Catholic Church to rediscover the deepest truths about its essentially evangelical character while developing a rich, complex proposal for ordering modern public life?

Sociologist Peter Rossi, a notable punster, used to quip that there were many ironies in the fire. The tale told here unfolds beneath that banner. For the history of modern Catholicism is, in fact, rather ironic. With modernity acting sometimes as midwife and at other times as amazed observer, Catholicism in its third millennium has reclaimed its birthright as a Gospel-centered, missionary enterprise. Rather than killing Catholicism, the encounter with modernity has helped the Catholic Church rediscover some basic truths about itself. Even more ironically, the Church's rediscovery of those truths might, just might, put Catholicism in a position to help secular modernity save itself from its own increasing incoherence.

To PUT IT another way: the received wisdom in this business of Catholicism-and-modernity has got hold of only one end of the stick—and the result is a unilinear analysis that misses a lot of the drama. According to the conventional telling of this history, modernity was always the drama's protagonist and the Church was always the reactive (even reactionary) force. That Catholicism may have been, on occasion, a creative and independent actor in this process, rather than a merely defensive one, is seldom considered. Modernity acts;

Catholicism reacts; end of story. The only tension in the drama is over the degree of reaction: How much should, or will, or can the Church concede to this, that, or the other modern claim, be that claim political, social, or cultural?

Modernity as active protagonist, Catholicism as defensive reactor: many historians, and virtually the entire Western mainstream media, frame the story that way, down to yesterday and today. Interestingly enough, both twenty-first-century Catholic traditionalists and twenty-first-century Catholic progressives share this conventional meta-narrative about Catholicism and modernity. The traditionalists of the nineteenth and twentieth centuries argued, and the traditionalists of the twenty-first century continue to argue, that there should be no Catholic accommodation to modernity, or at least as little as possible. Catholicism should always fight a stern rearguard action, surrendering as little ground as possible until that happy day when the modern project crumbles—after which the Church can help the chastened survivors pick up the pieces and start civilization again. By contrast, Catholic progressives throughout the nineteenth and twentieth centuries urged a fulsome embrace of cultural, social, and political modernity, and continue to do so in the twenty-first century. The traditionalists tend to think of the progressives as abject, even heretical, appeasers. The progressives return the favor by treating the traditionalists as merciless, anti-intellectual reactionaries frozen in ecclesiastical amber.

But suppose the story is more complicated? Suppose Catholic traditionalists and Catholic progressives (and conventional historians and the mainstream media) are all wrong, because they all think of modernity as the sole protagonist of this drama: a force to be resisted, accommodated, or embraced, but still the driving force of the historical action? Yes, there were indeed moments (even decades) of Catholic "reaction" to modernity, moments (or decades) that the progressives vigorously resisted, often at cost. Yes, there was a moment when the

Church seemed to offer social, cultural, and political modernity a warm embrace: an embrace the traditionalists loathed, and thought a terrible mistake. But amidst all that, suppose something else was going on: something that looks, from the second decade of the third millennium, like a surprising renewal of Catholic identity and mission, one that reaches back two thousand years to the Church's founding generation of believers and thereby hears a call not to resist or embrace modernity, but to *convert* it?

And suppose further that—in another irony—the Catholic Church helped the modern project to a deeper self-understanding? Suppose Catholicism helped modernity discover that it did not spring full-blown from the brow of Voltaire but had a longer, far more complicated, and much more interesting history that owed a great deal to biblical religion? Suppose Catholicism helped the postmodern West in the twenty-first century understand how things came to the point where the contemporary passion for equality became self-destructive, threatening free speech and open academic inquiry? At a curious (or ironic) moment, in which a pope insists that "the Church proposes; she imposes nothing," while proudly modern (and thoroughly secular) universities struggle to maintain free space for argument, might a differently configured idea of the relationship of Catholicism to modernity help the West find a more rational, humane path into the future?

Answering all those questions is beyond the scope of this modest experiment in revisionist historiography. But the claim here is not a modest one. The claim is that the conventional telling of the story of Catholicism-and-modernity is wrong. What follows is an attempt to start a conversation about how we might better understand that dramatic and ongoing encounter.

THE DRAMA TO be explored will unfold in five acts, the last two of which overlap chronologically, further complicating an already complicated story. So before getting into the drama proper, a modest *Playbill*, a plot summary to help orient what follows, is in order.

Act One: Political and cultural modernity mount a full-scale assault on Catholicism. Popes Gregory XVI and Pius IX respond by hurling anathemas. Several promising starts at reconciling Catholic faith and modern political aspirations come to unhappy ends.

Entr'Acte: Theologians working in the interstices of Catholic intellectual life try to build bridges of conversation between the Church and modernity even as, somewhat to everyone's surprise, Catholicism flourishes in the first great modern democracy, the United States of America.

Act Two: Pope Leo XIII, elected in 1878 as an elderly placeholder, launches what will become a revolution in Catholic thought by gingerly exploring the modern project in its political, economic, social, and cultural expressions. That Leonine Revolution continues through fits and starts (and often brutal political and ecclesiastical controversies) for the first six decades of the twentieth century. Meanwhile, the Counter-Reformation that began in the sixteenth century draws unexpectedly to a close.

Entr'Acte: While Catholicism struggles with the political turbulence of two world wars, and then the Cold War, creative Catholic thinkers in Europe and America extend the Leonine Revolution into virtually every field of Catholic thought, preparing the way for a future that will arrive with unanticipated rapidity—and turbulence.

Act Three: Another elderly pope thought to be a papal placeholder decides to focus the energies first set loose by Leo XIII through the prism of an ecumenical council. John XXIII opens that council, Vatican II, by calling the Church to convert modernity rather than deplore it. The Council advances the Leonine Revolution across the full spectrum of Catholic thought and practice, but is less successful in bringing the modern world and its immediate future into clear focus.

Entr'Acte: Amidst two decades of intra-Catholic turmoil over the proper interpretation of Vatican II, three key markers are laid down by a pope, a future pope, and a diverse company of theologians, suggesting the possibility that John XXIII's original, evangelical intention for the Council just might be recovered, and then acted upon.

Act Four: In sharp contrast to the anathemas of Act One, a bold Catholic critique of political and cultural modernity from inside modern intellectual premises is developed by John Paul II and Benedict XVI: two popes who, as younger men, had helped guide the Leonine Revolution through the contentions and controversies of Vatican II.

Entr'Acte: As the struggle to get Vatican II right continues, late modernity morphs into postmodernity, and the cultural crisis of the West intensifies, John Paul II challenges Catholicism to rediscover its originating purpose as a missionary enterprise, not least through the experience of the Great Jubilee of 2000.

Act Five: While Act Four continues to unfold in a new and bracing encounter between Catholicism and political modernity, the Church begins to grapple with the challenges of twenty-first-century evangelism—and is confronted by scandals that threaten Catholicism's capacity for public witness and for mission.

FINALLY, AND AS a last bit of orientation, a preliminary clarification of terms will be helpful.

By "Catholic Church," I mean primarily the teaching authority of Catholicism as embodied in the Bishop of Rome as universal pastor of the Church—and, at one significant moment (known here as Act Three), in the bishops of the Church gathered in ecumenical council with and under the Bishop of Rome. This definition certainly does not exhaust what "Catholic Church" means, and many other influential characters will come on stage during what are styled here the drama's entr'actes. Given the unique authority-structure of Catholicism, however, a close focus on the papacy and its teaching about modernity provides a clarifying angle of vision for considering the complex set of relationships and interactions being examined here.

By "modernity," I mean societies characterized by the decline of aristocratic authority based on inherited power and land-based wealth; the desacralization of power by the sharp differentiation of religious and political authority and the dominance of the latter in public life; industrialization, urbanization, and mass education; social mobility; popular participation in government; the rationalization and bureaucratization of virtually every aspect of life; great improvements in nutrition and medicine with a concomitant rise in life expectancy; and a vast expansion of the leisure time available to everyone.

Playing on the name of the eighteenth-century German thinker Ludwig Feuerbach, sociologist Peter Berger added one more piece to our understanding of "modernity" that will be useful to keep in mind in what follows. The turn into modernity, Berger proposed, was a matter of societies passing through the "fiery brook"—a boundary beyond which religious conviction becomes personal decision rather than cultural or ethnic inheritance. Because of that crossing, "modernity" also means societies deeply marked by pluralism, which Berger described as "the coexistence of different worldviews and value systems in the same society." Both modernity and Catholicism have struggled with "pluralism," in Berger's descriptive sense of the word. One question to be explored below is whether, in another of the ironies of Catholicism-and-modernity, certain aspects of Catholic thought might help a fractured and contentious postmodernity discover a normative, not merely descriptive, meaning of "pluralism" that reanimates civil conversation about the human future.

But enough of plot summaries and definitions. Now to the dramatic story of Catholicism-and-modernity: reconsidered, reimagined, and refocused.

Catholicism
Against Modernity

A Problematic Patrimony

T HE RELATIONSHIP BETWEEN Catholicism and modernity is such a complex business that it's often useful analytically to subdivide it along different lines of inquiry: the Church's relationship to the demise of the traditional political order and the rise of new forms of government (including, but not limited to, democracy); the Church's relationship to the passing of the traditional cultural order (the displacement of metaphysics at the center of Western intellectual life and the rise of the scientific method as the dominant paradigm of knowledge); the Church's relationship to the transformation of traditional society into new forms of community (including new forms of economic life).

But however the question is parsed, one determinative factor remains a constant. The often tense, even violent, relationship between Catholicism and modernity in the first eight decades of the nineteenth century was bound up with the fact that the pope was the absolute monarch of a Class C European power, the Papal States, whose territory covered a swath of central Italy from south of Rome to just south of Venice. That was the mega-issue.

Cultural and intellectual modernity certainly challenged the then regnant forms of Catholic intellectual life. The modern "social question" posed by the Industrial Revolution and the rise of an urban proletariat eventually compelled a new Catholic appraisal of modern economic life and its impacts on society. But it was the challenge of political modernity that was immediate and urgent for the two principal players in the first act of this drama, Pope Gregory XVI (1832–1846) and Pope Pius IX (1846–1878). As they saw it, the papacy was inextricably bound to the pope's temporal sovereignty over the Papal States; to challenge that sovereignty threatened the very existence of the papacy; and by threatening the papacy as they understood it, political modernity threatened the Catholic Church as they understood it. This bottom-line conviction, which seems odd to a twenty-first-century mind, takes a bit of explaining.

The Holy See—the juridical embodiment of the ministry of the Bishop of Rome as universal pastor of the Catholic Church—had been recognized for centuries as having legal, and thus diplomatic, personality. Long before the modern nation-state existed, the Holy See exchanged embassies and other forms of diplomatic representation with other sovereign actors: kings, and so forth. As subsequent history proved, the Holy See could exercise its unique form of sovereignty— and thus the pope could maintain the independence from all earthly sovereignties essential for his mission and ministry— from a tiny parcel of land. That was not how Gregory XVI and Pius IX saw things, however. The complex history of the Papal States is a fascinating story in its own right, involving such piquant characters as "the Warrior Pope," Julius II, patron (and bane) of Michelangelo. But it need not detain us here. The key point to grasp is that both Gregory XVI and Pius IX saw in political modernity—meaning representative, constitutional government and limited executive authority—a profound threat: first to papal authority within the Papal States, and later to the existence of the Papal States themselves. And to their minds, that threat was fraught with dire implications for the entire Catholic Church.

THERE WERE OTHER issues and events in play here, and they revolved around that complicated affair known as the Enlightenment. The Catholic Church of the nineteenth century (and the first half of the twentieth, for that matter) paid very little attention to the Anglosphere, and to the ways in which the English and Scottish Enlightenments created forms of political modernity quite different from those that were born from the French or Continental Enlightenment. From the point of view of Gregory XVI and Pius IX, which is what concerns us in Act One of this drama, "the Enlightenment" primarily meant the radical skepticism of Voltaire and other influential thinkers, which meant the French Revolution, which meant the "Civil Constitution of the Clergy," which meant the complete subordination of the Church to the French regime, which meant the Terror, the suppression of the monarchist Catholic revolt in the Vendée, the martyrdoms memorialized in Francis Poulenc's *Dialogues of the Carmelites*, and all the rest of that bloody business.

Nor was the Church's experience in France unique. For throughout continental Europe, the formation of the modern nation-state was typically undertaken *against* the Catholic Church. Two examples were the Italian Risorgimento, a deeply anticlerical affair, and the Bismarckian Kulturkampf, an attack on the Church that went (iron-fisted) hand-in-glove with the Iron Chancellor's assembly of the Second Reich and his early management of the new imperial Germany. As if that were not enough, there was the Catholic experience of "enlightened" monarchy in the Hapsburg lands (where Emperor Joseph understood the Church as a "department of [the] police"); there were recurrent anticlerical agitations in Spain and Portugal; and the 1834 Articles of Baden tried to separate Swiss Catholics from the authority of Rome. As post-Enlightenment Europe oscillated between revolution and restoration, until a measure of stability was established after the Franco-Prussian War of 1869–1870, the Catholic Church remained firmly in the crosshairs of European governments of various ideological stripes.

Europe in the nineteenth century also experienced the beginning of a secularization process that would eventually over-
whelm most of the western portion of the continent in the
twentieth century and early twenty-first. The nineteenth-century
process involved a kaleidoscope of social and intellectual
changes and their effects, ranging from the dismantling of the
old political regimes to the emergence of an urban proletariat
to the conceptual revolutions underway in science, history, and
philosophy. This was also the period in which the phenomenon
that Henri de Lubac dubbed "atheistic humanism" emerged to
dismiss the God of the Bible as a tyrannical shackler of human
freedom and a severe obstacle to humanity's maturation. In
the minds of many, if not all, senior Catholic leaders, though,
the decline of religious practice in nineteenth-century Europe
came down to two factors: Enlightenment thought and the Industrial Revolution. The former, coupled with the triumph of
the scientific method as the model of all true knowledge, resulted in what Max Weber would describe as a disenchantment
of the world and a contempt for religious belief among elites;
the latter uprooted millions from the rural environments their
families had known for centuries and from the pieties that had
given meaning to life in peasant societies. Like Matthew Arnold,
institutional Catholicism's nineteenth-century leaders heard the
retreat of the "Sea of Faith" and its "melancholy, long, with-
drawing roar"; they, too, felt themselves on a "darkling plain
/ swept with confused alarms of struggle and flight / where ig-
norant armies clash by night." And for most of the first eight
decades of the nineteenth century, the men at the tiller of the
Barque of Peter had little or no idea what to do about all that,
except to resist it and say, time and again, "No."

A BOVE ALL, HOWEVER, and always lurking in the background, there was the threat to the Papal States, which
Gregory XVI and Pius IX thought a threat to the very

existence of the Catholic Church. Their fear now seems to us overwrought: Why should these men imagine that being sovereign rulers over a chunk of the middle of Italy was essential to their functioning as universal pastors of the Catholic Church? But from their point of view, their sovereignty of the Papal States was bedrock, for it touched what they believed was their religious obligation before God as well as their political position in Italy, Europe, and indeed around the world. That conviction should always be kept in mind as essential background to the story that follows in this first act of the drama: the story of Catholicism's rejection of so much of the modern project in the mid-nineteenth century, and the often frustrated attempts by some Catholic reformers to find a path beyond intransigent rejectionism.

That story begins, as so much of modern history does, with the French Revolution.

Le Déluge

C ATHOLICISM IN EIGHTEENTH-CENTURY Europe was in a weak position to resist, or even temper, *le déluge* foreseen by the Sun King, Louis XIV: the historical tsunami of the French Revolution, the Napoleonic Wars, and the struggle to remake Europe after 1815.

The popes of the day were not corrupt men, as several of their Renaissance predecessors had been. Some were pious and ascetical; others were great patrons of scholarship and the arts, rebuilding Rome through their benefactions. But with the exception of the scholarly Benedict XIV (1740–1758), who corresponded with Voltaire, they were not equipped by training, experience, or inclination to comprehend, much less engage, Enlightenment thought.

Throughout Europe, the spiritual and moral authority of the Church was eroding, thanks in part to a vast array of riches and privileges—and the suspicion, fostered by the Church's Enlightenment critics, that the entire ecclesiastical enterprise was propped up by an untoward alliance between altar and throne. Many clergy did little or no pastoral work, yet lived well off ancient benefices. Monastic life was often more a comfortable sinecure than an ascetic vocation. There were exceptions to this clerical decadence and corruption, but the hard fact remained that the Catholic Church was closely identified with the privileges of the old regimes in the ancient states where Catholicism predominated.

Moreover, Catholic intellectual life had become desultory at precisely the moment when Europe began to cross that fiery brook on the far side of which lay religious-conviction-as-personal-decision rather than cultural inheritance. The Church had also lost the sharp, mission-driven evangelical edge that characterized the best parts of Counter-Reformation Catholicism in the late sixteenth and seventeenth centuries. The fiasco of the Chinese Rites controversy, in which an imaginative approach to the evangelization of a non-European culture—the transposition of traditional Chinese religious practices into a Christian key—was squashed in 1704 by Roman bullheadedness, demonstrated just how dulled the Church leadership's imagination had become.

These weaknesses are one reason why the French Revolution and its aftermath shook European Catholicism, which then accounted for well over one-half of the world Church, to its foundations. Within a few tumultuous and bloody years, France, Europe's largest Catholic country, was at war with itself, and its new revolutionary leadership was at war with the Church. When the armies of France sought to extend the revolution (and French hegemony) throughout Europe, the Catholic position in Germany, the Netherlands, and the Italian Peninsula was gravely compromised.

In its first decade or so, revolutionary France sought to make the Catholic Church a ward and instrument of the state, after failing to eradicate the Church in the Revolution's most violent early periods. As would be the case with twentieth-century totalitarianisms, the proto-totalitarians of the guillotine first sought to destroy monastic life: seizing monasteries and convents; forbidding anyone from taking the vows of poverty, chastity, and obedience that defined consecrated life; and dissolving all religious orders and communities not involved in educating the young or caring for the sick—those aspects of consecrated life the new French state deemed useful. Finally, in August 1792, even the "useful" communities were dissolved by legislative fiat.

The parish clergy and the normal religious life of the people were not spared. At the same time as all consecrated life was shut down, the French Assembly ordered the sale of whatever Church administrative properties remained in ecclesiastical hands, forbade the wearing of religious habits in public, banned religious processions in Paris—and shortly afterward ordered that all priests loyal to Rome be deported. A few weeks later, in September 1792, the three hundred priests and three bishops who had been languishing in Parisian prisons were massacred. Several thousand priests risked their lives to remain in France and minister to their flocks, but more than thirty thousand fled. Those who remained had to function without any institutional support.

After the "Thermidor" period had cooled the bloodiest revolutionary ardor, the situation eased a bit and some clergy returned from exile. But the French Church was now divided between those who had submitted to the demands of the revolutionary regime and those who had resisted or fled. The "eldest daughter of the Church" was in critical condition, which had an effect throughout Europe, given the influence that this largest of local Churches in Europe had exercised. And as revolutionary France sought to extend its power (and, theoretically, its ideals) throughout the continent by force of arms, the issue of the Papal States and the pope's temporal sovereignty came into play yet again.

G IOVANNI ANGELO BRASCHI, whom history would know as Pope Pius VI, was not the man to deal with this crisis, the greatest the Catholic Church had faced since the cataclysm of the sixteenth-century Reformations.

Born into the minor nobility in 1717, he was elected pope in 1775: a compromise candidate after a conclave that lasted four and a half months and was dominated by the question of what should be done about the suppression of the Jesuits by his predecessor, Clement XIV. Pius VI was a handsome man (and vain of it) who devoted time and resources to his building programs, including the Trevi Fountain and a colossal new sacristy for St. Peter's. His twenty-four-year-long pontificate was marked by conflicts with Joseph II of Austria: the Emperor sought to subordinate the Church to the enlightened, autocratic state; the Pope futilely tried to persuade him to reverse the policy. Bishops in Germany and Italy declared their independence from the papacy, and Pius seemed incapable of responding with anything more than documents condemning their ideas. Something of his barnacle-encrusted cast of mind (and that of those who served him in Rome) can be gleaned from the tack taken by the Holy See when a bishop had to be appointed in the newborn United States. Inquiries were made to Benjamin Franklin, then the U.S. ambassador in Paris: What did the American government have to say about this? Nothing, Franklin replied, to the papal representative's astonishment.

Pius VI's initial attitude toward the upheavals that began in France with the storming of the Bastille was cautious. But when the clergy were compelled in 1791 to take an oath of allegiance to the new revolutionary regime, he suspended the priests and bishops who complied with the directive from their functions, then doubled down by condemning, retrospectively, the 1789 Declaration of the Rights of Man and of the Citizen; as a result, the French Church was split in two. Pius VI's struggle with the Revolution came to a brutal end when Napoleon, in the name of the French Directory, invaded the Papal States in 1796, forcing the Pope to sign an abject surrender of most of his territories. After a French general was killed during a Roman riot, the Directory ordered the seizure of the remainder of the Papal States, and in February 1798 the French general Louis Berthier proclaimed the Roman Republic. Pius, gravely ill, was eventually kidnapped by French troops. After a painful journey from Florence to Turin and across the Alps into France, he was imprisoned in a fortress in Valence, where he died on August 29, 1799—and was left unburied for months before his embalmed remains were interred in a grave marked "Citizen Braschi."

The heroic way he faced his kidnapping and exile somewhat mitigated the extravagances, vanities, and failures of the first two decades of his pontificate. And Pius VI left behind a surprise for those who imagined that, with his death and burial in exile, the papacy had been consigned to the dustbin of history. For in 1797 and 1798, knowing that a conclave in Rome would likely be impossible while the city was under French occupation, he had made provisions for an emergency situation: the senior cardinal who survived him should convene a conclave, in a safe place of that cardinal's choosing, to elect his successor.

Lost Opportunity

ON CHRISTMAS DAY, 1797, the bishop of Imola in the Cisalpine Republic (one of the new French protectorates that included parts of the Papal States) preached a remarkable sermon. Democracy and the Gospel were not incompatible, taught Cardinal Luigi Barnabà Chiaramonte, a Benedictine monk and former theology professor; God favored no particular form of government, and there was no reason why a Catholic couldn't be a loyal citizen of a democracy. But democratic self-governance required a virtuous citizenry, and the deepest meaning of freedom and equality could be learned from Christ and the Gospel. This same Cardinal Chiaramonte used stationery inscribed with an interesting variant on the motto of revolutionary France: "Liberty, Equality, and Peace in Our Lord Jesus Christ."

Napoleon Bonaparte pronounced himself happy with the cardinal's Christmas sermon: "The Citizen Cardinal of Imola," he remarked, "preaches like a Jacobin." Cardinal Chiaramonte was no Jacobin, and Napoleon would soon enough turn on the man he had praised. But Chiaramonte was open-minded and able, and had Napoleon been less an aggressor, the drama of Catholicism-and-modernity might have taken a different course.

THE CONCLAVE TO elect a successor to Pius VI was held in Venice, with the roiling politics of revolutionary Europe foremost in the thirty-five cardinal-electors' minds. Fourteen weeks of deadlock were exacerbated by several European powers exercising their long-claimed right of tacit or overt veto in papal elections (a practice that continued throughout the nineteenth century and was only abolished after the conclave of 1903). Finally, a compromise was arranged, and, with one dissenting vote (his own), the unanimous choice fell on Cardinal Chiaramonte. Taking the name Pius VII, he quickly appointed as his secretary of state the man who had organized the conclave, Ercole Consalvi. It was an inspired choice.

Consalvi, a conservative reformer who would likely have found himself in considerable agreement with Edmund Burke about the sane management of political modernity, combined intelligence and devotion to the Holy See with diplomatic flexibility and a shrewdness in reading political situations. He was named cardinal in August 1800 (although, curiously enough, Consalvi was never ordained priest or bishop, and was only ordained a deacon in December 1801).

The new pontificate's first order of business was to try to settle the Church's affairs in France, and Cardinal Consalvi was dispatched to Paris to negotiate a concordat with Napoleon, a virtual dictator by this time. Once, when the aggressive French leader asked Consalvi if it were not true that "all Italians are thieves and liars," the papal ambassador is said to have stopped the bully in his tracks with a brilliant pun on Napoleon's surname: No, he replied, "*soltanto la buona parte* [just the greater part]." Napoleon was impressed, describing the mild-mannered Consalvi as "a lion in sheep's clothes."

The negotiation was difficult, but the resulting Concordat of 1801 had something in it for both parties. Pius VII recognized the Republic as the legitimate government of France, while the Republic, maintaining its commitment to no Church establishment, nevertheless acknowledged Catholicism as the religion of the majority of the French people. The French Church was reorganized: Napoleon essentially abandoned the "Constituent Church" that had formed in opposition to Rome, and Pius VII requested the resignations of the Old Regime bishops, so that the entire French episcopate could be re-created. Concessions were made to the government in the appointment of bishops, but the bishops could only be invested in their offices, and thus function, by authority of the pope. The laity were once again permitted to make financial gifts to the Church, and the state agreed to pay the salaries of bishops and priests as partial compensation for the nationalization of Church properties. The Concordat dramatically and paradoxically strengthened papal authority over French Catholicism, which had long chafed under the Roman bridle and had not infrequently toyed with schemes of a national Church that came to be known, wherever they appeared, as "Gallicanism."

But within nine months, Napoleon tightened state control over the Church by unilaterally appending implementing articles to the Concordat, and the relationship between Napoleon and Pius deteriorated from there—despite the Pope's willingness to travel to France to participate in Napoleon's coronation as emperor (during which Napoleon famously refused to be crowned by the Pope, but took the crowns from the altar to crown himself and the Empress Josephine). The new emperor evidently expected Pius VII to act as a kind of court chaplain, blessing his military adventures. When Pius declined the role, French troops once again occupied Rome, and Napoleon annexed the remainder of the Papal States. After excommunicating "the robbers of Peter's patrimony," Pius was arrested and held incommunicado in Savona, in northern Italy, before being transferred as a prisoner to Fontainebleau, outside Paris. There, in poor health and under intense pressure, he signed an abject "Concordat of Fontainebleau" in which, among other things, he implicitly surrendered his sovereignty over the Papal States. Within two months, however, he rallied and renounced what he had signed. A year later, in March 1814, Napoleon, who was in serious trouble on the battlefield, released Pius, who reentered Rome. When Napoleon escaped his exile on Elba the following year, Pius fled to Genoa before returning, at last and for good, to the Vatican in June 1815—a week before what the Duke of Wellington called that "damned near-run thing," the Battle of Waterloo, ended Napoleon's sanguinary career.

A T THE CONGRESS of Vienna, which redrew the political map of Europe in 1814–1815, Cardinal Consalvi deftly negotiated the restoration of virtually the entire Papal States. In the aftermath of that diplomatic triumph, he and Pius VII instituted internal reforms while they sought to rebuild the Church in those parts of Europe shattered by revolutionary upheaval and the Napoleonic Wars. Pius's suffering in captivity had drawn widespread sympathy, and his generosity in offering Roman refuge to Napoleon's relatives after the French emperor's fall enhanced his reputation as a man of courage and decency. Insofar as he and Consalvi were able, they tried to "fit" the papacy into the post–*ancien régime* world, although they were opposed by both Catholic proponents of full-blown restoration and secularists who could only imagine the Church as the enemy of progress. The papacy was held in low regard at the time of Pius VII's election in 1800. When he died in 1823, the Office of Peter was beginning to seem like a moral authority supported by popular sentiment and respect.

Yet the pontificate of Pius VII remains something of a "What if?" Given the position Cardinal Chiaramonte had taken at Christmas 1797, his election as pope might have resulted in a new Catholic engagement with political modernity. But Napoleon's determination to bring the Church to heel, which led to his brutal persecution of the Pope, prevented that outcome—and suggested to some influential Roman prelates the impossibility of any Catholic rapprochement with the new regimes. After the Congress of Vienna brought a measure of order to a traumatized Europe, the stage was set for a papal alignment with the forces of restoration. Those forces seemed to Pius VII's two successors, Leo XII (1823–1829) and Pius VIII (1829–1830), to be the guarantors of political stability, as well as of the pope's own position as a sovereign-among-sovereigns.

Missionary and Reactionary

T HE CONCLAVE OF 1830 was another drawn-out business. After more than seven weeks of failure and a political veto cast by Spain, the electors finally settled on Cardinal Bartolomeo Alberto Cappellari, who had taken the religious name "Mauro" on entering the strictest of Benedictine orders, the Camaldolese, in 1783, when he was eighteen. The election of the man who chose the regnal name Gregory XVI was supported by the *zelanti* (zealots), those cardinals who wanted religious reform coupled with a rejection of liberal politics. That Cappellari was also the preferred candidate of the Austrian proponent of postrevolutionary restoration, Klemens von Metternich, suggested the tack he would take toward political modernity during his papacy.

Pope Gregory's sixteen-year pontificate included initiatives that might not be immediately expected from someone whose politics were unashamedly reactionary. He supported the reform of religious orders and the creation of new ones. He condemned slavery and the slave trade. His artistic and archaeological interests helped revivify ancient Rome and make it accessible to both scholars and visitors, and he created new museums devoted to Etruscan and Egyptian art in the Vatican.

He was also a strong proponent of Catholic missionary activity, having served as prefect of the Vatican's missionary agency, Propaganda Fide, for four years prior to his election. Gregory XVI created seventy new dioceses and vicariates apostolic (mission territories preparing to be fully erected dioceses) all over the world and named some two hundred bishops for the missions. Most boldly, given the attitudes (and politics) of the day, he insisted on the development of a native clergy in mission territories, where the colonial powers had long been accustomed to maintaining control of the Church through importing clergy from the "old country." He also defied the

Spanish and Portuguese governments in the matter of appointing bishops within their colonial territories, challenging both imperial power and racism.

A T THE HEIGHT of Pius VI's travails in 1799, Fra Mauro Cappellari had published a tome whose title signaled the claims he would later press as pope: *The Triumph of the Holy See and the Church Against the Attacks of the Innovators.* A forthright defense of papal autocracy and the pope's sovereignty over the Papal States, it was also a defiant rejection of the claims of political modernity. That uncompromising, even reactionary, conservatism would guide his papal policy in dealing with post-Napoleonic Europe. He fought the anticlerical legislation being proposed by secularist regimes in Spain, Portugal, and Switzerland and decried the persecution of Catholics in Russia (to some effect). But the determination to uphold established political authority that commended him to Metternich led to actions that seemed strange, even incomprehensible, to his fellow Catholics struggling under foreign rule: he condemned the Catholic Poles for their revolt against Russian rule in 1830–1831, and thirteen years later, he had Propaganda Fide send a letter to the Irish bishops instructing them to stay out of British politics.

It was in reaction to intra-ecclesiastical and then political developments in France, however, that Gregory XVI issued the two incendiary encyclicals that would be his enduring legacy—and that set the foundation for the full-throated Catholic rejection of modernity in virtually all its forms that came to fruition in the pontificate of his successor.

One should try to understand the harsh positions Gregory XVI took in these two encyclicals from his point of view. He was a stubborn if often good-humored man. But he was singularly ill-equipped by his monastic experience and intellectual formation to grasp what was afoot in the emerging modern world, or to see how political modernity could be reconciled with the Gospel and the Church—which might even be able to offer the institutions of liberty a more secure foundation in a more carefully thought-out understanding of freedom. Given his limitations of formation and experience, Gregory could only see what was then styled religious "indifferentism"—the claim that one religious conviction is in principle as good as another—as the opening wedge toward hostility toward religion, and to the eventual breakdown of religious faith and the moral cohesion it provided society. Secularization would in turn lead to social anarchy and the kind of revolutionary violence that characterized the first decade and a half of the nineteenth century, and that Gregory feared as an ever-present danger thereafter.

So when French Catholic intellectual circles began arguing for freedom of conscience, the institutional separation of Church and state, freedom of the press and assembly, and voting rights for a wider electorate, Pope Gregory's own deeply conservative political instincts came into play, as did European power politics: Austrian troops were then garrisoned in the Papal States as protectors of papal prerogatives, and the Austrian chancellor, Metternich, urged the Pope to condemn these liberal ideas as inimical to both Christian faith and public order.

In the 1832 encyclical *Mirari Vos*, "On Liberalism and Religious Indifferentism," Gregory XVI did just that, and in some of the most strident language imaginable. Indifferentism was a "poisonous spring" from which had issued "the absurd and erroneous doctrine, or rather delirium, that freedom of conscience is to be claimed and defended for all men." Those who sought to "enslave the nations under the mask of liberty" were also condemned for the "detestable and insolent malice" of their "agitations against . . . the rights of rulers." Freedom of opinion, expressed through a free press and the publishing of books without fear of state censorship, was madness:

"Is there any sane man who would say poison ought to be distributed, sold publicly, stored and even drunk . . . ?" The state had a duty before God to ban the public promotion of "racial prejudice, or paederasty, or pornography, or adultery, or murder," which freedom of expression treated as if "these were not . . . sins." As for those who suggested that Catholicism needed renewal and reform to meet the exigencies of the present age, they were besotted by the "flock of errors" that characterized modernity. For the Church had been "instructed by Jesus Christ and his apostles and taught by the Holy Spirit": it would "be completely absurd and supremely insulting to suggest that the Church stands in need of restoration and regeneration."

For Gregory XVI, "a free Church in a free State"—the solution sought by liberal French Catholic thinkers searching for a path between the Scylla of Old Regime failure and the Charybdis of revolutionary violence and anarchy—was a snare and a delusion. Gregory's own struggles with regimes that were then trying to bring the Church to heel in Prussia, on the Iberian Peninsula, and in various colonies abroad might have inclined him to think more positively about the freedom of action the French liberals sought for a Church unencumbered by state patronage. But he could not make the connections. The result was to put official Catholic thinking about political modernity into a deep freeze that would take decades to thaw.

The Ultramontane Democratic Socialist

THE FOIL FOR Pope Gregory XVI's condemnation of political modernity, and the direct target of his second encyclical on the subject, *Singulari Nos*, "On the Errors of Lammenais"

(1834), was a French Catholic priest, intellectual, and publicist. Hugues-Félicité-Robert de Lamennais (1782–1854) was one of the tragic actors in the drama of Catholicism-and-modernity, a strong proponent of papal authority who ended up condemned by the papacy for his social and political views and who died outside the communion of the Church.

"Ultramontanism"—the vigorous defense of papal prerogatives within the Church—is often thought of as another nineteenth-century reactionary movement. The story of the ultramontanes is rather more complicated, as the case of Lamennais illustrates.

As a body of thought and a program, French ultramontanism (so called because of its emphasis on the powers of the pope, who lived *ultra montes*, "beyond the mountains" [the Alps]) was the product of several converging forces. It had some conservative roots, in that the ultramontanists believed that Enlightenment rationalism had so hollowed out the moral core of society that the horrors of revolutionary violence, including the Reign of Terror, inevitably followed. Thus the ultramontanists sought a deep religious renewal of Church and society, led by a strong papacy, as a barrier against a return to revolutionary anarchy and bloodshed. At the same time, they resented the attempts by Napoleon and the Austrian Emperor Joseph II to turn the Church into a department of the state; such a Church, they believed, could not ignite the spiritual renewal essential for France, and indeed for all of Europe. To prevent the creation of politically subservient, lapdog "national" Catholic Churches throughout Europe, it was necessary to defend the prerogatives of the pope as the supreme spiritual authority of Catholicism. To agitate for "a free Church in a free State"—which necessarily involved religious freedom—was to advance both the Church's evangelical mission and the ideal of political liberty.

Abbé Lamennais was the central figure in this movement, and it was through him that liberal ultramontanism came to prominence in France in the 1820s. Lamennais enjoyed a cordial relationship with Pope Leo XII, successor to Pius VII, and founded several influential publications. In 1828, he published *On the Progress of the Revolution and the War Against the Church*, which marked his final break with royalism and his turn toward becoming an advocate for religiously guided democracy. The journal *L'Avenir* (The Future), which he founded in 1830, promoted a full-blown liberal democratic agenda under the motto "God and Liberty." But its often sarcastic tone, its denunciation of state patronage for the Church, and the prominent role of laymen in its pages drew the wrath of more royalist and conservative churchmen. It also worried Metternich. The result was the 1832 encyclical *Mirari Vos*.

Lamennais, who was not mentioned in *Mirari Vos*, made clear that he, a good ultramontanist, accepted papal authority in matters of faith and morals, and as an act of deference to Gregory XVI (who had initially hoped that the controversies involving Lamennais could be handled privately), he shut down *L'Avenir*. But his critics were not satisfied, because he continued to hold and promote liberal political opinions. Finally, in response to attacks from his ecclesiastical and political enemies, he published a short and ill-tempered book, *Words of a Believer*, in which he rejected all forms of authority, Church and state, and advocated both liberal democracy and socialism. The book was a sensation throughout Europe, but the denouement of Lamennais's life as a liberal Catholic ultramontanist followed quickly.

L AMENNAIS'S BOOK APPEARED during a period of political unrest in the Papal States, and Gregory XVI was not long in responding. The short and rhetorically overwrought encyclical *Singulari Nos* condemned Lamennais and his views by name, denouncing *Words of a Believer* as "small in size [but] enormous in wickedness." Lamennais's work, the Pope thundered, "corrupts the people by a wicked abuse of the word of God. . . . [I]t arouses, fosters, and strengthens seditions, riots, and rebellions in the empires. We condemn the book because it contains false, calumnious, and rash propositions which lead to anarchy . . . and which are impious, scandalous, and erroneous." The encyclical ended with a plea that Lamennais return to the Church's fold, but Gregory's choice of words showed just how out of step the Pope was with the temper of the times:

> Let us beseech [God] with repeated prayer to give this man a docile heart and a great spirit to hear the voice of the most loving and most sorrowful Father. May he hasten the joy of the Church [and] the joy of this Holy See. . . . Certainly we shall provide an auspicious and happy occasion to take hold of him and embrace him as a son returning to the bosom of his Father. We are and we shall be very optimistic from his example that others will come to their senses, others who might have been led into error by the same author.

It was not to be. Abandoned by most of his friends, who refused to join him in breaking with the Church, Lamennais was in prison for debt in 1836 and for criticizing the government in 1840. Enthusiastic about the revolutions of 1848, he was elected to the French Constituent Assembly, which rejected his plans for a new constitution. He remained in the legislature until Napoleon III's coup in 1851, after which he occupied himself with a translation of Dante's *Divine Comedy*. Rebuffing all attempts to reconcile him to the Church, he died in 1854 and was buried in a common grave without a funeral.

His legacy was striking for several ironies. Lamennais was a liberal who made ultramontanism intellectually respectable, and who managed, at least theoretically, to align a strong papacy disentangled from worldly power with the *libertas ecclesiae*, the freedom of the Church. He sought religious reform and spiritual renewal in France and throughout Europe; he inspired the Benedictine monk who would later become one of the founders of the modern Liturgical Movement, Prosper Guéranger, the longtime abbot of Solemnes; and yet he died, seemingly unrepentant, outside the Church. He initially, and eagerly, sought the approval of the papacy for his program of Christian democracy, but he could not accept religious authority when it came into conflict with his politics.

In some of these characteristics, Lamennais was the archetype of a certain type of modern Catholic intellectual: he was impatient with God's patience with the Church and its sometimes stolid ways. In the final crisis—certainly exacerbated by the harshness of Gregory XVI's condemnations (tacit in *Mirari Vos* and explicit in *Singulari Nos*)—he could not, or would not, discipline his personal brilliance and keen insight by respectfully engaging criticism, well founded or stupid. When matters spiraled out of his control, this critic of Enlightenment rationalism chose autonomy over churchmanship.

Both Lamennais and nineteenth-century Catholicism lost as a result, although his concept of a "free Church in a free state" would have a major impact on the world Church a century after his death.

The Apogee of Reaction and the Beginning of the Modern Papacy

THE CARDINAL-ELECTORS OF the conclave of 1846 recognized, to some degree, that Pope Gregory XVI's intransigence had left the Church and the papacy in a bad way, not least in what had become the contentious and politically unstable Papal States. So in a two-day conclave they quickly found a candidate they thought could give the Church a fresh face and something of a new approach: the fifty-four-year-old Cardinal Giovanni Maria Mastai-Ferretti, who took the regnal name Pius IX. Mastai had been a successful local bishop in Imola and Spoleto, popular with everyone, including political liberals. And two years of work in Latin America as a young priest had given him a breadth of view not common among his colleagues. Warm and approachable, he was a man of great personal charm. In short order he remade the public aspects of the papacy by offering Mass in local parishes, visiting hospitals and children's homes, and opening up his general audiences to the public, which responded with enthusiasm.

Pope Pius IX was sympathetic to the stirrings of Italian patriotism that had been influenced by the Romantic movement, and that had arisen in no small part because of the decades in which the politically fragmented Italian Peninsula had been a pawn in the contests of the great powers, especially France and Austria. As a pastor and an Italian patriot, he was pained by the brutalities of Austrian troops in Italy; as a local bishop and later as pope, he resented the attempts by Austrian administrators to impose the Viennese notion of the Church as a ward of the state on the parts of Italy controlled by the Hapsburg monarchy. In 1861, when Camillo Cavour, the chief architect of Pius IX's eventual demise as a prince, died, the Pope, true to his warm-hearted nature, mourned him: "Ah, how he loved his country, that Cavour. . . . That man was truly Italian. God will surely pardon him, as we pardon him."

Yet for all his emotional sympathies with resurgent Italian patriotism, Pius IX was the absolute sovereign of the Papal States. And as before in this drama, that fact decisively shaped his approach to political modernity when it expressed itself in the quest for a unified Italian state in the mid-nineteenth century. He rejected the idea, bruited by some, that the pope should become the president of an Italian federation; this, he thought, was incompatible with his mission as the spiritual head of all Catholics. And he could not accept Giuseppe

Mazzini's idea of a unified Italian republic, for that would have meant, he believed, the end of the sovereignty he required in order to fulfill his pastoral mission. So Pius IX was stuck on the horns of a dilemma—the perennial dilemma of the pope as temporal sovereign of a considerable territory.

In the early years of his pontificate, Pius IX tried to deal with that dilemma by making modest if welcome reforms in the administration of the Papal States, granting an amnesty on his election, making plans for railroads, lighting Rome's streets with gas, creating local advisory councils, and eventually permitting a legislative assembly. But in his conception of his responsibilities, and, it seems, in his heart, he could never get beyond an ecclesiastical paternalism that took the political form of what he intended as a benign autocracy. That set in motion the struggle with the Italian Risorgimento that defined the public dimension of his pontificate for over two decades, leading him into an increasingly hostile stance toward modernity in all its forms.

Things began to unravel for Pius IX two years after his election. In 1848, when the forces of the Risorgimento rose in arms to expel the Austrians from Italy, Pius refused to join in their war, claiming that his office required him to remain neutral; his decision bitterly disappointed those who had believed him a friend of Italian nationalism. Then his liberal-minded prime minister, Pellegrino Rossi, was assassinated on November 15, 1848. In the tempest that followed, Pius was first besieged in his home in the Quirinale Palace before fleeing to Gaeta, where he remained for seventeen months under the protection of Ferdinand II, King of the Two Sicilies. The Roman Republic proclaimed by the forces of the Risorgimento in February 1849 lasted but a few months, and after a papal appeal for support, French troops restored papal control over Rome, to which Pius returned in April 1850.

The Pope deputed responsibility for political affairs, in the Papal States and abroad, to his secretary of state, Cardinal

Giacomo Antonelli. Like Ercole Consalvi, Antonelli was a deacon who was never ordained to the priesthood or the episcopate; unlike Consalvi, he was an inflexible and intolerant man whose attempts to maintain strict control in the Papal States exacerbated rather than relieved tensions. Positions thus hardened on both sides of what had come to be known as the "Roman Question"—the issue of the pope's temporal sovereignty—over the next twenty years. The demand for self-government became widespread throughout the Italian Peninsula. That popular sentiment fit well with the ambitions of the Piedmontese House of Savoy to lead a united Italy as well as those of Camillo Cavour to bring such a unification about. The emergence of a middle class in the Papal States, which chafed under papal autocracy and resented the fact that most of the important jobs in the papal administration of central Italy were held by clergymen, raised the political temperature even higher.

Pius, for his part, could only see popular sovereignty as an unacceptable challenge to papal sovereignty, and thus a threat to the spiritual authority of the papacy. That stance hardened even more when Cavour engineered the passage of anticlerical legislation, including the suppression of religious orders, monasteries, and convents not involved in teaching or nursing, in those parts of Italy controlled by King Victor Emmanuel II and the House of Savoy from its capital in Turin. As for Antonelli, his intransigence guaranteed that no compromise granting the pope a nominal state of his own would be reached.

The beginning of the end came in 1860 when the papal army, largely composed of volunteers from France, Belgium, and Ireland, was defeated by the forces of the Risorgimento at the Battle of Castelfidardo. Following the defeat, the Marches and Umbria were annexed to the new Kingdom of Italy, and the papal domains were reduced to Rome and the surrounding Lazio region. That much smaller state survived another ten years, and in 1868, Pius IX made another futile attempt to reverse the course of history with a decree banning Catholics from participation in the political life of the new Italy, which he deemed a kingdom of "usurpers." When the French soldiers protecting the much-reduced Papal States were withdrawn in 1870 because of the Franco-Prussian War, Italian forces conquered Rome after a token resistance from papal troops. The city was incorporated into Italy as its capital through a plebiscite held a month later. Pius refused the terms offered him in 1871 (personal inviolability, freehold of the Vatican and other properties, and an indemnity); left the Quirinale Palace to King Victor Emmanuel II (who was excommunicated for his role in depriving the pope of his temporal sovereignty); withdrew inside the Apostolic Palace; and never left the Vatican compound again.

Cardinal Antonelli, the papal secretary of state, whose policies had helped make a difficult situation worse, remained in office until his death in 1876.

THE PRESSURES ON Pope Pius IX that eventually led to the conquest of the Papal States by the forces of the Risorgimento had a boomerang effect in those parts of the Catholic world not directly affected by the struggle for Italian unification: they made Pius immensely popular and gave him that central position in the Catholic imagination that is readily associated with popes today, but of which he was in fact the first example. The jubilees of his ordination as a priest and bishop, the celebrations of his twenty-fifth and thirtieth anniversaries as pope, and the jubilee for the 1,800th anniversary of the martyrdoms of Sts. Peter and Paul drew unprecedented crowds of pilgrims to Rome. His many beatifications and canonizations were popular. And his definition of the dogma of the Immaculate Conception of the Blessed Virgin Mary in 1854 was a crucial moment in the development of the Marian piety that would shape world Catholicism over the next century and make Lourdes, where Bernadette Soubirous experienced apparitions of Mary in 1858, one of the world's great pilgrimage centers. (In one of her apparitions at Lourdes, Mary had declared herself the "Immaculate Conception," and the site became the place of many medically inexplicable cures.) Pius IX also encouraged devotion to the Sacred Heart of Jesus; originally promoted as a means of recovering a spiritual sense of the human nature of Christ, the Sacred Heart became a symbol of resistance to the French Revolution when it was displayed on the banner of monarchist rebels in the Vendée, and throughout the nineteenth century this form of popular piety became increasingly identified with a politics of restoration.

In the context of the times, however, the extraordinary popularity of Pius IX, the devotion he drew from ordinary Catholics throughout the world, and the resurgence in popular piety he fostered did more than reinvigorate the spiritual life of the Church. It also accelerated, even as it supported, the evolution of a conservative ultramontanism that, unlike the liberal ultramontanism of Lamennais and his followers, set itself against virtually the entirety of modernity, especially in cultural and intellectual life.

To the conservative ultramontanes, the theological analogue to the calls for self-government and popular sovereignty that characterized political liberalism was a religious liberalism that stressed free inquiry, the ultimate authority of reason in matters of faith, and a skepticism about many traditional religious and moral truth claims. The net result was a concept of religion as a matter of taste, even fancy or sentiment, rather than a matter of truth and falsehood, good and evil—which fit neatly with the arguments being advanced by such luminaries of nineteenth-century thought as Auguste Comte (the only truth is that which can be empirically verified), Ludwig Feuerbach (religion is a projection of humanity's noblest aspirations), and Karl Marx (religion is an opiate with which the dominating classes control the masses).

Thus, to conservative ultramontanes like England's Henry Edward Manning, a former Anglican archdeacon who became the Catholic archbishop of Westminster, to support the pope was to support the battle against the secularist bias of the Enlightenment and the French Revolution in the name of God's revealed truth, which was essential to the survival of civilization. And how better to support the pope in this cosmic struggle than to extol his teaching authority and invest it with both an irresistibility and a breathtaking range? How better to stand firm against the tidal waves of change sweeping across European society and culture than to lift up a figure who would be above history and its vicissitudes, and who would give such authoritative instructions in virtually every dimension of life that fallible mortals would be relieved of the burden of choice? How better to confound the skepticism of the age, the tendency of the new biblical scholarship to dismiss so many biblical events as myths, the claims of the Darwinists to have found the key to human evolution in the material world alone, and the revolutionary agitations of those who claimed to speak for the urban proletariat in the name of History, than to say that here, in this infallible man, is the divinely guaranteed repository of truth?

THE LIBERAL ULTRAMONTANIST cause espoused by Lamennais and his followers was energized by a journalism dedicated to controversy and polemics. In another irony, the conservative ultramontanists adopted the same modern public relations strategy, spreading their critique of intellectual and cultural modernity, advancing their campaign for a formal definition of papal infallibility, and denouncing fellow Catholics who took a more benign view of modernity through various journals: *L'Univers* in France, the *Dublin Review* in the United Kingdom, and *La Civiltà Cattolica* in Italy. These organs and the movement they represented and encouraged, strongly supported by many Roman officials and by the Jesuits, urged Pius

IX to issue a comprehensive catalogue of what they deemed the errors of the age. In 1864 he took their advice and issued the encyclical *Quanta Cura*, which included as an appendix a *Syllabus of Errors*.

The encyclical was quickly overshadowed by the *Syllabus*, whose eighty propositions became the occasion for great public controversy. Many of the condemned notions were, from a Christian point of view, eminently condemnable. No serious Christian would object to the sharp rebuke the *Syllabus* offered to the ideas that God does not exist, that God does not act in history, that Jesus was a mythical figure, that the miracles and prophecies recorded in the Bible are poetic fictions, and that faith is ultimately irrational. Defenders of the prerogatives of civil society would not object to the *Syllabus*'s condemnation of the notions that the Church could not exercise its authority without the let and leave of the state; that the Church did not have a right to own property; and that bishops could not promulgate letters from the pope without government authorization. One might even imagine Thomas Jefferson and James Madison agreeing with Pius IX when he blasted the claim that "the State, as being the origin and source of all rights, is endowed with a certain right not circumscribed by any limits."

So the *Syllabus of Errors* does not quite tally with its frequent caricature as a reactionary, even silly, catalogue of alleged horrors. It identified errors and lacunae in nineteenth-century thought that would later become painfully obvious: publicly, in the rise of totalitarianism, and culturally, in the breakdown of reason and the subsequent loss of the conviction that human beings can grasp the truth of anything with certainty. But the last condemned proposition—that "the Roman Pontiff can and should reconcile himself with progress, liberalism, and modern civilization"—was a blunderbuss formulation that seemed not so much boldly defiant of the nineteenth century's form of political correctness as simply mindless. Moreover, the format of the *Syllabus*, which did not so much refute as flatly condemn, was ill-suited to a cultural moment in which there remained some room for serious debate—and that therefore regarded those who refused debate as obscurantists dependent on authority rather than argument (presumably because they had no real arguments). The *Syllabus* also exacerbated tensions with the Church, as it was clearly intended as a rebuke to Catholics interested in exploring a rapprochement with modernity, and their opponents used its promulgation to ratchet up their polemics.

After *Quanta Cura* and the *Syllabus*, the conservative ultramontanists focused their campaign on securing a formal definition of the pope's infallibility. That the Bishop of Rome could, under certain circumstances, teach with infallible authority had long been held in the Catholic Church. But those circumstances had never been defined, nor had the scope of that infallible teaching authority been clarified. During the 1867 anniversary celebrations of the martyrdoms of Peter and Paul, Pius IX announced that he would summon a general council, the first since the Council of Trent in the sixteenth century, to begin on December 8, 1869. This was the opportunity the conservative ultramontanists had been seeking; Archbishop Manning and several other episcopal leaders of the conservative ultramontane party vowed, at St. Peter's tomb, that they would secure a definition of papal infallibility at the forthcoming council. Their efforts would ultimately be successful, but not in the form they sought or with the effects they anticipated.

P IUS IX'S ORIGINAL purpose in summoning the First Vatican Council was to continue the two projects that had come to define his pontificate: the battle against forms of rationalism that he was convinced led to the collapse of religious faith, and the struggle to disentangle the Church from the grip of state power. But the contest over infallibility eventually took over the proceedings. Extreme ultramontanes like Britain's William G. Ward, a convert (like Manning) from Anglicanism, wanted a sweeping definition that would have defined the pope as an infallible authority on virtually everything; as Ward famously said, he wanted a papal bull to read at breakfast every day along with the *Times*, and his views were mirrored in a less pithy way by various Roman officials and the Jesuit theologians involved in *La Civiltà Cattolica*. There were few disbelievers in some form of papal infallibility. But a considerable number of bishops believed that any definition of that charism was untimely or inopportune, because it simply could not be understood by the contemporary mind and would widen the gulf that had opened up between the Church and modern culture. Their concerns intersected with those of the bishops who were open to some form of definition of the pope's infallibility as a religious teacher but wanted it very narrowly drawn.

The Council thus turned into a political battle between the conservative ultramontanes and their diverse opponents, which included, on the inside of the Council, important figures such as the French bishop Félix Dupanloup, and, on the outside, the English historian Lord John Acton and the German theologian and historian Ignaz von Döllinger. The polemics were continual, as was the political maneuvering. Vatican I managed to produce a major document on the compatibility of faith and reason, the Dogmatic Constitution *Dei Filius*, but when the Council went on to consider a document on the Church, Pius IX moved the infallibility debate to the head of the agenda, at the request of Manning and his ultramontane allies.

The possibility of an infallibility definition roiled governments as well as the Church. More than a few political leaders assumed that any such definition would be so broad as to call into question their own authority within their countries, and ambassadors of various powers brought pressures to bear on the Council fathers. At the end of the day, however, the bishops made up their own minds and the moderate infallibilists prevailed, such that the definition agreed upon, in the Dogmatic Constitution on the Church *Pastor Aeternus*, was quite circumscribed:

> The Roman pontiff when he speaks *ex cathedra*, that is when in discharge of the office of pastor and teacher of all Christians, by virtue of his supreme Apostolic authority, he defines a doctrine regarding faith or morals to be held by the universal Church, by the Divine assistance promised to him in Blessed Peter, is possessed of that infallibility with which the Divine Redeemer willed that his Church should be endowed in defining doctrine regarding faith or morals, and that therefore such definitions of the Roman pontiff are of themselves and not from the consent of the Church irreformable.

In brief: Papal infallibility, which was an expression of the Church's infallibility as embodied in the pontiff and his office, rather than a quality of the human personality of the pope, only touched questions of faith and morals and was only exercised on those rare occasions when the pope spoke *ex cathedra* on some fundamental point that the entire Church had to hold as revealed truth. The definition explicitly did not say that the pope ought to act by himself, as if he were an oracle. Nor did *Pastor Aeternus* indicate how the pope should gauge the mind of the "universal Church" by discussion, consultation, and the like before making any such definition. Thus the definition did not reflect the views of the extreme ultramontanists, and despite the efforts of Manning and others to stretch the definition's applicability after its adoption by the Council, *Pastor Aeternus* remained the high-water mark of conservative ultramontanism, which began to recede in influence over the decades to come.

Vatican I never completed its work. It was adjourned *sine die* when the Franco-Prussian War broke out and was never reconvened, much to the dissatisfaction of those who wanted a reconvened council to complement the definition of infallibility with a reflection on the authority of the Church's bishops. And far from the Council having settled things once and for all by its embrace of infallibility, the last years of Pius IX were scarcely less contentious than those that had preceded the *Syllabus* and Vatican I. A small schism led by Ignaz von Döllinger, who was unreconciled to even a circumscribed definition of papal infallibility, broke the unity of northern European Catholicism. Another wave of anticlericalism led to German chancellor Otto von Bismarck's Kulturkampf against the Church, which resulted in the imprisonment of some bishops and the exile of others. Yet through it all, and despite his absence from public view as the "Prisoner of the Vatican," Pius IX maintained his popularity among masses of Catholics. When he died on February 7, 1878, he was certainly the best-known pope in history, and likely the most beloved.

WHILE THE PONTIFICATE of Pius IX is often reduced in memory to the loss of the Papal States, the *Syllabus*'s challenge to modernity in all its forms, and Vatican I's definition of papal infallibility, the longest reign in reliably recorded papal history included far more of considerable consequence to the drama of Catholicism-and-modernity.

Pius's tomb in the *confessio* of the Basilica of St. Lawrence Outside the Walls is decorated in mosaic with the coats of arms of the various dioceses and vicariates apostolic he erected over thirty-four years: some two hundred in all, indicating a vast expansion of the Catholic Church throughout the world under his leadership. Pius IX helped close out the Reformation by creating new Catholic hierarchies in England and Holland—and did so in the face of often aggressive Protestant opposition. He was a successful diplomat, with numerous concordats regularizing the legal position of the Church in various countries to his credit. Consecrated religious life flourished during the mid-nineteenth century, with the Pope approving dozens of new congregations; for the first time since the Revolution, France experienced a vibrant presence of priests and nuns in consecrated life, many of them in active apostolates. And there was a vast expansion of Catholic missionary activity in Africa and Asia. To be sure, a drive toward Roman centralization ran parallel to all this activity. But for all the chafing that centripetal force sometimes caused (not least among the Eastern Catholic churches, whose unique spirituality and methods of governance Pius could not seem to appreciate), it would also have unexpected and beneficial effects when local churches came under the lash of the twentieth century's totalitarianisms and authoritarianisms and found their lifeline in a strong papacy and Vatican.

Thus there is an ironic quality to the pontificate of Pius IX. On the one hand, it saw the apogee of papal anti-modern reaction, embodied in the last proposition condemned in the *Syllabus of Errors*. On the other, Pius IX created the modern papacy as an office with universal appeal and global impact. The pope mocked as "Pio No-No" never ceased to deplore the loss of his temporal sovereignty. But in another irony, the demise of the Papal States would prove to be the essential condition for the possibility of the papacy exercising politically effective moral authority in the twentieth century.

And while it is true that Pius IX remade the world episcopate in his own image over thirty-four years, it is also true that, in his last years, he rehabilitated the career of the man who would become his successor—a man with a very different cast of mind, who would open the second act of the drama of Catholicism-and-modernity by taking a grand strategic decision to engage, not simply repudiate, modernity in its various expressions.

Bridge Builders

Explorers and Pioneers

T HE "OFFICIAL" THEOLOGY of the Catholic Church in the first eight decades of the nineteenth century—the theology taught in the Roman universities and the theology that shaped thinking in the Vatican—tended toward the dry and dusty: a theology-by-syllogism little influenced by Scripture, the Fathers of the Church, or the history of Christian thought. That official theology was also marked by a strong combativeness. Its apologetics, aimed at both Protestant and secular Enlightenment thought, embodied the conviction of Popes Gregory XVI and Pius IX that it was more important to play good defense against these intellectual assaults on Catholicism than to go on offense and propose Catholic answers to the quandaries of the age. Yet there were theological explorers who were exceptions to this general rule.

As conservative or reactionary ultramontanism was driving the liberal ultramontanism of Lamennais's followers to the margins of Catholic life and preparing for what it hoped would be a decisive victory at Vatican I, intellectual bridges were nonetheless being built across the chasm between the Church and the modern world. The bridge-builders were determined to replace a Catholicism bent on rejecting modernity root and branch with a Church exploring modernity in the hope of converting it. Five of the most important of these thinkers bear brief examination. By taking us beyond the tight focus in our first act on the papal confrontation with political modernity, their stories help fill out the picture of nineteenth-century

Catholicism in a way that sheds light on what followed the rejectionism of Gregory XVI and Pius IX.

Each of these men was a controversial figure in his own day, and one of them found his works officially deplored. Yet all were true churchmen. None went into schism or abandoned Christianity. And they would all be vindicated by the next acts in our drama as the ideas and themes they developed moved from the peripheries to the center of Catholic thought and life.

Johann Adam Möhler (1796–1838), a German priest, historian, and theologian, made original contributions to ecclesiology, the Church's theological reflection on itself. The Roman theology of the day thought of the Church in primarily juridical terms. The Catholic Church was the *societas perfecta*, a "perfect society": ordered hierarchically, governed legally, and, if not immutable, then at least something close to that. Möhler, who as a young scholar was in conversation with the influential Protestant theologian Friedrich Schleiermacher, proposed a different, more organic view of the Church influenced by a close reading of the Church Fathers of the first millennium.

The Church was a living body enlivened by the Holy Spirit, Möhler taught, and its self-understanding developed over time. Yet the Church always remained centered on Christ, which meant that, in addition to its visible or juridical elements, Catholicism was shaped by its spiritual life. Mystics, contemplatives, and the Church's liturgy were as important as lawyers and jurists in understanding the Church's character and mission. Möhler also urged the Catholic Church to engage Protestantism rather than simply conduct jeremiads against it, in a proto-ecumenism shaped by his confidence in the divine origins of Catholicism and his belief in the abiding presence of the Holy Spirit in the Church over time. These themes, hotly contested by his fellow Catholics during his lifetime, would nonetheless prove fruitful for the theology of the twentieth century, which in many ways was the century of ecclesiology.

That fruitfulness would be evident in one of the two great Dogmatic Constitutions of Vatican II, *Lumen Gentium*, "On the Church," which in important respects complemented and completed the work of Vatican I.

Johann Adam Möhler died in Munich, three weeks short of his forty-second birthday, from a combination of cholera, pneumonia, and overwork.

Antonio Rosmini-Serbati (1797–1855) may well have been the outstanding Italian Catholic thinker of the nineteenth century. An intellectual polymath with an intense spiritual life, as well as a priest determined to engage modernity in order to convert it, Rosmini challenged both the reactionaries who denied any development in the life or self-understanding of the Church and the secular liberals who saw no value in the past. His philosophical work aimed to demonstrate that every branch of human knowledge developed from within, by growing "out" from fundamental, unchanging principles. Yet for all his rejection of the French Revolution and the rationalist Enlightenment, he also sought to rescue what he took to be their deepest and truest aspirations for public life, detaching the ideals from the destructive political and intellectual forms they often took and putting those aspirations on a firmer foundation.

This rescue operation required, among other things, a Church free to be itself: to get about the apostolic mission given it by Christ and invite the world into the liberating experience of the supernatural. In Rosmini's view, a Church freed from state patronage would fulfill that evangelical mission better than one tied to the apron strings of public authority. He buttressed that conviction with the Christian medieval concept of a richly textured, pluralistic society—an idea quite different from the one being proposed by the enlightened despots and Jacobins promoting an omnicompetent state. Defending the modern ideal of freedom, Rosmini also refused to concede that freedom was essentially willfulness.

For the Church to be modernity's tutor in the true meaning of the liberty to which modernity aspired, the Church herself had to be renewed and reformed. It must be a Church of persuasion: a Church that appealed to thought and conscience, rather than to coercive state power, to advance the truths it believed it could offer. Rosmini was also a visionary in imagining an important role for lay Catholics in the work of both ecclesial renewal and societal reform. He admired the philosophical and theological work of St. Thomas Aquinas, who was then not much studied in the original, but only through commentators. Rosmini's effort to rehabilitate the "Angelic Doctor" would be vindicated at the highest levels of the Church some three decades after his death, although, in another ironic turn, the Church's recovery of Thomas's work would lead to an ill-judged condemnation of some of (what was taken to be) Rosmini's thought.

Rosmini's most enduring work (and his most daring, given the ecclesiastical temper of the times) was *Le cinque pianghe della Chiesa* (*The Five Wounds of the Church*), written in 1832 but only published in 1848—after which it was, without explanation, put on the Vatican's Index of Forbidden Books. In it, Rosmini analyzed the defects of the Italian Catholicism of his day by analogy to the five wounds of Christ on the cross. The first wound was the gap between clergy and laity in the Church's worship, which he believed to be caused by poor catechesis of the people, who too often worshiped out of habit rather than conviction. The second wound was closely related to the first: the sorry state of the priesthood, which he attributed to an inadequate seminary education and formation that produced men unfamiliar with the Scriptures, uninterested in evangelism, and too susceptible to the temptations of a worldly lifestyle. The third wound, which Rosmini compared to the wound in the heart of Christ, involved the Church's bishops: their lack of effective communion with each other, their distance from their priests and people, and their lack of a sense of responsibility for the unity of the body of Christ. The fourth and fifth wounds were the bishop-as-political-leader and the bishop-as-property-manager, roles Rosmini thought incompatible with the bishop's consecration as a spiritual shepherd.

Rosmini was a saintly man with a remarkable capacity for friendship; among his interlocutors he could count Alessandro Manzoni, author of the classic Italian novel *I promessi sposi* (*The Betrothed*), and, prior to his election as pope, Cardinal Mauro Cappellari. He was in close contact with Pius IX before the political events of 1848 drove them apart. The religious community he founded, the Institute of Charity, spread throughout the world, despite the controversies in which the founder was continually engaged. He did not protest when *Five Wounds* was put on the Index, but retired to the north of Italy, where he died in Stresa, near Lago Maggiore. Despite decades of vilification, primarily by Jesuits, his reputation for holiness was such that he would eventually be beatified under Pope Benedict XVI in 2007. Nine years earlier, in the 1998 encyclical *Fides et Ratio* (*Faith and Reason*), Pope John Paul II saluted Rosmini as an important teacher of the Church, a prophet ahead of his time who had helped build a bridge between philosophy and scriptural revelation.

Matthias Joseph Scheeben (1835–1888) was trained in Rome at the Pontifical Gregorian University before his priestly ordination in 1858. Two years later he began teaching at the seminary in Cologne, where he remained until his death. A man of mystical inclination, considered by some the greatest German theologian since the Reformation, he enriched the theology he had absorbed in Rome by a deep reading of the Bible and helped Latin-rite Catholicism to rediscover the Greek Fathers of the Church, including Athanasius, Cyril of Alexandria, and Gregory of Nyssa. In an era when "theology" was often done by accumulating putative proof texts from the papal magisterium in order to conduct disputations with opponents, Scheeben dug deeply into the biblical and patristic roots of Catholicism in order to relate Church teaching to the lives of the men and women of his time.

In his teaching on human nature and divine grace, Scheeben anticipated and helped make possible the transition of Catholic theology that would become evident in the mid-twentieth century: a transition beyond a propositional form of explaining Christian truth and beyond a juridical understanding of Christ's redeeming work. God's supernatural love, Scheeben taught, permeated and transfigured the world in a spousal relationship. Thus creation and redemption were not two separate and distinct actions of God "on" the world. Rather, God's creating activity and God's redeeming activity in Christ were linked. The incarnation of the Son of God was not just a remedy for sin, as if man's "fall" in Adam had somehow "caused" the incarnation. Rather, the incarnation was the ultimate expression of God's purpose in creating the world and humanity, which was to draw men and women into being "partakers of the divine life" (as Scheeben put it in *Natur und Gnade* [*Nature and Grace*], published in 1861). The suffering, death, and resurrection of Christ demonstrated the superabundance of divine love that had flowed out from the Trinitarian God to create the world "in the beginning"; the divine relationship to the world was more akin to that of a lover who invited the beloved to communion than to that of a judge summoning a criminal to judgment. The witness of divine love displayed on the cross of Christ, not mere argument, was the proposal the Church should offer the modern world.

This understanding of the natural and the supernatural, of creation and redemption, and of the Christ-centeredness of the entire drama of history led Scheeben to conceive of the Church as the "Mystical Body" of Christ in the world: an image that would have a profound effect on the Church's self-understanding in the century after Scheeben's death. And by enriching the syllogistic thinking of his time with the concept of human "divinization" he had learned from the Greek Fathers, Scheeben became a pioneer of a renewed Christian anthropology that would become the Church's counterproposal to the Prometheanism of cultural modernity and to the charge that the God of the Bible was an enemy of humanity's maturation.

Wilhelm Emmanuel von Ketteler (1811–1877) began his career as a government lawyer but left the Prussian civil service in protest of its attack on the Catholic archbishop of Cologne, who was trying to free the Church from the grip of state power in the matter of marriage law. Persuaded by another bishop that he should consider the priesthood, he undertook theological studies in Munich, where he was influenced by Johann Adam Möhler and Ignaz von Döllinger. Service as a parish priest for six years, including a term as dean of St. Hedwig's Cathedral in Berlin, gave him a familiarity with the circumstances of working people and shaped his conviction that pastoral care had to include efforts to improve their social condition amidst the upheavals of the Industrial Revolution. In 1848, the same year that Marx and Engels issued the *Communist Manifesto*, Ketteler began to promote a radically different vision of the society of the future, which he elaborated in addresses to a Catholic congress in Mainz and in a series of Advent sermons in Berlin.

Ketteler was chosen as bishop of Mainz at the age of thirty-nine and served in that post for twenty-seven years. During that time he became the leading Catholic figure in Germany and a model bishop, energizing his priests for evangelism and service. As one of the intellectual architects of modern Catholic social thought, he accepted the fact that the world was changing and argued that the Church should try to shape and guide those changes, not merely criticize them. He firmly believed that Christian conviction, based on biblical concepts of charity and fraternal responsibility and elaborated in the social ethics of Thomas Aquinas, could set a firm foundation for the future of modernizing societies, which otherwise risked descent into brutalization or even anarchy amidst great human suffering. Ketteler also understood that the Church must do more than teach charity, as important as that was; the Church also had to become an advocate for justice in society, which meant Catholic involvement in shaping public policy. For, as he put it (in a phrase that would have shocked Catholics still dreaming of a return to a mythical *ancien régime*), "religion and morality by themselves cannot cure the plight of the worker." He followed his own counsel and was an engaged public personality, helping shape the German Catholic Center Party and serving for two years in the Reichstag, where he forcefully opposed Bismarck's Kulturkampf against the Church.

Ketteler's social doctrine and its insistence that religion had an important role to play in the modern world distinguished him from two prominent forces in the public life of his time: the Enlightenment liberals, who either dismissed religion intellectually or regarded it as a private affair of no public consequence, and the Marxists, who wished to destroy religion as part of their liberation of the proletariat. At the same time, Ketteler challenged Christians to understand that their faith was hollow if it did not shape public life according to Gospel norms and Catholic social thought. He was sharply critical of the laissez-faire economics of Manchesterian liberalism, a form of social Darwinism applied to economic life that bracketed all moral categories from economic reflection; he clearly saw how an economics driven solely by growth imperatives and the profit motive would wreak havoc on families, which he thought were the basic building blocks of society. But Ketteler did not condemn capitalism outright; he was not a socialist (not least because the socialists of his era were almost uniformly anticlerical and aggressively secular); and his critique of the emerging capitalist system focused on those forms of it that ignored the dignity of workers and the demands of justice.

Ketteler did not live to see the establishment of the social-welfare reforms he had championed, but the German social security legislation of 1891, which provided state support for workers who suffered from illness, disabilities, or the ravages of age, was recognized as bearing his stamp. Fourteen years after his death, a pope whose election he likely could not have imagined referred to Ketteler as "my great predecessor" and drew much of his own social doctrine from the German bishop's thought and proposals.

John Henry Newman (1801–1890) was arguably the most creative Catholic thinker of the nineteenth century—and suffered for it. A mesmerizing preacher, he held his Anglican congregations spellbound at Oxford's University Church of St. Mary the Virgin for fourteen years. And from his post at Oriel College, Newman was one of the leading figures in the reformist Tractarian movement, which challenged what the Tractarians (so called because their reform campaign was conducted through essays published as *Tracts for the Times*) believed to be the decadence of the Anglican Church and the "national apostasy" of England. Then his historical studies, which led to his seminal *Essay on the Development of Christian Doctrine*, convinced him that Anglicanism was not the *via media* he had long held it to be but another form of Protestantism, and thus cut off from the historical roots of the Christian Church.

After preaching one of the masterpieces of Christian homiletics in his valedictory sermon as an Anglican ("The Parting of Friends") in 1843, Newman was received into full communion with the Catholic Church in 1845; following studies in Rome, he was ordained to the priesthood in 1847. He then founded an Oratory and Oratory School in Birmingham on the model created by St. Philip Neri during the Counter-Reformation. In 1854, Newman left Birmingham for three years to serve as rector of the Catholic University of Ireland in

Dublin: a frustrating experience that nonetheless led to one of his most enduring works, *The Idea of a University*.

Newman's life as a Catholic was not an easy one. The prominent Anglican divine Charles Kingsley charged that Newman held the view that Catholic priests need not tell the truth if it conflicted with their mission; Newman's response, written in the white heat of controversy and not infrequently in tears, became one of the greatest of autobiographies, the *Apologia Pro Vita Sua*. But while Newman maintained cordial relations throughout his long life with Anglican colleagues of a different cast of mind than Kingsley, many of his new Catholic coreligionists, some prominently placed, distrusted him. The conservative ultramontanes in England, led by his onetime friend and fellow convert Archbishop Henry Edward Manning, thought of him as a crypto-liberal theologically and deplored his unwillingness to join their campaign for a sweeping definition of papal infallibility. Newman, for his part, believed that that effort, if victorious at Vatican I, would unsettle many converts and severely damage the Catholic mission in England. But he also thought that his age and his health precluded his participation as a theological adviser at the Vatican Council, a post he was offered by the French bishop Félix Dupanloup, the leader of what remained of the party first influenced by Lamennais. That decision did not, however, prevent Newman from participating in the Council at a distance through one of his favorite means of communication: his vast correspondence.

A month after the First Vatican Council convened, Newman wrote his bishop, William Ullathorne of Birmingham, deploring the political maneuverings of the conservative ultramontanists as the machinations of an "aggressive insolent faction" and warning that the debate was being warped by "a clique of Jesuits, Redemptorists, and converts" (such as William G. Ward and Manning). The letter leaked, and although there was an uproar for a moment, Newman felt that, however inadvertently, he had discharged his mind on the subject that was roiling the Church: he believed in papal infallibility but thought the attempt at the Council to define it as a matter of fundamental Catholic truth was unnecessary, imprudent, and potentially dangerous if the definition were cast as broadly as Manning and the other ultramontane leaders wished.

As it happened, the conciliar definition was narrowly drawn, and Newman had no difficulty accepting it (although he hoped it would be complemented by a further conciliar statement on the teaching responsibility of the world's bishops when the Council reconvened—which it never did). He also invested considerable energy in reassuring fellow Catholics who were finding it hard to accept the definition, in part because Manning persistently and publicly gave the definition a very expansive interpretation when he returned to England after Vatican I's adjournment. Then these intra-Catholic quarrels became a public matter.

The Liberal prime minister, William Ewart Gladstone, was defeated in the 1874 parliamentary elections, a loss that Gladstone attributed in part to the opposition of the Catholic bishops of Ireland. With perhaps more pique than prudence, the Grand Old Man (as he liked to be called) then penned an inflammatory pamphlet with the magnificently Victorian title *The Vatican Decrees in Their Bearing on Civil Allegiance: A Political Expostulation*. The *Expostulation* claimed that the Council's definition of papal infallibility (to which Gladstone gave the broadest possible interpretation) "equally repudiated modern thought and ancient history"; moreover, the definition and the obedience to papal judgments it enjoined made it impossible for British Catholics to be trustworthy citizens, because their fidelity to the infallible pope would always trump their loyalty to their country. Newman responded in an essay addressed to England's leading Catholic layman. In his *Letter to the Duke of Norfolk*, he brilliantly refuted Gladstone's *Expostulation*, demonstrating that Gladstone misconstrued what the Council had taught and misrepresented its implications for citizens of a democracy: the pope's infallible teaching authority, he said, was narrowly circumscribed; it had no reach into the electoral decisions of citizens or their views on public policies. It was an effective defense of Catholicism and Catholics that, in the British context, only Newman could have successfully mounted.

Newman's *Letter* helped set the stage for the development of the twentieth-century Catholic Church's teaching on democracy. Moreover, his *Grammar of Assent*, a highly original philosophical work published in 1870, demonstrated the compatibility of faith and reason in a more creative way than the apologetics and polemics offered by the Roman theologians of the day. Yet for all his originality, Newman held firmly to the truth of divine revelation, insisting, in 1879, that he had consistently opposed the "great mischief" he called "the spirit of liberalism in religion," by which he meant "the doctrine that there is no positive truth in religion . . . [that] revealed religion is not a truth but a sentiment and a taste . . . and [that it is] the right of each individual to make it say just what strikes his fancy."

Newman died in 1890 at the age of eighty-nine, having been vindicated, at the end of his eighth decade, by a pope with a very different intellectual formation. He was beatified by Pope Benedict XVI during his pastoral visit to Great Britain in 2010 and canonized by Pope Francis in 2019.

THANKS TO THE bridge-building work of Newman, and that of Rosmini, Ketteler, Möhler, Scheeben, and others, the door was thus far more open to a Catholic exploration of both political and intellectual modernity than might have seemed likely, or even possible, at the death of Pius IX in 1878. That exploration needed papal authorization to flourish, for the success of the conservative ultramontanists and the pressures mounted on the Church by the cultural and political forces of modernity had contrived, in ironic conjunction, to place the pope at the center of Catholic initiative. But as Newman had foreseen when writing to those who were disturbed by the power politics of Vatican I, a change of papacy could make a considerable difference.

The Novus Ordo *in the West*

DEVOUT CHURCHMEN OF Europe and Great Britain who were also creative and courageous thinkers were not the only ones building intellectual bridges between Catholicism and modernity in the nineteenth century. Another sort of bridge was being built at the same time, often beneath the Roman radar screen, by the Catholic Church in the United States.

In eighteen hundred years, Catholicism had never experienced anything like the young American Republic. The Church had evangelized, suffered, grown, flourished, decayed, gone into crisis, and reformed itself under tyrants, emperors, monarchies, and oligarchies. But prior to 1783, Catholicism had never lived within a constitutional democracy: a republic in which the state claimed no interest in the appointment of bishops; a regime in which, as Cardinal James Gibbons of Baltimore would put it in 1887, "the civil government holds over us the aegis of its protection without interfering in the legitimate exercise of our sublime mission as ministers of the Gospel of Jesus Christ." This was something new, and it was feared by some in Rome that the American regime would be inimical to religious faith, and especially to Catholicism. Yet the Catholic Church in the United States experienced explosive, exponential growth throughout the nineteenth century. And as European Catholicism felt the first effects of secularization and lost congregants among the new industrial working class of Marx's proletariat, the Church in the United States not only retained workers' loyalty, but built a vast institutional infrastructure unlike anything else in the world Church.

At the American founding, Catholics were a minuscule minority of the citizens of the United States: perhaps 1.2 percent of the national population, some 35,000 souls, primarily located in Maryland (founded in 1634 as a proprietary colony and refuge for Catholics), with scattered enclaves and individuals in Pennsylvania and New York. Penal laws prohibited Catholics from participating in public life in most of the original thirteen states when the American colonies declared their independence, although a prominent Catholic, Charles Carroll of Carrollton, was one of Maryland's signatories to the Declaration of Independence. In the years after American independence was secured, Carroll's cousin John, another native Marylander and a former Jesuit, took the lead in organizing the nascent Catholic Church in the new republic and was named the country's first Catholic bishop in 1789 by Pius VI. The Diocese of Baltimore, erected at the time, covered the entire United States.

Immigration played a considerable role in the growth of Catholicism in the new republic: first from Ireland and Germany, and later from central, southern, and eastern Europe. By 1850, there were 1.6 million Catholics across the United States, a number that tripled by 1890. The Church became a primary vehicle for assimilating the immigrants: one of the great nineteenth-century accomplishments of U.S. Catholicism was the "Americanization" of a vast and diverse body of immigrants who nonetheless remained staunch Catholics—and who built a parallel education and health-care system largely run by women, in this case religious sisters. Assimilation in the nineteenth century was not infrequently a rough-and-ready process, with conflicts between "nativists" and immigrants, and between the Irish and the Germans, flaring up from time to time. But despite those conflicts, the Church did not split into northern and southern factions during the Civil War, as many Protestant denominations did.

By the time of Pius IX's death in 1878, the original Diocese of Baltimore had given birth to some eighty other ecclesiastical jurisdictions spread across the continent. Even more strikingly, given the ultramontanism of the era, the bishops of the United States developed a conciliar tradition unique in the Counter-Reformation history of Catholicism. Between 1829 and 1884, the U.S. bishops held seven provincial councils (during the years when the Archdiocese of Baltimore was the sole metro-politan see) and three plenary councils (after other archdio-ceses had been created). Held in Baltimore's Cathedral of the Assumption, designed by the Moravian architect Benjamin Latrobe to embody, in the play of light from its pierced dome, the American republic's commitment to religious freedom, these councils legislated for the entire Church in the United States on questions of clerical discipline and marriage law while solving thorny problems involving the ownership of church property. Over more than a half-century, they also mandated the creation of parochial schools, authorized a national catechism, founded a national Catholic university, resolved some of the frictions caused by the clash of various immigrant groups, and provided for domestic missionary work and regional seminar-ies. In 1849, the bishops of the Seventh Provincial Council of Baltimore petitioned Pius IX to declare the Immaculate Conception of the Virgin Mary a dogma of the faith.

This remarkable record was built amidst recurring waves of anti-Catholic prejudice, some of which took violent forms. Yet despite the ingrained cultural prejudices of a natively Protestant country and occasional legal hurdles thrown up by legislators eager to appease Protestant bigots, Catholicism in America in the mid-nineteenth century was demonstrating that the Church could flourish under the conditions of modernity while remaining loyal to Catholicism's center of authority in Rome. The intellectual and political battles that absorbed so much Roman attention in those decades had little impact on Catholic life in the United States. What was being built in America, however, would later have a significant impact on Catholicism's wrestling with political modernity.

Act Two

Catholicism Explores Modernity, Gingerly

Pivot

PAPAL FUNERARY MONUMENTS in Rome often depict the deceased pontiff kneeling in prayer atop a marble casket or recumbent upon it, his hands peacefully folded as he awaits a glorious resurrection. A good example of the latter style is the tomb-monument of Pope Innocent III, the most politically consequential pontiff of the High Middle Ages, which is to the right of the sanctuary of the Papal Basilica of St. John Lateran as the visitor or pilgrim faces the high altar and apse. The tomb-monument on the left side of the sanctuary offers a striking contrast.

It depicts Pope Leo XIII (1878–1903) standing erect in pontifical vestments, tiara on his head, right foot thrust forward and right hand raised and extended, as if he were saying to the modern world, "We have something to talk about. We have a proposal to make." To the left, kneeling by the polished green marble coffin on which Leo stands, is a manual laborer; to the right is an allegorical depiction of Faith. Sculptor Giulio Tadolini's composition suggests that this pope was different.

Which is altogether appropriate. For Leo XIII, perhaps more than he knew or could imagine, was the pivotal figure in the multi-act drama of Catholicism-and-modernity: the man who would set the Church on the road to a sometimes skeptical, sometimes intrigued exploration of modernity, which would lead to developments in this drama that could not have been foreseen in Leo's time. Those developments, in turn, would accelerate the process by which the Catholic Church rediscovered its evangelical essence while becoming an intellectual force capable of engaging in a serious, critical, and history-changing conversation with modernity about its most cherished aspirations.

THAT THE SUCCESSOR of Pius IX would be the pivot between Counter-Reformation Catholicism and the Church of what the new pope's eighth successor would call the "New Evangelization" was not what the College of Cardinals expected when it quickly settled on Gioacchino Vincenzo Raffaele Luigi Pecci at its third ballot in 1878. No one at the time could imagine a "New Evangelization," and in any event there were other, actuarial motives behind the cardinal-electors' swift decision. Sixty-eight at the time of his election—an old man in that era—and of somewhat delicate constitution, Leo XIII was expected to be a competent, moderate place-warmer after the thirty-two-year reign of his predecessor, a tenure no one wanted to see repeated. His pontificate would last for a few years; Leo would put a different face on things, but then he would fade from the scene, opening the door, perhaps, to a younger, more dynamic personality.

Proving yet again that there are no guarantees to be found in the best-laid plans of cardinal-electors, Leo XIII, the senior citizen chosen to fill a gap, proceeded to have what was then the second-longest reign in reliably recorded papal history. And over twenty-five years, he set in motion a Leonine Revolution, the effects of which are still being felt throughout the world Church in the early twenty-first century. Had his brother-cardinals looked closely into his background, however, they might have intuited that this was a man determined to make a difference. For Leo brought to the papacy considerable experience in dealing with modernity in its many expressions, and he understood that the rejectionism of his two immediate predecessors, Gregory XVI and Pius IX, had exhausted itself.

Leo's grand strategy took a dramatically new tack. Building on the success the previous two popes had enjoyed in revitalizing the Church's spiritual and pastoral life and putting the pope at the center of the Catholic imagination, he would lead a Church that would neither reject modernity outright nor surrender to it, as much of liberal Protestantism was in the process of doing. Rather, the Church of the Leonine Revolution would engage modernity with distinctively Catholic tools in order to propose a surer moral and cultural foundation for the modern world's aspirations.

A BRILLIANT STUDENT IN his youth, when he became the accomplished Latinist who would write verse and puns in that language into his nineties, Pecci was ordained priest at age twenty-seven. He spent the next five years in the civil service of the Papal States, becoming the governor of Benevento and then Perugia and displaying skills as an administrator. Named archbishop in 1843 when he was only thirty-three years old, he was sent by Gregory XVI to Belgium as nuncio; from his base in Brussels, he visited London, Paris, and Cologne, acquainting himself with the new parliamentary democracies and the effects of the Industrial Revolution as he could not have done by remaining in Italy. After three years, however, Archbishop Pecci got himself cross-wired with King Leopold I in an argument over Belgian educational policy, and the King eventually requested that Pope Gregory recall him. Gregory complied with what amounted to a royal decree of *persona non grata* and named Pecci bishop of the comparatively inconsequential see of Perugia, a post he filled for thirty-two years. Pope Pius IX's hard-edged secretary of state, Giacomo Antonelli, disliked and mistrusted Pecci, and although the former nuncio was created cardinal in 1853, he was kept away from Rome and the Curia for almost a quarter-century, until

Antonelli's death in 1876. The following year, Pius named Pecci as camerlengo of the Holy Roman Church: the man who would oversee the Church's affairs during a papal interregnum. The tradition that the camerlengo is not elected pope tells against any notion that Pius regarded Cardinal Pecci as a likely or desirable successor.

The years he spent in Perugia, a kind of ecclesiastical exile, proved to be the training ground on which Pecci forged the convictions that shaped his new grand strategy for the Church. Always an able manager, he showed political nerve by challenging the anticlerical legislation that followed Perugia's incorporation into the Kingdom of Italy. He reformed and modernized his seminary. Most importantly, he founded the Academy of St. Thomas Aquinas to promote the study of the great medieval philosopher and theologian in the original texts—an institution he eventually moved to Rome when he became pope. Inspired by his own research into Thomas's social and political thought, Pecci issued a series of pastoral letters between 1874 and 1877 calling for a Catholic engagement with modernity; in those letters he insisted that the Church was a force for civilization, because it treated working people with the dignity they deserved, supported the poor through its charities, and worked to temper economic efficiency with economic justice. Pecci's evident willingness to engage the realities of modernity did not go over well with Antonelli or his compatriots, reactionaries who feared that any such engagement would weaken the papacy's efforts to reclaim the Papal States; they tried but failed to block Pecci's election as pope.

Leo XIII was not a liberal in any nineteenth-century sense of the word. His temperament was conservative and he was skeptical about many currents in intellectual modernity (as might be gathered from his support of Pius IX's *Syllabus of Errors*, which he had encouraged his predecessor to issue). He loved the High Middle Ages, brought Innocent XIII's body to Rome to be buried in the papal cathedral of St. John Lateran, and likely preferred that era to his own. But he also knew that, as pope, he had to deal with the world as it was, even as he tried to engage and change it. He was not as affable as Pius IX, who was always making jokes, and what would today be called Leo's "management style" was rather autocratic. He liked ceremony and saw to it that he was given the respect he thought due the Vicar of Christ on earth. Yet he would occasionally make fun of himself, as when (according to a famous story which is so good that it ought to be true) a pious nun told him she was praying that the nonagenarian pontiff would see his centenary and Leo answered, "My daughter, why place limits on the bounty of divine providence?" He worked hard, took a serious interest in scholarship, and was steeped in Italian high culture, which he esteemed and cherished.

Early on, Leo signaled that his pontificate would mark a break with the immediate past. With the Holy See now bereft of a port, he sold the last papal warship, the corvette *Immacolata Concezione* (*Immaculate Conception*), which was marooned in Toulon. He ended the practice of hiring castrati for the Sistine Chapel choir. He named one of the most liberal of Pius IX's cardinals, Alessando Franchi, his secretary of state. But these moves were trivial compared to the striking signal he sent when, fifteen months after his election, he named John Henry Newman a cardinal. That gesture of personal regard was also a clear indicator of the Pope's understanding that Catholicism evolved over time (Newman was, after all, the author of the *Essay on the Development of Christian Doctrine*), and it underscored the new pope's willingness to engage the modern world with Catholic intellectual tools (even if Newman's tools were not Leo's particular favorites).

THREE MONTHS AFTER Newman's cardinalate, Leo laid down his own intellectual marker with the encyclical *Aeterni Patris*, a thoroughgoing celebration of the philosophy and theology of Thomas Aquinas. During his Perugian exile, Leo had concluded that Thomism was uniquely fit for shaping Catholicism's intellectual engagement with a world dominated by the scientific method, philosophical skepticism about the human capacity to get at the truth of things, and political theories that tended to atomize society. Modernity's problems, Leo judged, were largely the result of a failure to grasp and then live by true first principles; his own intellectual passion was the analysis of contemporary issues by reference to those principles; and Thomas, whose thinking combined faith and reason in a powerful synthesis, could, Leo believed, be a reliable guide out of skepticism, relativism, and social incohesion.

Leo's embrace of Thomas and Thomism was not a matter of nostalgia for the Middle Ages, however. Rather, it was an important step toward a serious Catholic engagement with intellectual modernity. After almost a century in which the teaching authority of the Church had battled what it judged to be reductive and narrow Enlightenment rationalism, here was a pope extolling human reason and its capacity to grasp the truths God had inscribed into the world—a pope who believed that a revival of Thomism and the natural moral law Thomas outlined could help the modern world apply those truths to the just ordering of society under contemporary conditions.

The revival of Thomism that Leo tried to foster through *Aeterni Patris* would not fully flourish until after the Pope's death. But his own Thomistic studies and those of the academy he founded in Perugia played a major role in shaping what would be Leo XIII's most enduring contribution to Catholic thought and life: his social doctrine. That body of thought is sometimes reduced to the 1891 encyclical *Rerum Novarum*, which defended both the right of private property and the rights of labor, and endorsed trade unions as civil society institutions necessary for the promotion of economic justice. But as important as *Rerum Novarum* was, and is, Leo's social thought was first developed in other important encyclicals, such as *Diuturnum* (1881), *Immortale Dei* (1885), and *Libertas Praestantissimum Donum* (1888), where the Pope explored virtually every major facet of political modernity in light of his cherished first principles.

What did the Catholic Church have to offer the post–*ancien régime* social, economic, and political world? For Leo, modernity's dilemma might be summarized in one admonition: no *telos*, no justice. Or, alternatively: no metaphysics, no morals. Or, to leave the technical vocabulary of philosophy: no grounding of society, politics, and economics in the deep truths of the human condition, no society fit for human beings.

At the heart of political modernity as Leo XIII read it was an empty shrine: religious conviction had been reduced to a lifestyle choice of no public consequence, while philosophy had become self-referentially self-absorbed. That, he thought, was the concrete, historical result of a dramatic revolution in European intellectual life in which metaphysics had withered and epistemology, or thinking-about-thinking, had replaced thinking-about-truth. And because ideas had consequences, governance had come unstuck from the first principles of justice. The natural sciences, which had replaced metaphysics as the most consequential of intellectual disciplines, could provide no answer to the essentially moral question at the root of all political theory in the West since Aristotle: How ought we live together? Worse, when science stepped outside its disciplinary boundaries and tried its hand at social and political prescription, it let loose new demons such as Social Darwinism, which would prove lethal in the extreme when those demons shaped the national tempers that presaged the great slaughter of the First World War.

Leo tried to fill the empty shrine at the heart of political modernity with reason and with the deep moral truths that reason can discern. This was, to be sure, reason informed by biblical faith and Christian doctrine. But the genius of Leo XIII, a kind of nineteenth-century public intellectual, was that he found a vocabulary to address the social, political, and economic problems of his time (and ours) that was genuinely ecumenical and accessible to all—the vocabulary of public reason, drawn from the truths of the natural moral law embedded in the world and in us. In one of his great encyclicals on political modernity, *Immortale Dei*, Leo wrote that "the best parent and guardian of liberty amongst men is truth." Unlike the cynics who imagine that the question "What is truth?" ends all argument, the Pope understood that this question, which can be asked in a non-cynical and genuinely inquiring way, is the beginning of any serious wrestling with a further question, "How ought we live together?"

This analysis of the basic problem of political modernity then led Leo to pose a cultural challenge to the modern public life of the West: to think more deeply about law, about the nature of freedom, about civil society and its relationship to the state, and about the limits of state power, all through the prism of the natural-law truths he believed were accessible to anyone willing to reflect carefully, all the way down to first principles. In the course of issuing that challenge through his encyclicals, Leo erected the scaffolding on which successor popes would develop Catholic social doctrine over the next century.

Leo XIII's concept of law, drawn from Thomas Aquinas, challenged the legal positivist notion that "law" is what the law says it is, period. Legal positivism (which was shaped in part by the modern tendency to see civil laws as analogous to the "laws" of nature) emptied law of moral content, detached it from reason, and treated it as a mere expression of human willfulness. Leo offered political modernity a nobler concept of law: a true law, he proposed, is a rule mandated by reason and enacted by a properly constituted authority in service to the common good of society. Thus law is not mere coercion, as modern political theory in the Hobbesian tradition has it; law is authoritative prescription, grounded in reason. True law reflects moral judgment, and its power comes from its moral persuasiveness. Law appeals to conscience, not just to fear.

Leo also challenged political modernity to a nobler concept of freedom. Following Thomas Aquinas and his emphasis on reason, rather than William of Ockham and his emphasis on the will, Leo insisted that freedom ought not be construed as sheer, arbitrary willfulness. Rather, freedom is the human capacity to know what is truly good, to choose it freely, and to do so as a matter of habit or virtue. That concept of freedom had public consequences: society should organize itself so that the natural human talent or instinct for freedom, which Leo called "the greatest of gifts" at the beginning of his 1888 encyclical *Libertas*, grows in each of its members as a habit of excellence, not just a means of self-assertion against others.

Leo's thought on political modernity was also a challenge to the omnicompetence of the state. Leo was a committed defender of what the twenty-first century would call "civil society," or what were known in his day as "voluntary private associations." Society, according to Leo, was composed of a richly textured pluralism of associations, of which the state was but one (albeit an important one). But before there was the state in its modern sense, society included a plethora of voluntarily entered, free associations (which, to reduce the matter to its simplest form, included everything from the natural associations of marriage and the family to civic associations such as businesses, trade unions, civic groups, and religious communities). These natural and civic free associations were goods in themselves: communities expressing different forms of friendship and human solidarity. Thus the just state would take care to protect these societies, which contribute to the common good in unique ways—not least by forming the habits of heart and mind that make willful men and women, constantly tempted to selfishness, into good citizens.

Moreover, Leo proposed, the state's responsibility to provide legal protection for the functioning of free associations ought not be something conceded out of a sense of royal largesse or governmental *noblesse oblige*. That responsibility was also a matter of first principles: in this case, the principle of the limited, law-governed state. For the state that can recognize free human associations that exist prior to the state—not just as a matter of historical chronology but as a matter of the deep truths of the human condition—is a state that has recognized the boundary-markers of its own competence and thus the limits of its legitimate reach.

In *Rerum Novarum*, the first encyclical of the papal social doctrine tradition strictly speaking, Leo drew on these essentially Thomistic convictions about law, freedom, civil society, and the state to lay down the first two foundational principles of classic Catholic social theory. The personalist principle, which would be called the human rights principle today, holds that all right thinking about society, polity, culture, and economics begins with the inherent, built-in dignity and value of the individual human person, not with the state, the party, the tribe, the social class, the ethnic group, or the gender group. The second principle is the principle of the common good, which in twenty-first-century parlance would be called the communitarian principle. The principle of the common good, which complements and completes the personalist principle and thereby distinguishes the classic social doctrine from any form of libertarianism, teaches that rights should be exercised in such a way that an individual's actions in the spheres of politics, economics, and culture contribute to the general welfare of society, not simply to his or her aggrandizement. For the individual is not a monad for whom society is merely a means of protection, as in Thomas Hobbes's conception; society itself is a natural phenomenon, and living one's inalienable dignity in and for the general welfare of society is essential for the integral development of the human person.

Thus, under Leo XIII, what would later be known as Christian Democracy was born. And while "Christian democracy" was not a phrase Leo would have used to summarize his view of the ideal society, he was also prepared to recognize that, under certain conditions, constitutionally ordered and popular self-government had its advantages, as did constitutional arrangements that kept a prudent distance between the institution of the Church and the institutions of the state. Thus, in his 1895 letter to the bishops of the United States, *Longinqua Oceani*, Leo acknowledged the benefits that had come to Catholicism in America as a result of its independence from state power; and while holding theoretically to the old preference for a Church that enjoyed the protection and patronage of civil authority, he made clear that (as a later generation of theologians would put it), the American arrangement *tolerari potest* (could be tolerated). As he had first taught in *Immortale Dei*, the Church could thrive under various constitutional arrangements, including those of modern democracies. And so the door was opened to the development of Catholic social doctrine that would result in the late twentieth-century Catholic human rights revolution: an evolution, unimaginable to Gregory XVI or Pius IX, in which religious freedom would be celebrated as the first of civil rights, and Catholicism would become a global proponent of democracy—not by surrendering to modernity, but by retrieving and renewing elements of its own intellectual patrimony.

THE LEONINE REVOLUTION in Catholic intellectual life extended far beyond Leo XIII's social thought and his promotion of Thomistic philosophy and theology. Leo reenergized the Vatican Observatory, thereby opening a Catholic dialogue with science as it was becoming the center of the Western intellectual world and challenging understandings of the universe previously thought to be matters of divine revelation. He permitted scholars of all faiths and none to use the resources of the Vatican Library and Archives, showing an openness to historical scholarship that he must have known would eventually demonstrate, against the claims implicit in the stances taken by his two predecessors, that the Church's self-understanding and thinking about the world developed over time. In 1892, he gave his blessing to the first Catholic institution of higher learning dedicated to the historical and critical study of the Bible, the École Biblique in Jerusalem, and his 1893 encyclical, *Providentissimus Deus*, became a kind of Magna Carta for modern Catholic biblical studies. While a skepticism about many modern methods of exegesis would dominate the early work of the Pontifical Biblical Commission that he founded in 1902, and lead to not a few intellectual tensions, *Providentissimus Deus*, like the École Biblique, fostered a renaissance of Catholic studies in biblical languages, archaeology, and history that would serve the Church well later in the twentieth century, helping prepare the way for the Second Vatican Council's efforts to restore the Bible to the center of Catholic theology and spirituality. Of all the currents in twentieth-century Catholic intellectual and pastoral life that would converge at Vatican II, perhaps the only important dynamic not launched during the pontificate of Leo XIII was the Liturgical Movement—but that, in another irony of this drama, had been set in motion by the ultramontanism of Pius IX and its influence on the French Benedictine liturgist and abbot of Solesmes, Prosper Guéranger.

Leo XIII's admiration for Innocent III suggests that he imagined himself playing a similarly large role on the world stage. His diplomacy had both successes and notable failures, however. Not without difficulty and compromise, he negotiated an end to the Kulturkampf in Germany and its lesser imitation in Switzerland. In 1885, he successfully mediated a dispute between Germany and Spain over the Caroline Islands in the southwestern Pacific; the resolution of this flap was not of great historical consequence, but it did return the Holy See to the world diplomatic stage for the first time since the debacle of 1870. He had further success sorting out the Church's affairs in Belgium and Russia. But the initiative on which Leo staked the most—his attempt to rally French Catholics to the support of the Third Republic—was a failure, thanks to the embittered obstinacy of French Catholic royalists, the poisoning of French politics by the Dreyfus affair, and the intransigent anticlericalism of the French political leadership. As for Italy, neither the increasingly anticlerical governments of the Kingdom nor Leo himself showed any interest in proposals for the reasonable solution of the Roman Question that was being bruited in some circles: the pope would recognize that Rome was the capital of Italy; papal sovereignty over a microstate, centered on the Vatican complex and with an outlet to the sea, would be acknowledged; an indemnity would be paid for the properties seized by Italy during the Risorgimento and the absorption of the Papal States into the newly unified Kingdom. Yet for all that, some of the bitterness accruing from the last years of Pius IX was drained from the relationship between the papacy and Italy. And if Leo's great ambitions as a diplomat were not fulfilled, he had considerable success building up the Church around the world. In all, he erected almost three hundred new dioceses or vicariates apostolic, and he secured the governmental agreements necessary to restore or create the ordinary structures of Catholic pastoral life in Scotland, North Africa, India, and Japan.

THE FIRST POPE since Charlemagne who did not, on his election, become a temporal sovereign with lands to rule, Leo XIII nonetheless completed the remaking of the papacy begun by Pius IX. Pius's accomplishment was to make the papacy the center of the Catholic imagination around the world. Leo's was to make it relevant again in the modern world—not as one among many power players, but as a global moral authority with intellectual heft and important things to say about the modern project in all its dimensions. From the perspective of the twenty-first century, he may seem a cautious figure. But in his time he was regarded as an innovator. And while he was conservative by conviction and temperament, he was also the pope who broke the spell of what the ultramontane Cardinal Manning had styled "the beauty of inflexibility." Inflexibility may have been romantically attractive to Catholic anti-moderns. But it was not the path toward a serious intellectual engagement with modernity, and it was not conducive to the Church's mission of witnessing to the Gospel.

Yet there were some who still wanted an inflexible and intransigent Church, even after a quarter-century of Leo's determined efforts to set a different course. Because of that, the next six decades of the drama of Catholicism-and-modernity were a contest, sometimes bitterly fought out, over his legacy. He took the Chair of Peter declaring "I want to carry out a great policy," and did so. Its effects, a century after his death, were not those he could have foreseen. But a well-founded suspicion suggests that, on reflection, he would have approved.

Sanctity, Sacraments, and Repression

I N MARKED CONTRAST to the aristocratic Leo XIII, whose pontificate was perceived by many cardinal-electors to have been a "political" one, the conclave of 1903 chose a pope of peasant stock who was a parish priest at heart. Getting Giuseppe Melchiorre Sarto onto the Chair of Peter as Pius X was no easy business, though. The conclave was sharply divided between the partisans of Leo's relatively open-minded approach to both Church and world and those who favored a return to the intransigent rejectionism of Pius IX. The Leonine party's prime candidate was Cardinal Mariano Rampolla del Tindaro, a skillful diplomat who had been Leo's secretary of state since 1887, and who had the lead in the early balloting. But then Cardinal Jan Puzyna of Kraków (which in those days was part of the Austro-Hungarian Empire) pronounced the veto of the Emperor Franz Joseph against Rampolla, whom the Hapsburgs thought too friendly to France. Many electors were angered with this intrusion of state power into their affairs, but the Austrian veto finished Rampolla's candidacy (which in any event was sharply opposed by the cardinals opposed to the Leonine Revolution). The electors eventually settled on the Patriarch of Venice, Sarto.

The new pontiff's choice of regnal name was no accident. Pius X was a holy priest and a friendly person with some insight into the dynamics of early twentieth-century history: he predicted the European catastrophe of the First World War—*una guerrone*, a "great war"—years before it broke out. But Sarto was also a convinced anti-modern who admired Pius IX's inflexibility, resented what he thought modernity had done to simple people, their lives, and their faith, and thought that things in the Church had come a bit unstuck during Leo XIII's quarter-century tenure. At the same time, Pius X was determined to lead a great spiritual renewal in Catholicism, and it is for his initiatives toward that end that he is best remembered today.

Sarto was a practical man who set about his reformist efforts with specific goals in mind: canon law would be codified and thereby simplified; seminary education would be enhanced so that better-educated priests would become real catechists in their parishes, teaching the faith to their people; the Church's worship would be reformed, its liturgical music cleansed of operatic excess; and all the people of the Church would be encouraged to receive Holy Communion—then a rare experience for most Catholics—as frequently as possible.

To that end, Pius IX lowered the age for the reception of First Communion from twelve or fourteen to seven: the "age of reason," as it was called, when a child could understand the difference between ordinary bread and the Eucharist. It may have seemed at the time a simple change, but it dramatically transformed the religious landscape of the Church and deepened the sacramental aspects of popular Catholicism, which in the nineteenth century had been characterized by devotional piety often detached from the Eucharist. In all of this, Pius X was a forerunner of the Liturgical Movement, which would reach the apex of its influence during the pontificate of his third successor, Pius XII, and at the Second Vatican Council.

For all his reformist instincts in terms of the Church's spiritual life, however, Pius X was unwilling to bend even an inch to political modernity. He had no use for the Kingdom of Italy and did virtually nothing to ease tensions with the reigning House of Savoy. His intransigence toward France, and the clumsiness of his secretary of state, Rafaelle Merry del Val, were factors in the Third Republic's draconian 1905 anticlerical legislation, which barred Catholic religious orders and their charitable and educational works and sent the French Church into deep crisis, its bishops at cross-purposes with the pontiff who would have no truck with the secularist French Republic and its laws. And while his emphasis on spiritual, catechetical, and liturgical renewal was aimed at forming a laity that could transform society, he was deeply skeptical of, even hostile to, "Christian Democratic" movements and parties. Indeed, in another irony of this drama, this popular, and in some respects populist, pope, fondly remembered today for having brought children into the Eucharistic fellowship of the Church, was steeped in clericalism. All Catholic organizations had to be under the firm control of the Church's hierarchy, as Pius saw it. That, for him, was a matter of basic ecclesiology: "The Church is by its very nature an unequal society; it comprises two categories of persons, the pastors and the flocks. . . . The duty of the multitude is to suffer itself to be governed and to carry out in a submissive spirit the orders of those in control."

I F LEO XIII's pontificate marked a real if modest opening to intellectual and cultural modernity—one that was sometimes more a question of tone than substance but that nonetheless had real effects in the Church's intellectual life—Pius X's papacy set in motion an intellectual pogrom in world Catholicism: a crusade in defense of orthodoxy that would reverberate in the drama of Catholicism-and-modernity down to the twenty-first century. At issue was the "compendium of all heresies" that Pius condemned as "Modernism" in the 1907 decree *Lamentabili,* and in the encyclical of that same year, *Pascendi.*

Modernism was and is not easy to define. For despite Pius X's strictures and fears, Catholic Modernism was more an ensemble of intellectual tendencies than a cohesive movement. Its principal figures—the French biblical scholar Alfred Loisy, the English Jesuit theologian George Tyrrell, and the Austrian philosopher Friedrich von Hügel—disagreed with each other on numerous points. There was no coordinated Modernist campaign in intellectual journals, of the sort that both liberal and conservative ultramontanists had conducted in the previous century. Moreover, the Modernists had no monopoly on reformist Catholic thought. In fact, their principal intellectual claims were rejected by prominent Catholic thinkers interested in the renewal and reform of Catholic philosophy and theology, including John Henry Newman and the French philosopher Maurice Blondel, whose "philosophy of action" sought a new Catholic metaphysics for the modern world.

The cast of mind prevalent in the loosely affiliated Modernist camp, and that Pius X found wholly unacceptable, reflected currents of thought that were already having a profound effect

on European Protestant theology. Like their Protestant con-
freres, the Catholic Modernists believed that modern methods
of textual analysis had eviscerated the reliability of the Bible
as conveying historical truth. Like their Protestant colleagues,
the Catholic Modernists were deeply influenced by the subjectivism that Ludwig Feuerbach and Friedrich Schleiermacher
drew out of the philosophy of Immanuel Kant, a turn in-
ward in the philosophy of religion and theology that tended
to reduce religion to personal sentiment. And again like their
Protestant fellow-intellectuals, the Catholic Modernists had a
very weak sense of the supernatural, a respect bordering on
the naïvely idolatrous for the natural sciences, a tendency to
think Darwin unassailable, and, perhaps most importantly, the
Hegelian conviction that History Is All. From that historicism,
they drew the conclusion that contemporary experience stood
in judgment on divine revelation, such that the Church must
adapt itself to the spirit of the age even if doing so meant a
rupture with the past.

Catholic Modernism also showed a deep, even arrogant,
contempt for ecclesiastical authority. That, and its tendency
to think of the Church as a society of good works rather than
a sacramentally centered community called into being by the
Son of God for the conversion of the world, could not but
put on high alert someone with the character and formation
of Pius X, who brought a country pastor's skepticism about
intellectuals to the papacy.

The tragedy of the Modernists, and the tragedy that followed their condemnation by Pius X, was that their thinking
reflected—albeit in an extreme form dangerous to the integrity of Catholic faith—currents of reformist thought that had
begun to flower during the pontificate of Leo XIII. Nineteenth-
and twentieth-century Catholic thinkers like Newman, Rosmini, Möhler, Scheeben, Ketteler, and Blondel understood that
Catholic philosophy and theology were in need of development, that faith could not be reduced to a chain of syllogisms,

and that the Bible had to be read in light of what history, archaeology, and the study of ancient languages and literary forms could teach the Church. Reformist Catholic intellectuals of the nineteenth and early twentieth centuries had begun to explore religious experience as a locus of theological reflection, thereby offering the Church an enriched spiritual anthropology in which the act of faith was not simply an assent to propositions, important as the truths of the Creed are. Ketteler and Leo XIII had set the Church on the path of engagement with political and economic modernity, and the vital Catholic organizational life that had emerged after the chaos of the Napoleonic Wars augured a development of the Church's self-understanding in which the ordained and the laity worked together for the renewal of society and the conversion of culture. Had these reformist currents been appreciated by Pius X and those closest to him—and had the Thomist philosophical and theological revival sought by Leo XIII borne fruit more quickly—the reformers' ideas might have been grasped, and then proposed, as an alternative to the deconstructive tendencies of the Catholic Modernists that eventually led Loisy to abandon Christianity and Tyrrell to abandon Catholicism. But it was not to be, and the results were severe.

In addition to condemning what it took to be the intellectual program of Modernism, the encyclical *Pascendi* set up what amounted to intellectual vigilante committees to root out supposed Modernist tendencies in university and seminary faculties and to enforce the 1910 Anti-Modernist Oath enjoined by Pius X on all clerics and religious. This campaign led to the ruination of scholars' reputations by small-minded and vindictive monitors, whose espionage on the intellectual work and teaching of others was coordinated by what was known as the *Sodalitium Pianum* (Fellowship of Pius), a network of ferrets led by an Italian zealot, Monsignor Umberto Benigni, who reported purported Modernist miscreants to the Vatican authorities after receiving confidential information about their alleged heresies. Threats and bullying replaced serious intellectual debate (much less the charitable and fraternal exchange of views) as the worst excesses of ultramontanism were brought to bear on Catholic intellectual life by frightened and unscrupulous men. The net result was to put the life of the Catholic mind into something of a deep freeze, even when the anti-Modernist campaign was effectively shut down after the death of Pius X.

Pascendi saw conspiracy and a coordinated movement of doctrinal deconstruction where there were only intellectual tendencies that deserved to be challenged and corrected. Yet it is also true that the trajectory *Pascendi* foretold for Modernist thought was borne out in Pius's time—and in ours. Catholic Modernism, as embodied by Loisy and Tyrrell at least, was not compatible with either Catholic orthodoxy or Newman's criteria for the authentic development of doctrine. The brutality with which Pius X (and Benigni) handled the Modernist crisis, however, deferred serious Catholic thought about some of the major intellectual challenges posed by cultural and scientific modernity until the middle of the twentieth century. And the anti-Modernist campaign left a harvest of bitterness over lives wrecked by innuendo and ecclesiastical power politics that lingers into the Church's third millennium.

The Leonine Revolution Revived

THE GUNS OF August 1914 initiated the *guerrone* Pope Pius X feared; he died on August 20, just three weeks after the shooting began. The conclave to elect his successor thus took place in exceptionally fraught circumstances and could be held in Rome only because Italy had not yet entered the war. Something of its atmosphere can be gleaned from a

sharp exchange before the balloting, when the German cardinal Felix von Hartmann, archbishop of Cologne, met the
Belgian archbishop of Malines-Brussels, Cardinal Désiré Mercier. Hartmann said, rather haughtily, "I hope that we shall
not speak of war." To which Mercier—a leader of Leo XIII's
Thomistic revival and a former professor at the University of
Louvain, whose renowned library had been destroyed by the
invading German army on August 25—replied, "And I hope
that we shall not speak of peace."

The national divisions among the cardinals were not the defining dynamic of the conclave of 1914, however. The deeper
dividing line between the electors was defined by their attitudes toward the Leonine Revolution: some wanted the next
pope to return to the Leonine approach, while others, sympathetic to, or even enthusiastic about, Pius X's anti-Modernist
campaign, wanted a pope who would continue on the path
of intransigence. The leader of the latter camp was Pius's secretary of state, Merry del Val. The candidate of the Leonine
reformers was Giacomo Della Chiesa, archbishop of Bologna
and former chief aide to Mariano Rampolla, the reformist
cardinal vetoed by Austria-Hungary in 1903. Shortly after his
election, Pius X had abolished what was known as the *ius ex-
clusivae* (right of exclusion) and decreed excommunication for
any Catholic sovereign trying to lay down a veto in a future
conclave, so that option for blocking a reformist candidate
was off the table. But Della Chiesa had only been a cardinal
for three months.

The balloting was close and bitter, and its end game reflected that. When Cardinal Della Chiesa was announced as
the victor after the tenth ballot, it seems that he had reached
the two-thirds majority required by a single vote. Merry del
Val challenged the validity of the election, claiming that the
archbishop of Bologna might have voted for himself and demanding a reexamination of the ballots to determine whether
that was true. Della Chiesa sat in the Sistine Chapel in a frame

of mind that can only be imagined while the scrutineers, the cardinals charged with reading and counting the votes, went through every single ballot again—and determined that the archbishop of Bologna had not cast a winning, self-serving vote. The tiny Della Chiesa then retired to the Sistine Chapel's "crying room" to be vested as pope—none of the pre-prepared cassocks fit him, he was so slight—and returned to the chapel to receive the homage of the cardinals. When Merry del Val approached, and, as was then customary, knelt and kissed the new pope's foot, knee, and hand, the man who was now Benedict XV looked at him frostily and said, "The stone that the builders rejected has become the cornerstone." To which the seemingly unshaken Merry del Val replied (with the next verse from Psalm 118), "This is the Lord's doing, and marvelous in our eyes." Benedict XV was neither amused nor mollified, and Merry del Val was ejected from his Vatican apartments the next day—although he was later given a lower-ranking job at the Holy Office, the Church's doctrinal agency.

B ENEDICT XV IS the most understudied and underappreciated pope of the twentieth century. His pontificate was much briefer than anticipated (he died of pneumonia in 1922 at the age of sixty-seven), and his seven years and four months on the Chair of Peter were dominated by the First World War and its immediate aftermath. By taking the position that the pope must remain neutral in the war, not only because Catholics were engaged on both sides of the trenches, but in order to be available as a mediator, he brought down on himself the opprobrium of all the powers. Della Chiesa was an experienced and skillful diplomat and, with Merry del Val shunted off to the Holy Office, he chose as his secretary of state the equally skillful Pietro Gasparri. It is not all that difficult to imagine Benedict and Gasparri forming a team, like Pius VII and Consalvi, that would have made a useful contribution to the postwar settlement negotiated at Versailles, as had happened at the Congress of Vienna a century earlier. But at the Italian government's insistence, a secret clause in the Treaty of London that brought Italy into the war on the side of Britain, France, and Russia barred the Holy See from any postwar negotiations.

In August 1917, Benedict XV proposed a seven-point peace plan to the warring parties that was rudely dismissed by all concerned. Britain and France thought it too solicitous of Germany. The Central Powers paid some initial attention; but when the Bolshevik Revolution and the Treaty of Brest-Litovsk knocked Russia out of the war and German forces could be redeployed en masse to the Western Front, it seemed to Germany and Austria-Hungary that they might win, so why negotiate? Woodrow Wilson, a lifelong anti-Catholic bent on accelerating American involvement in what H. G. Wells had dubbed the "war to end all wars," paid no attention.

Frustrated as a mediator, Benedict XV nonetheless insisted that the Holy See take an active role in humanitarian relief, principally by providing aid to and information about prisoners of war. In doing so, he virtually bankrupted the Vatican, and at Benedict's death, Gasparri, who was camerlengo as well as secretary of state, had to borrow money from the Rothschilds to finance the conclave. (The cardinal-electors slept on beds and cots borrowed from Roman hospitals and schools.)

Benedict was critical of the Versailles peace treaty, which he thought more an act of retribution than of statesmanship, but he was mildly supportive of the new League of Nations and worked successfully to restore the Holy See's relations with various states. In 1915, Great Britain sent a diplomatic representative to the Vatican for the first time since the seventeenth century. The diplomatic breach with France that had begun under Pius X in 1905 was healed in 1921, the reconciliation having been accelerated by the Pope's highly popular canonization of Joan of Arc the year before. Benedict and Gasparri also sought concordats with the new states created by the Treaty of Versailles, and their surprising decision to send the Vatican librarian, Achille Ratti, to newly independent Poland as papal representative would have far-reaching consequences. Benedict XV did not manage to solve the Roman Question of the pope's temporal sovereignty, but he set in motion the process his successor would see through to a successful conclusion. And by affirming the work of the Popular Party, a new Italian political configuration that embodied some of the ideas and ideals of Christian Democracy, he brought Italy's Catholics back into the political life of their country, thus taking another step toward a serious Catholic engagement with political modernity.

Like several of his predecessors, Benedict XV was deeply interested in the missions. He urged the formation of a native clergy and insisted that bishops in European colonies in Africa and Asia put the interests of the colonized people they served ahead of the interests of the imperial powers where those bishops had been born. Benedict also completed the codification of canon law begun by Pius X, thus bringing a welcome degree of order into the Church's internal life. The new Pio-Benedictine Code, largely the work of Pietro Gasparri, was widely admired as a masterpiece of legal architecture and writing.

Benedict XV's most important contribution to the drama of Catholicism-and-modernity came at the very beginning of his pontificate. Two months after his election, in his inaugural encyclical, *Ad Beatissimi Apostolorum*, he called an immediate halt to the anti-Modernist campaign, urging Catholics in the contending camps within the Church to treat each other with charity and respect. The *Sodalitium Pianum* of Monsignor Benigni (who would later become a fellow-traveler of Mussolini and Italian fascism) was dismantled. And while the chilling effects of the pogrom that had afflicted the Church's intellectual life would continue to be felt, the worst of the repression stopped and the door was once more open to a Catholic engagement with cultural and intellectual modernity.

Throughout his pontificate, Benedict XV demonstrated his sympathies for the trajectory of the Leonine Revolution, confirming that the intransigents at the conclave of 1914 were quite right in their assessment of him. That it was Pius X who made it possible for all of this to happen, by giving Della Chiesa the red hat he had denied him for seven years and creating him cardinal just twelve weeks before Pius's own death, was one more irony in the fire in the drama of Catholicism-and-modernity.

THE CONCLAVE OF 1922 was another donnybrook, in part because no one expected Benedict XV to die when he did and in part because the battle over the Leonine Revolution continued within the College of Cardinals. As Rampolla had been seen as the natural successor of Leo XIII by that pope's devotees, Pietro Gasparri was seen as the natural successor to Benedict XV by many who applauded Benedict's decisive action in halting the anti-Modernist pogrom. But Gasparri could not make it past the two-thirds hurdle, and neither could the preferred candidates of the intransigents, the resilient Merry del Val and the Patriarch of Venice, Pietro La Fontaine. So on the conclave's fourth day and fourteenth ballot, a compromise was reached: the former Vatican librarian and recently created cardinal-archbishop of Milan, Achille Ratti, was elected, taking the regnal name Pius XI.

The son of a silk-weaver, Ratti was a distinguished academic whose work at the Ambrosian Library in Milan and the Vatican Library had made him an expert in medieval paleography. As a personality, however, and despite his high-myopia rimless glasses, he defied the stereotype of the donnish, mild-mannered scholar. His chief recreation was mountaineering; he had climbed several of the Alps' most challenging peaks;

and he was given on occasion to describing himself as "part mountain goat." Mystery surrounds his unexpected choice by Benedict XV as apostolic delegate to Poland, but in that post he showed more nerve and grit than veteran diplomats. When the Red Army of Leon Trotsky and Mikhail Tukhachevsky was closing in on Warsaw during the Polish-Soviet War of 1920, the ambassadors accredited to the new Polish Republic fled. But not Ratti, who stayed at his post and developed a lifelong respect for Polish Catholic heroism; later, as pope, he would have scenes from the Polish resistance to the Swedish invasion of 1655–1660 and from the 1920 Battle of Warsaw painted on the walls of the chapel at the papal summer residence, Castel Gandolfo.

He may have been a compromise candidate, but Pius XI— a name he chose in part because he said he wanted "a Pius" to settle the Roman Question, which had been created under Pius IX—immediately displayed the forcefulness with which he would govern the Church for seventeen years. After accepting election, he declared that he would give his first blessing *Urbi et Orbi* ("to the city and the world") facing Rome from the exterior central balcony of St. Peter's, which, in protest of the seizure of the Papal States, had not been done since Pius IX's election in 1848. There were objections from the intransigents; Pius XI brushed them away. It was a preview of his management style, which is perhaps best described as ultramontane papal autocracy in service to driving the Church forward.

He did not brook dissent. And when he decided to put an end to the recalcitrant anti-republicanism of French Catholics— which in the 1920s centered around the extreme reactionary and anti-Semite Charles Maurras, his Action Française movement, and its eponymous newspaper—he did not negotiate: he acted. Resisting pro–Action Française sentiment in Vatican circles, Pius engineered a critique of Maurras by the French bishops; when that did not break the movement, Pius put *Action Française* and Maurras's other writings on the Index of

Forbidden Books. In 1927, he finally excommunicated anyone involved in the movement. When the French Jesuit Cardinal Louis Billot, a major figure in the anti-Modernist campaign, sent a sympathetic letter to *Action Française* (which, naturally enough, published it), Pius called Billot on the carpet, and by the time Billot left the papal library after a pontifical tongue-lashing, he had agreed with the Pope's demand that he resign his membership in the College of Cardinals—a strong disciplinary act signaled to the world by the brief notice in the Vatican newspaper, *L'Osservatore Romano*, that Father (i.e., not Cardinal) Billot had been received in audience by the Holy Father.

That kind of decisiveness squelched whatever internal Vatican resistance there might have been to Pius XI's determination to settle the Roman Question, which was resolved by the Lateran Treaties of 1929. Vatican City State was recognized as a sovereign entity, to include the 108-acre plot around St. Peter's and the Vatican complex, as well as several noncontiguous extraterritorial properties, including hospitals, offices, universities, and Castel Gandolfo; Italy recognized Catholicism as its official religion and agreed to the teaching of the catechism in the state-run schools; and the Italian state paid the Holy See a large indemnity, chiefly in government bonds, for the properties seized during the Risorgimento. It was the deal that Pius XI's predecessors might have made, but neither Leo XIII nor Pius X would consider it, and while Benedict XV laid the groundwork for it, he did not live long enough to see it through.

The independence necessary for the pope's global mission was thus guaranteed, and the albatross of governing the Papal States was removed from the necks of Pius XI and his successors. The Lateran Treaties came at a cost, however, and the loser was the Catholic Partito Popolare Italiano (Italian Popular Party), which Mussolini, for whom it was a potential rival, wanted to see dismantled—and so it was. Papal support for the party was withdrawn, and its leader, Don Luigi Sturzo, was sent into exile in London.

Relations between the Holy See and fascist Italy quickly soured, however. Pius XI cherished Catholic youth organizations, one of whose chaplains was the young Monsignor Giovanni Battista Montini, a future pope. Fascist harassment of these groups brought the quick-tempered Pius to a boil, and the result was the 1931 encyclical *Non Abbiamo Bisogno*, a stinging rebuke to the "pagan worship of the state." The encyclical had to be smuggled out of Italy to be published abroad; the smuggler was a then obscure American working in the Vatican named Francis Spellman, who would later play a considerable role in Church affairs as archbishop of New York.

Pius XI's diplomacy got into similar trouble with the new government in Germany. Whatever his dubieties about democracy and the liberal political order, Achille Ratti detested Nazi racial theory and was under no illusions about what Hitler represented. Trying to secure the Church's position under the new Nazi regime (the character and durability of which seems to have been miscalculated by some Vatican diplomats), Pius's second secretary of state, Eugenio Pacelli, negotiated the German Concordat of 1933—and another Catholic party, the Center Party, was sacrificed as the price of a legal agreement thought to protect the Church under a totalitarian regime. Hitler, of course, had no intention of honoring the pledges of Catholic organizational independence in the Concordat. After some three dozen strongly worded diplomatic notes (drafted by Pacelli) failed to reverse the deterioration of the Church's position, Pius XI, on meeting the German cardinals in Rome in 1937, asked the archbishop of Munich and Freising, the anti-Nazi Michael von Faulhaber, to draft an encyclical. *Mit Brennender Sorge (With Burning Anxiety)* was then printed surreptitiously in Germany and read from all German pulpits. Pius's denunciation of an "idolatrous cult" that replaced belief in God with a "national religion" and a "myth of race and blood," and his insistence on the perennial value of the Old Testament, made it unmistakably clear what he thought of the swastika and what it represented.

Similar papal critiques were directed at regimes of the totalitarian left, including the anti-communist encyclical *Divini Redemptoris* (issued just five days after *Mit Brennender Sorge*). There, Pius XI blasted the persecution of the Church in the Soviet Union, republican Spain, and Mexico, which had been of concern to him throughout the 1930s. In 1938, Pius was preparing an encyclical on the unity of the human race—another critique of racial ideology—with the assistance of an American Jesuit, John LaFarge, a pioneer of interracial pastoral work in the United States. But despite pleas to his doctors to keep him alive long enough to deliver it to the annual meeting of the Italian bishops, the Pope died in February 1939, before it could be issued.

I T WAS IN this context—the rise of totalitarian power as one expression of political modernity—that Pius XI made his most original and enduring contribution to Catholic social doctrine. Mussolini's definition of the totalitarian project ("Everything within the state, nothing outside the state, nothing against the state") was not only idolatry, in Pius's view, but a prescription for a tyranny in which there would be no place for the "voluntary civil associations" Leo XIII had cherished. Thus, in *Quadragesimo Anno*, an encyclical he issued in 1931 for the fortieth anniversary of Leo's *Rerum Novarum*, Pius XI (with an intellectual assist from the German Jesuit Oswald von Nell-Breuning) cemented a third principle into the foundations of modern Catholic social doctrine, building on the personalist and common good principles Leo had defined. This was the principle of "subsidiarity," and on it the Catholic defense of civil society against the encroachments of the modern state in all its forms was built.

According to the subsidiarity principle, decision-making in society should be left at the lowest possible level commensurate with the common good (i.e., the level closest to those directly affected by the decision). American federalism, with its division of federal, state, and local authority, is a good example of subsidiarity at work: the federal government does not run the local fire department; the local police are not responsible for national security; the states run the highways, which the federal government helps fund. In Pius XI's conception, there is far more to the modern political community than the individual and the state: there are intermediate or mediating institutions, both nongovernmental and governmental, and it is the responsibility of the highest authority, the national authority, to respect the prerogatives of and provide help (*subsidium*) to the "lower authorities." Subsidiarity gave an anti-totalitarian, even anti-statist, inoculation to Catholic social doctrine and thought, by warning against the tendency of all modern states to extend the reach of their power while lifting up the moral and political importance of what Edmund Burke had defended as society's "small platoons."

If articulating the subsidiarity principle was Pius XI's chief contribution to a Catholic exploration of political modernity at the level of social and political theory, his creation of the Feast of Christ the King in the Church's liturgical calendar was a parallel effort in the sphere of the spiritual life. As the shadows of the totalitarian project began to lengthen across Europe, Pius wanted to remind the Church that all Christian thought about politics and public authority begins, in a sense, with Christ's injunction in Matthew 22.21 to "render to Caesar the things that are Caesar's and to God the things that are God's"—a powerful reminder that if God is God, Caesar (in whatever guise he appears) is not God. The 1925 encyclical that lifted up the image of Christ the King and fixed the new feast in the Church's liturgical calendar, *Quas Primas*, was cast as a critique of "the plague of secularism." In the drama of Catholicism-and-modernity, however, "Christ the King" was the liturgical and spiritual complement to the subsidiarity principle and its defense of civil society against the overreaching King Caesar.

P IUS XI ALSO advanced the Catholic exploration of modernity by his vigorous missionary policy, which pointed toward a world beyond colonialism and a Church detached from the old regimes. Against the kind of internal Curial opposition that he brushed aside (quietly, or, more typically, sharply), he personally consecrated the first six indigenous Chinese bishops in St. Peter's in 1926, and in 1927 did the same for the first Japanese-born bishop of Nagasaki, the historical center of Catholicism in the Land of the Rising Sun. Later, he would consecrate native bishops for India and Southeast Asia. There were no native bishops governing missionary dioceses when Ratti was elected pope in 1922; at his death there were forty, and because of his insistence on the training of a native clergy, the number of native-born priests in the parts of the Church overseen by the Vatican's mission department, Propaganda Fide, tripled during his pontificate to more than seven thousand. This would not have happened without the impetus provided by his 1926 encyclical on the missions, *Rerum Ecclesiae*; his insistence that all religious orders send priests, brothers, and sisters to mission work; his creation of mission studies departments in pontifical universities; and his determination to fight the old-guard approach to missions inside the Roman Curia, which was more than tinged with colonial paternalism. Pius's mission policy was thus an ironic example of ultramontanism and papal authoritarianism at the service of the modernization and internationalization of the Church.

Pius was not an easy personality, and his legendary irascibility was likely a factor in there never being a beatification cause bruited after his death on February 10, 1939. Yet his battle with totalitarianism won him the respect of the West and set some of the foundations for the Catholic human rights revolution that would come to full flower under the Polish pope whose earliest papal memories were of Pius XI. At a moment in history when Jew-hatred was rising—always a barometer of lethal political sickness—Pius embraced Christianity's Jewish roots and declared that "spiritually, we are all Semites." He exhausted himself in his final struggle against fascism and Nazism, which won him a reputation among traditional anticlericals as a defender of freedom. In that sense he died a heroic death, fighting to the end—and vindicating the Leonine Revolution, whose cause, on balance, he advanced considerably, both theoretically and in the pastoral and public life of the Church.

The Hinge

THE PONTIFICATE OF Pope Pius XII, Pius XI's successor, has become so inextricably enmeshed with the debate over his role during the Second World War that it can be easy to forget that, in the sixteen documents of the Second Vatican Council, the second-most-cited source after the Bible is his teaching. In that important respect, the man who was first falsely charged with Nazi sympathies by communist propagandists as the Red Army moved into East-Central Europe in 1944–1945 was the papal hinge between the second and third acts of this drama: between a Catholicism exploring modernity gingerly and a Catholicism embracing modernity. It is quite unlikely—perhaps even certain—that Pius XII ever imagined himself in that role. But that is simply another irony in a drama replete with ironies in the fire.

N O ONE IS born to be pope, but if anyone were, it would be Eugenio Maria Giuseppe Giovanni Pacelli, a Roman of the Romans, who entered the world on March 2, 1876, a younger son in a family of lawyers distinguished by its service to the Holy See. Unusually for someone of his background, he attended a state-run high school before studying at several pontifical universities and earning three doctoral degrees. Ordained at twenty-three, this gifted linguist and brilliant ascetic began working in the Vatican in 1901 and spent twelve years at the side of Pietro Gasparri in the great project of codifying canon law; he also taught courses on international law at the Vatican's training school for papal diplomats, then known as the Pontifical Academy of Noble Ecclesiastics.

Consecrated bishop in 1917, Pacelli, who would develop a deep respect for German culture and was fluent in the language, was sent to Munich as nuncio to Bavaria, and his remit was extended to the entire Weimar Republic in 1920. After twelve years in Germany, during which he faced down communist thugs during the political chaos that followed the dissolution of the Hohenzollern monarchy, Pacelli was recalled to Rome, where he was created cardinal in 1929 and succeeded his mentor, Gasparri, as secretary of state in 1930—a position he held until Pius XI's death in February 1939. Pius became another mentor and patron and sent Cardinal Pacelli on numerous missions around the world, cueing him up as *papabile*. On one of these international forays, he was hosted to lunch at Hyde Park by President Franklin D. Roosevelt on the day after FDR's 1936 reelection (the historical record does not reveal whether, like King George VI, Cardinal Pacelli was served presidential hot dogs).

With another *guerrone* on the horizon, the cardinal-electors at the conclave of 1939 wasted little time in settling on the Church's most accomplished diplomat, Eugenio Pacelli, as the next pope, and the secretary of state was duly elected on the third ballot. His apprenticeship under Gasparri clearly

marked him as a man in the Leo XIII–Benedict XV line of reformers, and Pius XII's first decade as pope was, in the main,
an expression of that heritage. In that period, he made three
signal contributions that would accelerate the Church's thinking about its life and mission and bear fruit at the Second
Vatican Council.

The first was the June 1943 encyclical, *Mystici Corporis
Christi* (*The Mystical Body of Christ*), whose very title signaled a development beyond the notion of the Church as,
above all, a "perfect society." Drawing on themes from Johann
Adam Möhler and others, Pius XII re-centered Catholic thinking about the Church on Christ himself, describing Catholicism as Christ's living body in the world. Grace, he taught,
is not simply something that happens within the Church, for
the Church's own sake; the Holy Spirit, promised by Christ to
the first disciples, empowers the Church for its mission in the
world, which is a mission of conversion. Each of the members
of the Mystical Body has a distinctive role, and all of those
roles, not just the roles played by the clergy, serve to build up
the Body and accomplish its mission.

Three months later, in the encyclical *Divino Afflante Spiritu*
(*By the Spirit's Divine Inspiration*), Pius XII pushed Catholic biblical studies into more extensive contact with modern
critical methods of exegesis, extending the approach taken by
Leo XIII in *Providentissimus Deus* on that encyclical's fiftieth
anniversary. He underscored the importance of doing exeget-
ical work on biblical texts in their original languages rather
than simply working from the Latin Vulgate; he urged biblical
commentators to help the Church grasp the text's literal sense
as the author intended the text to be understood; and he endorsed the use of "form criticism," the study of the patterns
in which the biblical authors wrote, in Catholic exegesis—a
marked advance beyond the boundaries formerly set by Leo
XIII and Pius X. The encyclical's embrace of modern exegeti-
cal methods, and its concluding admonition to charity on the

part of all those involved in biblical studies (an echo of Benedict XV's inaugural encyclical, *Ad Beatissimi Apostolorum*, and the dismantling of the *Sodalitium Pianum*), likely reflected the views of Pius's confessor and confidant, the Jesuit biblical scholar Augustin Bea, who was rector of the Pontifical Biblical Institute; Bea later became a link between the pontificate of Pius XII and Vatican II, in which he would play a major role as head of the Secretariat for Christian Unity.

The third of Pius XII's great encyclicals, *Mediator Dei* (*The Mediator Between God and Man*), was issued in November 1947 and gave an important papal endorsement to the Liturgical Movement, which had gained momentum in the 1920s and 1930s in Europe—and in American circles influenced by St. John's Abbey in Collegeville, Minnesota, where, under the leadership of Father Virgil Michel, OSB, liturgical renewal was linked to the promotion of Catholic social doctrine. While cautioning against extremes of liturgical innovation, Pius endorsed active lay participation at Mass, for laypeople offer themselves to God in union with Christ when the Eucharist is celebrated in community. *Mediator Dei* also urged lay Catholics to pray the Divine Office, the breviary, which had hitherto been regarded as the virtually exclusive preserve of priests and consecrated religious. Over against conceptions of the Church's liturgical life that begin and end with issues of obligation, *Mediator Dei* described the liturgy as the vital center of Catholic life and mission and called all Catholics to make the rhythms of the Church's worship and liturgical year the pattern of their lives and religious practices. A few years after issuing the encyclical, Pius XII gave it practical effect by relaxing the rules for Eucharistic fasting, authorizing the celebration of Mass in the evening, reforming the celebrations of Holy Week, and reestablishing the ancient Easter Vigil, the apex of the Church's liturgical life for centuries, which had fallen into desuetude.

These three encyclicals were reformist, not radical, and each was hedged with cautions about this, that, or the other extremist tendency. But taken together, they represented a real liberation of Catholic thought and practice after the constraints felt in the aftermath of the Modernist crisis. And while Pius XII would himself give the reins a hard jerk in the 1950 encyclical *Humani Generis* (*On Human Origin*), which sharply criticized certain tendencies in contemporary theology, resulting in the withdrawal from public debate of several theologians who would later shape the thinking of Vatican II, his pontificate, as a whole, accelerated the Catholic exploration of cultural and intellectual modernity.

THAT PIUS XII wrote no social encyclical is somewhat surprising given that 1941 was the fiftieth anniversary of *Rerum Novarum*. Nonetheless, he significantly advanced the Church's engagement with the modern democratic project, most prominently in his 1944 *Christmas Message*. World War II was drawing to a close, and the Pope evidently wanted to influence the discussions already underway about the structure of the postwar international order, calling for a "new era of far-reaching renovation" involving the "complete reorganization of the world."

During the last twelve years of his pontificate, Pius XII was a strong and vocal advocate of European integration and the emerging transnational structures of European unification—when the Treaty of Rome was signed in 1957, a year before his death, he received the heads of state or government of the six signatory nations creating the European Common Market, the foundation on which the future European Union would be built. In 1944, however, his primary concern was to identify the moral and cultural prerequisites for flourishing democracies, for, as he put it in his *Christmas Message*, the peoples of the world yearned for "a system of government more in keeping with the dignity and liberty of the citizens." And to his mind, that yearning would be best satisfied in the future by democracies, be they constitutional monarchies or republics.

The Church was not in the business of designing govern-ments, he said, and, quoting Leo XIII in *Libertas*, he reiterated that "the Church does not disapprove of any of the forms of government, provided they are per se capable of serving the good of the citizens." That ruled out tyrannies, because tyr-annies do not have citizens, but subjects. Yet democracies, the Pope insisted, were not simply electoral machines that could run by themselves, toting up majority sentiment and then ac-tualizing that sentiment through public policy. For a democ-racy to flourish, virtuous leadership was imperative, and so was the citizenry's clear understanding that freedom did not mean license. The "equality" that was promoted by political modernity, and that was a fundamental principle of any dem-ocratic polity, had to be an equality of responsibility. And that responsibility could only be lived by citizens who were both inwardly governed by the moral law and free from arbitrary or absolute state power.

Pius XII's social doctrine thus embraced the notion of Christian Democracy theoretically, and Vatican diplomacy embraced Christian Democracy practically. The crucial mo-ment was Italy's 1948 general election, in which the Vatican put the full weight of its then considerable local authority be-hind the Christian Democratic Party as the best alternative to what seemed a real possibility—the victory of the Italian Communist Party as the hub of a coalition of the left. In the event, the Christian Democrats (financed in part by clandes-tine funds provided by the Truman administration and the U.S. government) won 48 percent of the vote under the leadership of Alcide De Gasperi.

De Gasperi had been a founder of the Partito Popolare Ital-iano with Luigi Sturzo and was one of Italy's leading theore-ticians of Christian Democracy. An anti-fascist, he had been domiciled in Vatican City and given a cataloguer's job in the Vatican Library between 1929 and 1943 to protect him from Mussolini. During the war years, he helped organize a new

Christian Democratic party, of which he was the leading figure. In addition to serving as Italian prime minister from 1945
to 1953, De Gasperi was also one of the founding fathers of
European integration, along with the French Catholic foreign minister Robert Schuman and the Catholic chancellor of
the newly constituted Federal Republic of Germany, Konrad
Adenauer.

PRIOR TO THE illnesses that plagued him in the last five
years of his life, Pius XII was an active public figure, speaking on virtually every topic imaginable to various associations
and organizations; his 1951 address to a congress of midwives
remains one of the touchstones of twenty-first-century Catholic medical and sexual ethics. He met vast crowds of pilgrims,
including the millions who came to Rome for the Holy Year
of 1950, and defined as dogma the Assumption of the Blessed
Virgin Mary—itself a step into the future, as it would come to
be understood as the Church's formal acknowledgment that a
layperson and a woman was the first beneficiary of the fruits
of the redemption won by Christ. Slender, almost ethereal, and
looking like someone who had just stepped out of an El Greco,
Pius XII, the first pope of the television age, seemed to most
Catholics of his era the quintessence of what a pope should be.

The controversy over his role in World War II has focused,
at least among reasonable people, on the soundness of his pru-
dential judgment that a vocal condemnation of the Holocaust
would have made matters worse for both Jews and Catholics
under Nazi rule. And on that, there is surely room for honest
debate. No serious student of this period thinks Eugenio Pacelli
was an anti-Semite or a Nazi sympathizer. His role as middle-
man in various plots to assassinate Hitler (none of which got
very far) has been documented, as have his orders to Catholic
institutions in Rome to hide Roman Jews about to be trans-
ported to extermination camps—an act that saved thousands

of lives. Jewish families were hidden at the papal summer villa at Castel Gandolfo, and Jewish babies (often named Eugenio or Eugenia) were born in Pius XII's bedroom. The pope whose older brother had helped draft the Lateran Treaties believed himself legally bound to a scrupulous political neutrality in the war. But that did not bind him to moral neutrality, and his was understood, at least in his own time (and by both Jewish organizations and the *New York Times*), as a voice of protest against Nazi genocide.

Pius XII's postwar international involvements centered on what he regarded as an apocalyptic battle against communism. His 1949 excommunication of all Catholics involved in or supporting communist parties was a blunt instrument, however. And like Pius V's excommunication of Queen Elizabeth I in 1570, it gave the Church's enemies a tool with which to charge Catholics with the crime of treason, simply for who they were. After the death of Cardinal Luigi Maglione in 1944, Pius acted as his own secretary of state, guiding Vatican diplomacy through the worst years of the Stalinist repression of the Church in East-Central Europe. He and his associates were originally skeptical of the approach taken immediately after the war by the primate of Poland, Stefan Wyszyński, who tried to find a modus vivendi with the Polish communist regime so that the Church could rebuild its strength after the devastation of World War II. But when the tough-minded Polish archbishop of Gniezno and Warsaw drew the line of firm resistance in 1953 and spent three years under house arrest as a result, he had Pius XII's full support. And over time, as the Church became the chief opponent of the regime and the safe deposit box of Polish identity, Wyszyński's conviction that he was a better judge of his situation than the Pope and his diplomats was fully vindicated. When Soviet tanks crushed the Hungarian Revolution in 1956, Pius XII protested with three encyclicals issued over the course of a week and a half. He could do nothing for the Hungarians, of course, any more than he could do something for the Greek Catholic Church in Ukraine, which was legally liquidated by the Soviet Union in 1946. But his constant, vocal support of the local churches behind the Iron Curtain was of immense psychological and spiritual importance in keeping Catholicism alive, vital, and resistant for decades, under the most difficult circumstances.

THE LAST YEARS of Pius XII were not happy ones. Beset by ill health and incompetent physicians, and surrounded by an increasingly febrile atmosphere within the walls of the Apostolic Palace, he seemed less the creative personality he was at his election and had proven to be for the first decade or so of his pontificate. In 1954, palace intrigue led him to exile his longtime right-hand man, Giovanni Battista Montini, to Milan as archbishop, but without the cardinalate that traditionally went with appointment to Italy's most prestigious diocese. Montini had been Pius's link to Catholic reformist movements, ecclesiastical and political, and support for those causes may have eventually brought him into disfavor; in any case, his departure removed a moderating voice from the Pope's immediate surround. Pius XII died at Castel Gandolfo on October 9, 1958, and was promptly betrayed by an unscrupulous physician who took photos of his death agonies and sold them to the press. His botched embalming led to embarrassing episodes before his funeral and became a sad metaphor for an era that had come to seem stagnant and ossified.

Viewed from the distance of the early twenty-first century, and judging him through the prism of the drama of Catholicism-and-modernity, it is Pius XII's first decade on the Chair of Peter that had the most enduring consequence. *Mystici Corporis*, *Divino Afflante Spiritu*, *Mediator Dei*, and the 1944 *Christmas Message* signaled that there would be no turning back to the anti-modern rejectionism of Pius X (who was nonetheless canonized in 1954, becoming the first pope to be declared a saint since Pius V in 1712). Moreover, during the pontificate of Pius XII, and despite the tremors sent through Catholic intellectual life by *Humani Generis*, the theological forces that would lead the Church into the third act of the drama of Catholicism-and-modernity achieved critical mass.

The second act was over, and the curtain had been drawn by Eugenio Pacelli.

Theological Renaissance

Unshackled

NOTWITHSTANDING THE INTELLECTUAL chill created by Pius X's 1907 anti-Modernist encyclical *Pascendi*—which was replicated in less arctic form in the years immediately following Pius XII's 1950 encyclical *Humani Generis*—the first six decades of the twentieth century were a period of great creativity in Catholic theology. During those years, themes that would become prominent in the third, fourth, and fifth acts of the drama of Catholicism-and-modernity were first articulated and then contested, before finally being worked into the texture of Catholic life and practice through an ecumenical council, the debate over its reception, and the authoritative interpretation given that council by Popes John Paul II and Benedict XVI. In this theological renaissance, one of whose roots was *Aeterni Patris*, the Leonine Revolution came to its first full flowering in Catholic intellectual life.

It might even be argued, admittedly in retrospect, that the anti-Modernist strictures that shadowed imaginative theological work from 1907 until 1962 played an important role in this creative process. For whatever the exaggerated fears that influenced Pius X, the package of tendencies known as "Modernism" did threaten to detach theology from reason. Thus the anti-Modernist polemics of the early twentieth century served to defend the prerogatives of reason and to underscore the Catholic Church's commitment to a theology that did not decay into subjectivism or emotivism, losing its tether to Scripture and tradition as so much of liberal Protestantism did. The men whose work shaped the twentieth-century renaissance of Catholic theology were all convinced that theology is a science: even if its subject matter and methods were distinctive, theology is an exercise in reason and a pathway to truth. And they were committed to a theology that reclaimed the biblical witness for Catholic thought and practice even as it explored the dynamism and development of the Church's tradition.

Were this theological renaissance to be summed up in one claim—if there is one thread that links the vast majority of the theologians whose work will be sketched briefly here—it is the conviction that, in order to be of service to the Church under the conditions of modernity, theology had to break free of the tendency in influential Catholic circles to reduce the discipline to a subset of logic. Rigorous thinking was crucial in theology; but theology could not be reduced to syllogisms. There was far more to theology than that.

The French term *ressourcement*—a "return to the sources"—was adopted by one school of reformist Catholic theology to describe its program, but it can also be used to describe twentieth-century theological renewal as a whole. The "sources" that theology was to reclaim included the Bible, the writings of the Fathers of the Church in the middle of the first millennium, and the full array of medieval thinkers who worked in the same milieu as Thomas Aquinas, such as Bonaventure and Duns Scotus. The *ressourcement* theologians also put theology into conversation with literature and modern philosophy (especially that of Maurice Blondel). This, and the attempt to wrestle with the profound influence of Immanuel Kant on Western thought, expanded the philosophical bandwidth of Catholic theology's reflection while seeking to make sense of Catholic faith in a culture becoming skeptical of the human capacity to grasp the truth of anything with conviction.

Two German theologians and a French philosopher were precursors to *ressourcement* theology in its broadest sense.

Karl Adam (1875–1966) picked up themes from Johann Adam Möhler and Matthias Scheeben while retrieving the theology of the Church and the sacraments that was central to the reflection of the Church Fathers. Adam's two principal works, *Christ Our Brother* and *The Spirit of Catholicism*, written during his professorship at Tübingen, were basic texts in what came to be known as "kerygmatic theology," which stressed the reality of the Church as a community of believers sacramentally united in Christ—a challenge to the then dominant, juridical image of the Church as a "perfect society." In the latter book, Adam proposed an understanding of the disenchantment of intellectual modernity that would be shared, in various degrees, by most reformist theologians:

> The individualism of the Renaissance, the dismemberment of man and his relations in the age of Enlightenment, and finally the subjective idealism of Kant, whereby our minds were taught to relinquish the objective thing, the trans-subjective reality, and to indulge in boundless subjectivism: these influences tore us from the moorings of our being. . . . We became imprisoned within the walls of our own selves. . . . The category "humanity" became foreign to our thought, and we thought and lived only in the category of self.

Romano Guardini (1885–1968) was a humanistic genius with a keen insight into modernity and its discontents and a parallel conviction that the Church must engage the modern world in order to convert it. He also forged a link between the world of creative theology and the Liturgical Movement; his 1918 book, *The Spirit of the Liturgy*, was influential in its time and remains so a century later. A sharp critic of the dry, syllogistic theology he found hard to digest during his seminary studies, his theological reflection often took place in response to poets, novelists, and unconventional philosophers, including Dante, Dostoevsky, Hölderlin, Pascal, and Rilke. In writings from the mid-1950s, when he held the Chair of Catholic Thought at the University of Munich, Guardini brilliantly analyzed what he called the "interior disloyalty" of the times: modernity's denial of the truths built into the human condition for the sake of a radical subjectivism arrogantly certain that it could build a utopia in history. The task of the Church was to offer Christ, the Son of God who reveals the full truth of our humanity, as the alternative to the twentieth-century Prometheanism that, Guardini believed, had shown its lethal face in German National Socialism and communism.

Karl Adam and Romano Guardini are not forgotten in twenty-first-century Catholicism, but **Maurice Blondel** (1861–1949) is rarely referenced—although he may have been the most influential of the thinkers who made the renaissance of twentieth-century Catholic theology possible. As a philosopher and a devout Catholic, his passion was to make the supernatural credible in a disenchanted world, and he did so in a highly original way that, at first, drew the critical attention of the anti-Modernist forces in the Vatican. But despite the suspicion in which his work was held throughout his life—both *Pascendi* and *Humani Generis* were thought by some to have cast a shadow over Blondel's thought—his steady development of a philosophy of "action" that displayed the human openness to transcendence, and thus to the world of the supernatural, had a profound impact on the renewal of Catholic thought.

Both Blondel's philosophical studies and his own intense spiritual life convinced him that modernity was not going to be persuaded, much less converted, by the syllogistically driven theology that had become a quasi-official Catholic way of thinking in the wake of the Modernist crisis—especially when that way of doing theology was allied with reactionary political forces like Action Française. Thus, in addition to his intellectual efforts to heal the fracture between faith and reason, and to show how the deepest aspirations of humanity, properly understood, display an openness to divine revelation, Blondel also worked with those who were trying to develop a Christian way of social action that met the needs of the twentieth-century human condition— and that was not bent on restoring an *ancien régime* that was beyond reclamation. The two projects, Blondel believed, were interconnected. A Catholicism reliant on proof texts and assertions of ecclesiastical authority to make its proposals could only produce an authoritarian, coercive political community. By contrast, a Catholicism that could show, both intellectually and in the quality of its service to society, how God's revelation in Christ spoke to the liberty and fraternity to which political modernity aspired was a Catholicism capable of converting the world—and offering an alternative, in the political sphere, to both fantasies of royalist restoration and secular anticlericalist regimes like the French Third Republic.

Blondel was a patient man who combined urbanity and charity, and who did not fall prey to bitterness when the highest authorities in the Church seemed to censure his work. He was also persistent, and his persistence would be vindicated in an ecumenical council.

Renewal in Several Keys

THREE THEOLOGIANS, TWO French Dominicans and a French Jesuit, formed the core of the *ressourcement* movement, strictly defined.

Marie-Dominique Chenu, OP (1895–1990), argued that Thomas Aquinas had been decontextualized and ossified, and that to grasp the penetrating thought of Leo XIII's favorite thinker meant relocating Thomas's teaching in the mystery of Christ, present in the Eucharist and in contemplative prayer. Those were Christian realities that Thomas took for granted, given his theological and cultural milieu. But the sacramental and spiritual foundations of Thomas's thought had become detached from his work as it was systematized after his death by generations of commentators. Rediscovering the Christological, sacramental, and contemplative roots of Thomism would, Chenu proposed, breathe new life into truths that had been reduced to conclusions at the end of a syllogism.

Chenu's Dominican confrere, **Yves Congar**, was a pioneer in several fields of twentieth-century theology. In *True and False Reform in the Church*, he adopted a strategy first deployed by John Henry Newman in discussing the development of doctrine. Whereas Newman proposed seven "notes," or characteristics, of a genuine development of doctrine (in contrast to a heresy), Congar's reading of the history of theology and ecclesiastical renewal suggested that authentic reform displayed four characteristics: charity, unity, patience, and a return to the sources. True reform was always re-*form*: a reclaiming of some facet of the Church's constituting "form," given it by Christ, that had gotten lost or forgotten. By these criteria, Congar asserted, Modernism was indeed a heresy, but so was the extreme ultramontanist reaction to Modernism, which had become known in French as *intégrisme*, or integrism. Congar (a decorated veteran of World War I) also produced groundbreaking works on ecumenism and the role of the laity in the Church and wrote a massive study of the Holy Spirit that restored the Third Person of the Trinity to a prominent place in Western Catholic theology.

If any one of the creative Catholic minds of the mid-twentieth century embodied the quintessence of the *ressource-*

ment project, it was the Jesuit **Henri de Lubac** (1896–1991). De Lubac put the "return to the sources"—the Bible, the Fathers, and the full range of medieval thinkers—into conversation with the philosophy of action of Maurice Blondel to paint a portrait of human nature, redeemed by Christ, as a nature that always seeks the beatific vision of God. Here, he thought, was the Catholic answer to the false anthropologies embodied in what he dubbed "atheistic humanism" (the post-Enlightenment philosophies in which the God of the Bible was the enemy of human maturation and liberation). Here was the answer to the mid-twentieth-century totalitarianisms that were wreaking human havoc in Europe (and which de Lubac challenged at risk of his life in his underground work with the French resistance during World War II). And here, too, was a compelling counterproposal to those forms of Catholic theology that sometimes seemed to mimic Calvinist views of human nature as totally depraved.

More than one prominent Catholic intellectual considered de Lubac's first great work, *Catholicism: Christ and the Common Destiny of Man* (in the 1938 original, *Catholicisme: Les Aspects sociaux du dogme*), the most important book of Catholic theology in the entire twentieth century, for its restoration of the balance between personal faith and ecclesial experience, the demands of individual freedom and the demands of the common good. Then, in *Surnaturel: Études historique* (*The Mystery of the Supernatural*, in the English translation), de Lubac analyzed the human person as the creature who seeks God with an "absolute desire"—and thereby launched a theological civil war that was one factor in Pius XII's writing of *Humani Generis*. De Lubac also did original work on the history of biblical exegesis and the sources of revelation; the latter helped pave the way for a creative Catholic resolution of the Reformation-era argument about the relationship of Scripture and tradition in conveying divine truth to humanity. De Lubac's theology of the Church reached back to Origen and Cyprian in the patristic era to emphasize *mater ecclesia*—the Church as mother—in another development beyond the notion of Church as *societas perfecta*. Yet in one more irony, Henri de Lubac would be both a crucial figure in the third act of our drama—the embrace of modernity by Catholicism—and a pivotal thinker in moving the Church beyond Act Three to Acts Four and Five.

THE LEONINE REVOLUTION's promotion of Thomas Aquinas came to its fullest flower in the mid-twentieth century as a variety of Thomistic tendencies and schools made their contributions to the renaissance of Catholic theology.

The "strict observance" Thomism associated with **Reginald Garrigou-Lagrange, OP** (1877–1964), a powerful figure in Rome during the Pius XII years, held firmly to the conviction that both the deductive theological method it used and the vocabulary it employed could not be changed without threatening the truths of Catholic faith. This was the propositional approach to theology that Guardini and the *ressourcement* theologians found objectionable—and incapable of enlivening a Church committed to the conversion of the world. Garrigou seemed to have won the first round of this debate when *Humani Generis* (which he likely helped draft) was issued; Chenu, Congar, and de Lubac disappeared from public debate for several years. But the "sacred monster of Thomism," as he was dubbed, was no mere logician. He did original work on mysticism and the theology of the priesthood, and that work would shape the thinking of a young Polish priest who studied in Rome during the immediate post–World War II years—a priest who would become a major figure in the fourth and fifth acts of the drama of Catholicism-and-modernity.

"Transcendental Thomism" was that branch on the Thomistic tree that sought to "read" Thomas through the philosophy of Immanuel Kant, thus arriving at a new Thomistic synthesis for the modern world. While its origins lay in the philosophical work of a Belgian Jesuit, **Joseph Maréchal** (1878–1944), its most prominent figure was **Karl Rahner, SJ** (1904–1984). Rahner stressed that divine revelation was first and foremost God's self-revelation to humanity: God revealed himself, not just information or propositions about himself. Humanity could "hear" this revelation, Rahner contended, because there was an instinct for the divine, a "supernatural existential," built into us, such that every human being is, in principle at least, an "anonymous Christian." The Incarnation of Jesus Christ, Rahner taught, was the point at which God's self-revelation and man's receptivity to that revelation met "absolutely."

The "Neo-Thomism" of two French laymen, the philosophers **Jacques Maritain** (1882–1973) and **Étienne Gilson** (1884–1978), did not begin from the philosophical premise that drove the transcendental Thomists: the conviction that Kant's critique of metaphysics was an insuperable obstacle that had to be acknowledged in any truly modern Catholic thought. Rather, the French Neo-Thomists sought the renewal of Thomism from within Aquinas's own philosophy, unfiltered by commentators. Maritain presented Thomism as an "existential realism" distinguished from the nihilistic existentialism of Jean-Paul Sartre by its firm tether to the truths embedded in the world and in human nature. Against the individualism of the Enlightenment and the modern tendency to reduce the essence of humanity to self-assertion, Maritain proposed a philosophical anthropology of personalism that displayed the individual in his or her full material and spiritual dimensions, which include reason and will, our yearning for transcendence and our capacity for relationships. Under the impact of the Second World War, Maritain also helped reshape Catholic thinking about political modernity, especially in terms of human rights and democracy.

Gilson, for his part, made original contributions to the history of philosophy and, like Maritain, sought to reconnect philosophy and theology in a dynamic synthesis. Perhaps the crucial insight in Gilson's work is that the God who reveals himself to Moses as "I am Who am" is Thomas's *ipsum esse subsistens*: Being itself. God is not, in other words, one super-being among other beings; God is sheer Being. God is "to be" absolutely, and that makes all other being (and beings) possible. God is not, as de Lubac's "atheistic humanists" would have it, in competition with the world; God in his very "to be" is what makes the world, and us, possible.

S WISS THEOLOGIAN HANS Urs von Balthasar (1905–1988), a singular figure in his intellectual dexterity, was allied to the *ressourcement* theologians in their determination to renew Catholic thought, although his own theological project is not easily categorized. Like Guardini, he sought a theology in touch with multiple literary interlocutors and wrote important studies of Dante, Gerard Manley Hopkins, Vladimir Soloviev, and Charles Péguy as theological "sources." Like de Lubac, he plumbed the Fathers and Bonaventure for theological insights pertinent to modern humanity. Amidst modernity's disenchantment, Balthasar insisted that Christians, still caught up in the "wonder of being," are the people who can take the "mystery of being"—why there is something rather than nothing—seriously. Perhaps most insightfully, Balthasar, who understood how and why modernity had gotten itself detached from the transcendentals of truth and goodness, proposed that reflection on the third transcendental—beauty—might offer a post-Kantian, post-Nietzschean, post-Freudian culture a way back into contact with truth and goodness, beyond the subjectivism of "your truth and my truth" and the solipsism of "I did it my way." This led to Balthasar's six-volume study, *The Glory of the Lord*, a massive propaedeutic to theology that would have a profound effect on Catholic thought for decades. Balthasar also reintroduced to the center of Catholic ecclesiology the notion that Christ's relationship to the Church is spousal or nuptial. And his Marian theology was both distinctive and influential: Balthasar stressed Mary as the model or "form" of all Christian discipleship, proposing that this Marian "profile" was what allowed all the other aspects of the Church to make sense. Authority in the Church (modeled on St. Peter), evangelization (modeled on St. Paul), and contemplation (modeled on St. John) all exist to foster discipleship, which is first and foremost modeled in Mary—Balthasarian themes that would be papally proposed to a startled Roman Curia in 1987.

Personalism and Political Theory

THEN THERE WERE the **Catholic Personalists,** under which rubric could be included not only important Thomists like Jacques Maritain and Étienne Gilson but also a diverse and contentious cast of characters such as the German philosophers **Dietrich von Hildebrand** (1889–1977) and **Max Scheler** (1874–1928), and the French philosopher and political activist **Emmanuel Mounier** (1905–1950).

Von Hildebrand and Scheler were among the first disciples of Edmund Husserl, founding father of phenomenology—a philosophical method aimed at rescuing the discipline from subjectivism and getting thinking reconnected to the truth of things. Scheler would later influence the philosophical work of Karol Wojtyła, and while the young Polish scholar ultimately judged that Scheler's phenomenology did not reestablish a secure philosophical basis for ethics, Scheler's analytic method would shape several papal encyclicals—which would undoubtedly have been to his great surprise.

Unlike several other major figures in the twentieth-century renaissance of Catholic philosophy and theology, von Hildebrand was never seduced by the anti-pluralistic allure of fascism and German national socialism; indeed, he was a fierce anti-Nazi who eventually fled to the United States. Mounier was a charismatic proponent of the claim that Christian personalism, and its emphasis on the inherent dignity and value of each individual human being, was the answer to modernity's discontents. In sharp contrast to von Hildebrand, however, Mounier had little political sense; he was first taken in by Vichy France's claims to be building a truly Christian polity, and, after the war, he flirted with the possibility of Catholic collaboration with Stalinist communism in building the just society.

Von Hildebrand, Scheler, and Mounier illustrate the breadth of ferment in European Catholic intellectual life in the latter part of the second act of the drama of Catholicism-and-modernity; the personalist stream of thought they embodied in their different ways would play a significant role in the next act of this drama, if not in the precise form in which they articulated it. All three continue to engage the interest of Catholics grappling with modernity and its challenges in the twenty-first century. The political naïveté of Mounier, for example, is a constant reminder of the dangers inherent in a Catholic approach to the challenges of modernity that seeks an answer to the problems of plurality and the quest for authentic modern community through a new and radical *integrisme*.

A S THESE NAMES and brief sketches suggest, the twentieth-century renaissance of Catholic theology was primarily European (although both Maritain and Gilson spent significant time during World War II in the United States, where von Hildebrand had settled in 1940). The native American exception to this Eurocentrism was the Jesuit theologian **John Courtney Murray** (1904–1967). Murray, who did his doctoral work in Rome on Matthias Scheeben's concept of faith, taught dogmatic theology at Woodstock College, a Jesuit seminary in rural Maryland, for decades. His most creative scholarship, however, was in the field of Church-state relations.

In the years immediately following World War II, Murray published a series of articles on Leo XIII in the quarterly review *Theological Studies*. There, his close reading of Leo's political thought in *Diuturnum, Immortale Dei*, and *Libertas* stretched the trajectory of Leo's thought toward a Catholic affirmation of religious freedom as a fundamental human right—and to a Catholic endorsement of the institutional separation of Church and state as a good in itself, not just something that could be tolerated for reasons of historical contingency. Murray was also something of a *ressourcement* thinker, in that he reached back to a patristic-era pope, Gelasius I, for a deeply rooted Catholic understanding of the distinction between religious and political authority in a properly ordered society. In his encyclicals on modern political life, Murray argued, Leo XIII was retrieving the Gelasian distinction between sacerdotal and kingly authority. Thus a reform of Catholic Church-state theory in favor of religious freedom and Church-state separation would not mean a concession to modernity or Enlightenment political thought. It would be a retrieval of something the Church had once known, on the basis of Christ's distinction between what is owed to God and what is owed to Caesar, but had lost sight of.

L IKE CHENU, CONGAR, de Lubac, and Rahner, Murray drew critical attention from the Roman authorities in the last years of Pius XII and for a time was forbidden to publish on Church-state questions. (The Neo-Thomism of Maritain and Gilson was also suspect in Roman circles, but they were laymen, and thus of less consequence in Curial eyes.) But all these creative thinkers were churchmen. They chafed under censorship and discipline, but they understood that God's patience with the Church must be mirrored by their own. Their vindication was not long in coming, if from a most unexpected quarter.

Act Three

Catholicism
Embracing Modernity

Another Presumptive Placeholder, Another Bold Decision

WHEN POPE JOHN XXIII's spiritual diaries were published in 1965, two years after his death, more than one reviewer found them surprising, even disconcerting. *Journal of a Soul* revealed the inner life of a man of quite traditional piety, which ill fit the portrait of the pontiff that had been created by the world media and a host of Catholic commentators: the image of John XXIII as a radical reformer who turned the Barque of Peter hard to port. "Good Pope John," as he was quickly dubbed, was taken to be the very antithesis of the austere, aristocratic Pius XII, and in one sense that contrast rang true: Angelo Giuseppe Roncalli was a warm-hearted man who loved being with people, had a keen sense of humor, and kept his ego very much in check, even in high ecclesiastical office. But his spiritual notebooks made clear that, in terms of the interior life, he was no radical. And indeed, why would anyone have expected this son of peasant farmers, born in 1881, to be something other than a man of old-fashioned, devotional piety?

Something else was also missing from the "Good Pope John" image, which sometimes reduced the man to an affable *nonno*, a portly Italian grandfather of no intellectual heft. And that was certainly not true. Young Father Roncalli had been attracted to the theology of Antonio Rosmini, to the point that the anti-Modernist ecclesiastical police rapped his knuckles and warned him off such dangerous speculations. He was a

131

keen student of Church history whose scholarly specialty was the reforming episcopate of St. Charles Borromeo in Counter-Reformation Milan. His ecclesiastical mentor was an open-minded Italian bishop, Giacomo Radini-Tedeschi of Bergamo, who put Leo XIII's *Rerum Novarum* into action by supporting Catholic trade unions.

Moreover, Roncalli was no otherworldly naïf. After being conscripted into the papal diplomatic service by Pius XI (whom he had met while working on Borromeo's papers at the Ambrosian Library), Roncalli successfully completed some very tough assignments in largely non-Catholic countries: apostolic visitor to Bulgaria, then apostolic delegate to Turkey and Greece. In the latter post, he issued false baptismal certificates to Jews fleeing the Holocaust. Sent to Paris as nuncio in 1944, he deftly navigated the fractiousness of a French Church riven by divisions between wartime collaborators and resisters, supported some early pastoral experiments with worker-priests (who lived as manual laborers in order to re-evangelize an increasingly communist-oriented industrial proletariat), and dealt ably with the postwar government in regularizing Catholicism's legal situation in France—a thorny issue since the days of the Bastille. In 1953, Pius XII sent him to Venice as patriarch and gave him the cardinal's red hat: an end-of-career plum for a man then in his early seventies. He charmed the Venetians and tried to breathe life into the ancient see of St. Mark, which, like much of the rest of Italy, was falling into the pastoral doldrums.

Roncalli's career had thus been somewhat unconventional, and his deep interest in history marked him as a man of a different intellectual formation than many of his brother cardinals, steeped as they were in neo-scholasticism and its syllogistic way of thinking, which tended to discount history. Since the dustup over Rosmini, Roncalli had not strayed into the sights of the guardians of orthodoxy, and in 1958 he was thought by the cardinal-electors to be a safe pair of hands, an elderly man who could put a more accessible human face on the Church for a few years. Then the actuarial tables would come into play, and he would make way for the successor to Pius XII that many wanted but couldn't elect because he was in Milan without a cardinal's red hat: Giovanni Battista Montini.

T HAT, OF COURSE, had also been the view of the cardinal-electors of 1878 toward Gioacchino Pecci: after the lengthy pontificate of Pius IX, Pecci would serve as a place-holder for a few years. But that was not the only or most sig-nificant parallel between the election of Leo XIII and the 1958 election of Cardinal Roncalli as pope on the eleventh ballot, after two days of a deadlocked conclave. For, during a prayer service at the Basilica of St. Paul Outside the Walls a mere three months after his election, the new Pope John XXIII stunned the Church and the world by announcing his intention to sum-mon the twenty-first ecumenical or general council in the his-tory of the Church, the first since Vatican I in 1869–1870.

The thought of a council, he later said, came to him al-most as an unbidden inspiration: "*Un concilio!*" But he was a shrewd peasant, a knowledgeable historian, a courageous dip-lomat, and a warm-hearted pastor. And his opening address to what would be known as the Second Vatican Council, or, more popularly, as "Vatican II," made it clear that, like Leo XIII, he had begun his pontificate with a deliberate, bold decision.

John XXIII knew in his bones the tensions and riptides that had roiled Catholicism (often below the surface) because of its encounter with modernity and the dynamics set loose by the Leonine Revolution. He also knew that in the last years of Pius XII, the Church seemed becalmed, running more or less efficiently but in familiar grooves, chary of anything new (es-pecially in the world of ideas) and lacking evangelical energy. His years as nuncio in France and his patriarchate in Venice had taught him that something different was needed in the shattered postwar world. He was a covert disciple of Rosmini, who wanted Catholicism to engage modernity in order to convert it. And thus the grand strategy of John XXIII: focus the energy that had been let loose in the Church by the Leonine Revolution through the prism of a general council of all the world's bishops, and call the Church to a new engagement with the world, precisely for the sake of the world's conversion.

He would only live to see his council begin its work: on June 3, 1963, six months after its first session ended, he died of stomach cancer. In four and a half years, though, the brief pontificate of John XXIII opened the third act of the drama of Catholicism-and-modernity, thereby moving the Church toward a rendezvous with, and a recovery of, the evangelical impulse from which it was first born.

What John XXIII Wanted

MORE THAN A half-century after the Second Ecumenical Council of the Vatican was solemnly closed on December 8, 1965, the meaning of the Council remains sharply, and sometimes bitterly, contested within the Catholic Church. As the now published conciliar diaries and memoirs of such influential Vatican II theologians as Henri de Lubac, Yves Congar, and Louis Bouyer make clear, that interpretive battle began during the conciliar years themselves: concerns about currents of thought being set loose in Catholicism began to be expressed during the Council's third and fourth periods in the fall of 1964 and 1965—and by some of those who had been most active in Vatican II's reformist camp during the years of preparation and the Council's first two periods in 1962 and 1963. As this is not a history of Vatican II but an exploration of its role in the drama of Catholicism-and-modernity, there is no need to try to adjudicate here the ongoing disputes between those who invoke the "spirit of Vatican II" and those who insist that the Council's teaching is to be found in its texts: which is also a dispute between those who interpret the Council as a rupture with the past and those who interpret it as a reformist Council that developed the Church's tradition, often by recovering elements of that patrimony that had been forgotten, lost, or underplayed. Those arguments can, and will, go on.

I T WILL BE helpful, though, in locating Vatican II in the drama of Catholicism-and-modernity, to revisit John XXIII's opening address to the Council on October 11, 1962. That address, known from its first three Latin words as *Gaudet Mater Ecclesia* (*Mother Church Rejoices*), is typically remembered in the twenty-first century for its criticism of those churchmen whom John XXIII called "prophets of doom who are always forecasting disaster, as if the end of the world were at hand." There was far more to *Gaudet Mater Ecclesia* than ecclesiastical smackdown, however. For Pope John's speech marked another hinge-point in turning the Church toward a new self-understanding and a new relationship to modernity in all its forms.

Gaudet Mater Ecclesia was manifestly the work of a historian who called his brother bishops to "look to the past and listen to its lively and encouraging voices." It also reflected John XXIII's familiarity with the Christocentric reconfiguration of Catholic ecclesiology that had been underway since the days of Johann Adam Möhler and Matthias Scheeben: a re-centering of the Church's self-reflection on Christ, the "divine Redeemer" from whom the Church "takes her name, her grace, and her total meaning." Moreover, as some of the more adventurous theologians of the 1950s had underscored, this same Christ was not just a redeemer for Christians alone. He was, as St. Paul had taught, "the center of history" and the cosmos, an image the Pope drew not from the controversial Jesuit theologian Pierre Teilhard de Chardin, but from the Christo-logical hymn in Colossians 1.15–20.

"History . . . is the great teacher of life," John XXIII con-tinued, and that is why the Church would draw from Vatican II "the strength of new energies" and therefore "look to the future without fear," reaching out in evangelical mission to "individuals, families, and nations." To do what? To lead them to encounter "the glory of Christ the Lord, unconquered and immortal King of ages and of peoples." And in order to take up that mission, the Church of the second half of the twentieth century had to reclaim the truth that God is the lord of his-tory: that history, rightly understood, is His-story, God's story.

So there was no need to be afraid of the present and the future; there was no need to fear modernity: for "in the present course of human events, by which human society seems to be entering a new order of things, we should see . . . the mysteri-ous plans of divine Providence which through the passage of time and the efforts of men, and often beyond their expectation, are achieving their purpose and wisely disposing all things" for the proclamation of the Gospel. In the last years of Pius XII, others in the Church may have seen only the shadow side of modernity, focusing largely on its determination to complete the demolition of the old regimes and the close alliance of Church and state. John XXIII saw the history of the last century and a half through a different optic. For, as he put it, "no one can deny that these new conditions . . . have this advantage, that those countless obstacles have been taken away with which . . . the world once used to impede the free activity of the Church." So whatever else political modernity had done to the Church, it had liberated the Church for its mission.

And that was precisely what John XXIII wanted Vatican II to do: the "greatest concern of the Ecumenical Council is this, that the sacred deposit of Christian doctrine should be more effectively defended *and presented*" (emphasis added). The truths of Catholic faith were intended to be given away, offered to others. For those truths were not just matters of soulcraft for Catholics only; rather, the Church's faith "embraces the whole human person," who has a supernatural destiny far grander than what modernity often imagined. Mission and truth could never be separated, for the Church owes the world the truth it "has received from those who went before." Yet new means of proclaiming those truths must be devised, for the Church recognized "those wonderful discoveries of human genius . . . which we use today," even as she constantly reminded the world that humanity should not shut itself off in a technologically constructed habitation without windows, doors, or skylights.

Previous councils had been concerned with the clarification of doctrine. This council would be different. The Church certainly had to "transmit whole and entire and without distortion" the patrimony of truth it had received. But in the modern world, the Church's "task is not only to guard this precious treasure, as if we were concerned only with an antiquity"; nor was it sufficient for Vatican II to "discuss some of the chief articles of the Church's doctrine or to repeat at length what the Fathers . . . have handed on." "What . . . is necessary today," Pope John insisted, "is that the whole of Christian doctrine . . . be more fully and more profoundly known." And that meant that the truths the Church proposed "must be presented in a way demanded by our times."

Then the Pope, three and a half weeks short of his eighty-first birthday, made a crucial distinction that bade farewell to the notion that the truths of Catholic faith could be locked for all time into certain fixed formulas: "The deposit of faith, the truths contained in our venerable doctrine, are one thing; the fashion in which they are expressed, but with the same meaning and the same judgment, is another." This work of explication would take time, the Pope continued, and perhaps "much patience." But it was necessary: not in order to make concessions to intellectual and cultural modernity in the hope of achieving some sort of truce, but to engage modernity on terms that could lead to a serious conversation—the kind of engagement depicted in Leo XIII's monument in the Lateran Basilica. Above all, the Church of the future should offer its proposal to the world pastorally, for the Church's teaching authority "is primarily pastoral in character": the Church teaches so that the world may learn its true dignity.

This "translation" of the ancient truths of faith into conceptual schemes that modern men and women could understand would require a new approach to ideas and practices the Church thought erroneous. John XXIII was too knowledgeable a historian to imagine that the world had ever experienced some sort of golden age from which modernity had fallen: "Indeed, as age succeeds age, we see the uncertain opinions of men take one another's place and newborn errors often vanish as quickly as a mist dispelled by the sun." So modernity was not all that different from what had preceded it: human beings had been making a hash of things ever since the Garden of Eden. In the past, the Church had addressed errors with severity. Now, however, "the spouse of Christ prefers to use the medicine of mercy rather than the weapons of severity. And she thinks she meets today's needs by explaining the validity of her doctrine more fully than by condemning." Not that there weren't things that deserved reproach; but the Church of the future would be a truth-proposing Church and a Church that witnessed to the truth through Christian charity, not primarily as a naysayer. That was the path of evangelical mission, and it ought to invite a new conversation with a modernity beginning to grasp, after two world wars and amidst a cold war, that "the dignity of the human person and his appropriate perfection are [both] a matter of great importance and most difficult to achieve."

The Second Vatican Council, John XXIII urged, should help the Church "to show herself as the most loving mother of all, offering all the riches of "heavenly grace," which empowers men and women to live "a more human life." And in that life enlightened by Christ, the children of modernity can "thoroughly understand what they themselves really are, what dignity distinguishes them, what goal they must pursue." Human beings are not just congealed stardust; humanity's destiny is not oblivion; the Church of the future should help modern men and women grasp that.

While the Second Vatican Council would "earnestly strive . . . to have people accept more favorably the message of salvation," it would also make its contribution to a more just world, in Pope John's view of things. For in becoming once again a Church of evangelical mission, a Church in which "everything . . . stirs up joy," the Church will be "preparing and consolidating the path that can bring about that unity of the human race which is the necessary foundation if the earthly city is to be ordered into a likeness of the heavenly city, 'whose king is truth, whose law is love, and whose length is eternity' (St. Augustine, *Epistle 138, 3*)."

I N GAUDET MATER *Ecclesia*, then, Pope John XXIII, scholar of the great Counter-Reformation bishop Charles Borromeo, called the Catholic Church beyond the Counter-Reformation. For more than four hundred years, the Church had been on the defensive: first, against the Reformation; then, against the Enlightenment; most recently, against aggressive secularist powers with lethal capacity and purpose. A good defense had been necessary, especially when those powers sought to destroy biblical religion or drive it to the margins of modern society. Now, the Pope insisted, that defensive phase was over. Counter-Reformation Catholicism had built a strong, institutional foundation for the Church of the future. The task now was to turn those institutions into launching pads for a mission in which Catholicism would propose the truth of the dignity of the human person revealed in Christ, and witness to that dignity by its works of solidarity and charity.

The Counter-Reformation was over. *Gaudet Mater Ecclesia*, an address by a pope who was a keen student of the Counter-Reformation at its best, was the Counter-Reformation's eulogy— and a clarion call to recover the missionary impulse that had given birth to the Church in the beginning. Moreover, the Pope's opening address announced what he wanted his council to be: he wanted it to be a new experience of Pentecost, not for the sake of transient spiritual euphoria, but so that the entire Church might re-experience the evangelical zeal that had been the primary effect of the first Pentecost.

The Leonine Revolution had been vindicated by Leo's fifth successor, and the third act of the drama of Catholicism-and-modernity had begun.

Setting the Course

VATICAN II WAS a different kind of ecumenical council in several ways. It was not summoned to resolve a question of dogma that was dividing the Church, like the First Council of Nicaea or the Councils of Ephesus and Chalcedon, which had to settle questions of the Trinitarian God and the relationship of humanity and divinity in the Second Person of the Trinity. Nor was it called in a time of ecclesiastical crisis like the Council of Constance, which ended the Great Western Schism and elected Pope Martin V in 1417. When John XXIII summoned Vatican II, the Catholic Church seemed to many a rock of stability, although wiser churchmen knew there was a lot of tension beneath the apparently tranquil surface of Catholic life. (As Giovanni Battista Montini, the future Pope Paul VI, said on the night John XXIII announced his intention to call a council, "This holy old boy doesn't know what a hornet's nest he's stirring up.")

And unlike its twenty predecessors, the Second Ecumenical Council of the Vatican would not provide an authoritative key or keys to its proper interpretation: it would write no creed, define no article of faith, condemn no heresy, insert no canons into the Church's legal system, and authorize no catechism—all means by which previous councils had said, "*This* is what we meant." Rather, Vatican II gave the Church sixteen documents of varying levels of teaching authority, ranging from very weighty dogmatic constitutions to less weighty but still authoritative declarations.

Read through the prism of *Gaudet Mater Ecclesia*, the sixteen documents of the Council begin to come into focus as attempts to chart a course toward the post-Counter-Reformation Catholicism that John XXIII outlined in his opening address. In doing so, Vatican II also resolved several outstanding questions in Catholic thought and practice. These achievements of the Council *ad intra* can be briefly summarized before tackling the question of what the Council did *ad extra*, or facing the world, in response to Pope John's call for a new approach to modernity.

The Council's documents addressed virtually every facet of Catholic life: the Church's worship; the ministry of bishops and priests; the renewal of the consecrated life among vowed religious priests, brothers, and sisters; Catholic education, for both laypeople and seminarians; the Church's relationship to and use of modern media; the Catholic role in the quest for Christian unity; Catholicism's relationship to other world religions, and especially to its Jewish parent; the Church's missionary activity. Vatican II was thus completing the ecclesiological work of Vatican I, which had been truncated by its suspension at the outbreak of the Franco-Prussian War. That suspension had left a kind of imbalance in the conciliar record, given Vatican I's sharp focus on the teaching authority of the papacy. Vatican II tried to redress that imbalance by filling out the picture of the Catholic Church in all its component parts.

O F PARTICULAR IMPORTANCE in this "rebalancing" was Vatican II's most significant document, *Lumen Gentium*, the Dogmatic Constitution on the Church.

As its very title, "The Light of the Nations," suggests, the constitution took up where John XXIII had left off in *Gaudet Mater Ecclesia*. Drawing on the creative theological work of the past century and a half and developing themes from Pius XII's encyclical *Mystici Corporis Christi*, *Lumen Gentium* presented the Church in richly biblical and patristic terms while always keeping the focus on Christ: the Church *is* because of Jesus Christ, the "light of the nations." And while the Church has a structure willed by Christ, the Church is first and foremost Christ's living body in the world: a People of God called into being by the paschal mystery of Christ's passion, death, and resurrection, and sent on mission to share the gifts of faith and sanctity it has been given. God "imagined" the Church from the beginning, if you will. For as *Lumen Gentium* taught, God in creation "decided the raise human beings to share in the divine life," and did so first by gathering to himself the people of Israel and then calling the Church into being, as the Holy Spirit descended on the apostles at the first Pentecost.

Thus the Church manifests the reality that Jesus preached and that was confirmed by his Resurrection: the Kingdom of God is here, *now*, within history. Once, the first Christians could experience that in-breaking of the Kingdom—the inauguration of God's triumphant reign over the world he brought into being—through Christ himself. Now, through the Church, the men and women of every age experience that Kingdom through the Church's sacraments, the visible signs (like Baptism and the Holy Eucharist) by which Christ is present to his people.

Lumen Gentium taught that this Church is holy by its nature as the Body of Christ, yet in its human dimension it is always in need of renewal and reform, which takes place through the ongoing work of the Holy Spirit. The Spirit's outpouring at the first Pentecost was not a one-off event. It was the beginning of the Church's ongoing sanctification, which is essential to the Church's work of proclamation and its evangelical witness. The Church has been given a mission; that mission is evangelization; and evangelization is possible because the Spirit creates and sustains the Church in the truth.

Thus in its very first chapter, *Lumen Gentium* moved Catholicism beyond the pyramidal, juridically conceived image of the *societas perfecta*, the "perfect society," that had become the preferred concept of the Church during the centuries of the Counter-Reformation. The next seven chapters of the Dogmatic Constitution completed the Church's revitalized self-portrait.

The second chapter reflected more deeply on the Church as the "People of God": a dynamic reality prepared by God through the covenant with Israel and now, through Christ and the Spirit, offered to all who affirm that Jesus is Lord. Because those who make that affirmation are drawn from all the peoples of the earth, this new People of God is a "sacrament," or anticipatory sign, of the unity of the human race. That unity will finally be achieved in the Kingdom of God in its fullness, which is the true end of history and the beginning of what the Book of Revelation calls the "wedding feast of the Lamb." Every member of this new People has a priestly character: all have been empowered by the sacrament of Baptism to worship in truth. And it is the task of the ordained priesthood to serve the priesthood of all believers by drawing all the people of the Church into mission and service.

Lumen Gentium next takes up the hierarchical structure of the Church, which exists to foster discipleship and empower mission. Here, the "completion" of Vatican I by Vatican II is most evident, for the Dogmatic Constitution teaches that bishops are not the local branch managers of Catholicism, Inc., underlings of the one CEO in Rome. Rather, the bishops of the Church form a college that, with and under the Bishop of Rome, exercises full authority in the Church and shares responsibility for the Church's evangelical mission. *Lumen Gentium* also makes more explicit a point implicit in the definition of papal infallibility at Vatican I, by teaching that the pope's infallible teaching office touches only on matters of divine revelation. That charism of infallibility is, like the office of bishop, ordered to evangelization and mission: the Holy Spirit preserves the Church in truth so that the Church can proclaim and offer that truth to the world.

An English priest of John Henry Newman's time once said that the function of the laity in the Church was "to hunt, to shoot, and to entertain." The fourth chapter of *Lumen Gentium* took a rather different view. Not only does the laity, through Baptism, have a priestly character, meaning that rebirth by water and the Spirit empowers the Christian faithful to worship God truly; it also has a prophetic character that empowers its members to speak the truth, and a kingly character that enables them to be servants of their brethren by offering them friendship with Jesus Christ and binding up their wounds. These qualities of the baptized are all ordered to mission, for the primary task of the laity is to evangelize the world from within the world: the world of the family; the worlds of work and the professions; the worlds of culture and politics. In this work of evangelization, the laity cooperates with the Church's pastors, but laypeople require no permission to be evangelists: that is implicit in, and indeed required by, their baptism. The Great Commission of Matthew 28.19 was intended for all.

That point is further developed in *Lumen Gentium*'s fifth chapter, which deals with the "universal call to holiness." Sanctity, the Council fathers insisted, is not for the sanctuary alone. Sanctity is for everyone, for everyone is to practice that charity which characterizes those who abide in God; as God is himself love, so the People of God are to be love. Then, after delineating the special way of Christian life lived by those who are consecrated by formal vows of poverty, chastity, and obedience, *Lumen Gentium* presents the new People of God as pilgrims in history: again, not as members of a static institution, but as a dynamic communion of believers for whom the structures of the Church are means to sanctification and enablers of mission. This pilgrim Church includes, beyond its living members on earth, both those who have died and are being purified for the vision of God and those who already enjoy that vision in heaven.

Lumen Gentium concluded with a reflection on the Blessed Virgin Mary, the model of Christian discipleship and the Mother of the Church—the title Pope Paul VI formally bestowed on her the same day the Dogmatic Constitution on the Church was officially ratified and confirmed: November 21, 1964, the closing day of the Council's third period. The title, like the placement of the eighth chapter of *Lumen Gentium*, underscored Mary's role within the Church, and thus opened the door to a contemporary Mariology that was at once more biblically grounded and oriented toward mission: as Mary's role in the economy of salvation was always to point beyond herself to her son (as in John 2.5), and thus to the Incarnation and the Trinity, so Mary's fellow-disciples are always to offer others the possibility of friendship with the one who is both son of Mary and Son of God.

THE FINAL TEXT of the Dogmatic Constitution on the Church was approved by 2,151 votes in favor to 5 opposed, which suggests that the development in the Catholic Church's self-understanding begun by the Leonine Revolution had taken firm hold in the minds of the Church's leaders. A similarly overwhelming vote of approval (2,174 to 4) ratified the Council's Constitution on the Sacred Liturgy, known by its Latin title as *Sacrosanctum Concilium*, which was formally promulgated at the end of Vatican II's second work period, on December 4, 1963.

The liturgy wars—the battles over how that constitution should be implemented in practice—have been such a feature of post-conciliar Catholic life that, for purposes of reimagining the drama of Catholicism-and-modernity, it is crucial to remember that the twentieth-century Liturgical Movement always intended to foster both sanctity and mission, including the Church's social witness. That is why the Council, building on and developing the teaching of Pius XII's encyclical *Mediator Dei*, sought to recover an understanding of the liturgy as the entire Church's participation in the mystery of God's presence through the sacraments, after a period in which "liturgy" meant, primarily, the performance of rites at which the laity were spectators who attend because of legal obligation. That participation, both the Liturgical Movement and the Council fathers hoped, would be an energizer of mission, for at the center of the liturgy is Christ, and it is Christ who sends his people out as heralds of the Gospel. Or, as the Council fathers began, "The sacred Council has set out to impart an ever-increasing vigor to the Christian life of the faithful . . . [and] to strengthen whatever can help call all mankind into the Church's fold."

The Constitution on the Liturgy also sought to reestablish the celebration of the Eucharist, and especially Sunday Mass, as the enlivening, evangelical center of Catholic life, after centuries in which devotional practices, such as the rosary and novenas of prayers, were the principal markers of Catholic piety and the primary means by which the Church's people participated in the Church's worship. Drawing on Pius XII and *Mediator Dei*, the fathers of Vatican II taught that the laity should understand themselves as inwardly offering themselves with Christ to the Father in the sacrifice of the Mass, not simply watching the priest consecrate the Eucharistic elements. What the "full, conscious, and active participation in liturgical celebrations" by "all the faithful" enjoined by *Sacrosanctum Concilium* entailed would be debated for more than a half-century after the constitution was approved. But that it was intended to give Catholics a sense of themselves as a people on pilgrimage through history, and on mission in history, seems clear from the constitution's crucial eighth paragraph:

> In the earthly liturgy we take part in a foretaste of the heavenly liturgy which is celebrated in the Holy City of Jerusalem toward which we journey as pilgrims, where Christ is sitting at the right hand of God, Minister of the holies and of the true tabernacle. With all the warriors of the heavenly army we sing a hymn of glory to the Lord; venerating the memory of the saints, we hope for some part and fellowship with them; we eagerly await the Savior, Our Lord Jesus Christ, until he our life shall appear and we too will appear with him in glory.

This Christ-centered focus on the Kingdom to come was also intended as a Vatican II "rebalancing" of what had become somewhat unbalanced in the Church's worship. The people of the Church are to participate in the Church's liturgical worship, not only to fulfill an obligation, but to be sanctified for mission by a more thorough immersion in the paschal mystery of Christ's death and resurrection, which is made present every time the Church celebrates the Eucharist. By making themselves gifts to the Father along with the Eucharistic Christ, the people of the Church are empowered to make their lives into gifts for others in charity, service, and evangelization. By worshiping in truth here and now, the Church's people participate in an anticipatory way in the eternal banquet, and in so doing find renewed energy within history.

The Catholic Case for Religious Freedom

T HE SECOND VATICAN Council addressed the question of the Catholic Church's relationship to political modernity in several of its documents. *Gaudium et Spes*, the Pastoral Constitution on the Church in the Modern World (which will be discussed further below) took a sectoral approach to mid-twentieth-century society, describing modern public life as the interaction of culture, economics, and politics and giving priority to culture as that which makes a truly humane economic and political life possible. The Council's Decree on the Pastoral Office of Bishops in the Church (*Christus Dominus*) put an end to the ancient *ius patronatum* by which kings and others claimed rights in the matter of episcopal appointments, teaching that, "for the future, no rights or privileges [are to] be conceded to the civil authorities in regard to the election, nomination, or presentation to bishoprics." The most important statement of the Council in regard to political modernity, however, was its Declaration on Religious Freedom (*Dignitatis Humanae*).

Four overlapping groups of Council fathers saw this document—perhaps the most disputed of Vatican II—through the rocks and shoals of ecclesiastical debate and politics.

The first group involved those bishops whose primary concern at Vatican II was Christian unity, and who understood that disentangling the Catholic Church from various schemes of ecclesiastical establishment was important for ecumenical dialogue and reconciliation among Christian communities. Their concern explains why a conciliar statement on religious freedom was first proposed as a chapter of, or appendix to, what became the Council's Decree on Ecumenism (*Unitatis Redintegratio*).

Then there were the Council fathers from the United States, who came to Vatican II determined to see the Council affirm the American constitutional arrangement on Church and state as something good in itself, not simply a contingent arrangement to be tolerated because of historical circumstance. This was not to argue that the American solution of the ancient problem of the right relationship between religious and civil authority was universalizable; the Americans understood that there were different ways in which the principle of religious freedom could be instantiated in public life. But they wanted the principle affirmed, and to that end Cardinal Francis Spellman of New York brought with him as a *peritus*, or theological adviser, John Courtney Murray, SJ, who, as we have seen, had been developing an argument for religious freedom based on the encyclicals of Leo XIII. Murray's work had come under critical scrutiny from the Holy Office, the Vatican's doctrinal agency, during the latter years of Pius XII; and Spellman, no mean ecclesiastical tactician, likely thought that having Murray (who was painfully familiar with the arguments of the dominant Roman theologians on this question) would be helpful in meeting Roman objections. Murray's historical work was certainly important in shaping Vatican II's debate on religious freedom. But his preference (and that of the American bishops) for a lean conciliar affirmation of religious freedom as a civil right, based on a political theory of the limited state with echoes in Thomas Aquinas and the Counter-Reformation theologian Robert Bellarmine, would not win the day, as the Council finally looked to the Christian personalism developed in the mid-twentieth century by such Neo-Thomistic thinkers as Jacques Maritain and Yves Simon as theological and philosophical ballast for what became *Dignitatis Humanae*.

That perspective also informed the third group of Council fathers interested in an affirmation of religious freedom at Vatican II: the European bishops who wanted to see the Church make a definitive break with the altar-and-throne alliances and Church-state arrangements of the *ancien régime*. These bishops seem to have had both political and evangelical concerns. Politically, they wanted to put an end to the fratricidal war among European Catholics that had gone on since the French Revolution; in France, especially, that fight between old-regime restorationists and defenders of constitutional democracy had been deeply enervating—and publicly embarrassing (or worse) when it played out in the Dreyfus affair and Catholic collaboration with the Vichy regime during World War II. Evangelically, these bishops believed that any reconversion of Europe after the rapid secularization that had begun in the nineteenth century would be impeded by putting the coercive power of the state—whether exercised benignly or sharply—behind the truth claims and proposals of the Church.

Finally, there were the bishops from Central and Eastern Europe, who were locked into a mortal struggle with their respective communist regimes, and who hoped Vatican II could give them another weapon for the fight against aggressive, atheistic totalitarianism. Some of these bishops, including Karol Wojtyła of Kraków, were familiar with and sympathetic to the personalism of Maritain and Simon, in which religious freedom was understood first and foremost as a right of persons and a theological imperative: the act of faith was only legitimate when it was freely made, and that meant there could be no state coercion of conviction or conscience. Others, less intellectually attuned to the personalist development in Catholic philosophy and theology, were looking for the Council to give them an instrument by which to rebut the communist claim that the Church was the enemy of human rights and freedom; these bishops also wanted the Council to affirm the legitimacy of independent civil society institutions, such as religious communities, in communist states where the party-state worked overtime to fill up all the available social space. In that sense, these Council fathers saw a conciliar affirmation of the Church's religious freedom as a development of the principle of subsidiarity that had been cemented into the foundations of Catholic social doctrine by Pope Pius XI in *Quadragesimo Anno*.

The opponents of the Declaration on Religious Freedom included those Council fathers still committed to the Roman theology of the 1950s; those bishops from Iberia and Latin America who remained fond of the old altar-and-throne arrangements of the Counter-Reformation; and those determined to keep fighting the French Revolution. The latter group, led by the French archbishop Marcel Lefebvre, was perhaps the strongest in its opposition to a conciliar affirmation of religious freedom, and precisely on political grounds. Lefebvre would eventually go into schism over this and other issues.

In the end, *Dignitatis Humanae* was approved by the Council on a final vote of 2,308 in favor with 70 opposed. The document itself—and its "legislative history" in the debates of the 1940s and 1950s—rebuts the claim of its opponents that this affirmation of religious freedom was a concession, and a disastrous one at that, to political modernity. Thanks to the work of Murray and others in interpreting and extending the thought of Leo XIII in *Diuturnum*, *Immortale Dei*, and *Libertas*, Catholicism at Vatican II could reach back into its history and recover the distinction that Pope St. Gelasius I made between religious and civil authority—a distinction ultimately rooted in Matthew 22.21 and Christ's distinction between what is owed to Caesar and what is owed to God. Thanks to the development of Catholic philosophical anthropology in the twentieth century, the bishops of Vatican II could reappropriate the ancient truth that one of their theological advisers, Joseph Ratzinger, would later express in a simple, luminous formula: "God wishes to be adored by people who are free." Thanks to the experience of a vibrant American Catholicism under a constitutional democracy, the fathers of the Council could disentangle themselves from the notion that a close alliance between altar and throne (or legislature) is essential for the Church's mission. And thanks to its experience of twentieth-century totalitarianisms, the Church's leadership could grasp the fact that religious freedom was essential for Catholicism's institutional survival, and its affirmation was essential in challenging the claims of various forms of political modernity to omnicompetence. For when the totalitarians claimed a kind of theological competence—the competence to pronounce belief in the God of the Bible an obstacle to human liberation that must be expunged—something deep in the nature of the human person was being violated.

Political modernity certainly accelerated the development of Catholicism's official thinking about the relationship of Church and state. Political modernity did not, however, force the Church to concede to its claims. Rather, it created the conditions for the possibility of Catholicism's recovery of truths that were already its own—truths that were important for the Church's own evangelical mission; truths that, proclaimed and defended by the Church, could provide a check against political modernity's worst instincts.

The Encounter with God

FROM THE THEOLOGIANS' point of view, and in terms of the Catholic encounter with intellectual modernity, the crucial document of Vatican II was its Dogmatic Constitution on Divine Revelation, *Dei Verbum* (*The Word of God*). In it, the Catholic Church fully embraced modern methods of reading ancient texts and resolved a theological question that had vexed world Christianity since the Reformation: Does the God who reveals himself to humanity do so through Scripture alone, or through Scripture and Church Tradition? Is there one source of revelation, or two? That was how the question had typically been posed since Martin Luther insisted on the principle of *sola Scriptura* (Scripture alone). Vatican II solved that puzzle—and created new openings to ecumenical theological work—by affirming in *Dei Verbum* that there is but one source of revelation, God, who reveals himself through his covenant with Israel and then decisively through his Son:

> Christ the Lord, in whom the entire Revelation of the Most High God is summed up . . . commanded the apostles to preach the Gospel, which had been promised beforehand by the Prophets, and which he fulfilled in his own person and promulgated with his own lips. In preaching the Gospel they were to communicate the gifts of God to all men. This Gospel was to be the source of all saving truth and moral discipline. This was faithfully done: it was done by the apostles who handed on, by the spoken word of their preaching, by the example they gave, by the institutions they established, what they themselves had received—whether from the lips of Christ, from his way of life and his works, or whether they had learned it at the prompting of the Holy Spirit; it was done by these apostles and other men associated with the apostles who, under the inspiration of the same Holy Spirit, committed the message of salvation to writing. . . . Sacred Tradition and sacred Scripture, then, are bound closely together, and communicate with one another. For both of them, flowing from the same divine wellspring, come together in some fashion to form one thing, and move towards the same goal. Sacred Scripture is the speech of God as it is put down in writing under the breath of the Holy Spirit. And Tradition transmits in its entirety the Word of God which has been entrusted to the apostles by Christ the Lord and the Holy Spirit. . . . Sacred Tradition and sacred Scripture make up a single sacred deposit of the Word of God, which is entrusted to the Church.

Dei Verbum also marked a decisive moment in the Catholic Church's understanding of how the people of the Church come to faith. The Catholicism of the Counter-Reformation had stressed the act of faith as the submission of mind and will to a set of propositions: God revealed truths about himself, which the Church taught in propositional form and to which men and women submitted as to the self-evident logic of a syllogism. Vatican II, while certainly underscoring that what is revealed by God is true, emphasized that the act of faith is fundamentally a personal encounter with God, and that in encountering God in Christ modern men and women are offered truths about God, and truths about humanity, its origins, redemption, and destiny, to which they freely assent.

Vatican II understood that modernity can be an experience of silence, an experience of a cosmos without meaning. Into that silence, the Council fathers affirmed, God spoke, and continues to speak. God broke the silence, first by revealing himself through word and deed to Israel, later by entering history in a definitive way in the person of the Son, the Second Person of the Trinity.

To meet the God of the Bible is, then, a matter of encountering a personal mystery of love before it is a matter of entering into a system of thought. The conceptual understanding of that mystery, which is never once-and-for-all but always unfolds in that dynamic continuity that is the Church's Tradition, is important: For how could those who have encountered the mystery proclaim their experience of it to others without ideas of what the mystery means? That is why the Church has creeds and doctrines. Those creeds and doctrines, however, exist so that men and women of all time, including that "silent" time that is modernity under the shadow of atheistic humanism, can encounter God and "become sharers of the divine nature," as *Dei Verbum* puts it.

Facing the crisis of humanism in a twentieth century that had, in six decades, seen two world wars, the greatest slaughters in history, and the threat of nuclear holocaust, the Catholic Church must offer an alternative to a silence that had become lethal. The Church must always proclaim and witness to its belief that Jesus Christ, the risen Lord, is the definitive revelation that "God is with us, to deliver us from the darkness of sin and death, and to raise us up to eternal life." The truth of humanity's origin and destiny had been revealed in history: first in God's covenant with Israel, which is freed from slavery and then given a moral code to prevent its falling back into the bad habits of slaves; then in God's Son, whose Resurrection is the definitive sign that humanity is not congealed stardust and that our common destiny is life within the light and love of God himself.

In *Dei Verbum*, Vatican II said to intellectual modernity, and to that "turn to the subject" that began with Descartes, "Yes, we agree"—but we are going to propose a nobler, grander vision of human nature and human destiny than you have offered. That proclamation, which is based on God's self-revelation in Christ, is what we, the Church, exist for.

Reading and Misreading Modernity

F OUR DAYS AFTER Pope John XXIII opened the Second Vatican Council with *Gaudet Mater Ecclesia*, President John F. Kennedy was shown definitive photographic evidence that the Soviet Union was surreptitiously emplacing offensive nuclear missiles in Cuba, whose warheads could destroy Washington, New York, and every other major city on the East Coast of the United States in a matter of minutes. Histories of the Council and post-conciliar Catholicism rarely remark on the fact that the first three weeks of Vatican II—weeks of high ecclesiastical drama in which John XXIII called the

Church to a new evangelical activism in the modern world, and the bishops who were gathered in Rome wrested control of the Council's agenda from the Roman Curia—coincided with the Cuban Missile Crisis: by most accounts, the closest the world ever came to a nuclear holocaust. Yet this was a coincidence with consequences.

That juxtaposition of the Council's opening with the terrifying high point of the Cold War had several effects on the Church's life in the years immediately following. The experience of the Cuban Missile Crisis, which threatened to preclude the work of the Council before the Council had really begun, accelerated the Holy See's quest for a new *Ostpolitik*, a new strategy vis-à-vis the communist-dominated nations of Central and Eastern Europe that would be designed and implemented by Archbishop Agostino Casaroli during the pontificate of Paul VI. This strange coincidence—a world "one minute from midnight" at the opening of a Council intended to create conditions for the possibility of new Pentecost throughout the world Church—was undoubtedly one motive behind John XXIII's April 1963 encyclical on the imperative of peace, *Pacem in Terris*. It just as certainly formed part of the historical, even psychological, background for the emergence of one of Vatican II's most controversial documents, the Pastoral Constitution on the Church in the Modern World, known during its lengthy developmental phase as *Schema XIII*.

*S*CHEMA *XIII* HAD distinguished ecclesiastical parentage, in that numerous influential churchmen had urged that Vatican II write something like it: Pope John XXIII himself; his successor, Cardinal Giovanni Battista Montini of Milan, who would be elected as Pope Paul VI on June 21, 1963; and Cardinal Leo Jozef Suenens of Belgium, one of the Council's four cardinal-moderators. These churchmen wanted the Council to issue a document that would initiate a pastoral dialogue with modernity—with modern man, full of confidence in his new scientific and technological powers, yet now fearful of his self-induced obsolescence (as the editor Norman Cousins had put it in *Saturday Review* in August 1945, immediately after the first use of an atomic bomb). *Schema XIII* was also intended to be the model of a new style of ecclesiastical rhetoric. The formality of logical propositions and citations of ecclesiastical authority would give way to a more conversational tone, one in which the Church would make respectful proposals to the "modern world" aimed at eliciting a dialogical response from rapidly secularizing societies and cultures.

After four years of gestational travail (in which the archbishop of Kraków, Karol Wojtyła, and the *ressourcement* theologians Henri de Lubac, SJ, and Yves Congar, OP, played significant roles as midwives), *Schema XIII* was finally born at the end of the Council's fourth period and christened *Gaudium et Spes*. Its famous opening sentences signaled that this was going to be a document with a difference: "The joy and hope, the grief and anguish of the men of our time, especially those who are poor or afflicted in any way, are the joy and hope, the grief and anguish of the followers of Christ as well. Nothing that is genuinely human fails to find an echo in their hearts."

This was, to put it gently, not the tone of Gregory XVI and Pius IX; it was not even the tone of Leo XIII, Benedict XV, Pius XI, or Pius XII. *Gaudium et Spes* embodied a Catholicism that, while aware of modernity's challenges and defects, had ceased bewailing the demise of the old order of things and now identified itself with the strivings of the age. Nor was this a Church thinking of itself as a *societas perfecta* over against the lamentable condition of "the world": a Church whose primary teaching function was to tell "the world" what it was getting wrong. On the contrary, the Church of *Gaudium et Spes* "cherishes a feeling of deep solidarity with the human race and its history" and "can find no more eloquent expression of its solidarity and respectful affection for the whole human family . . . than to enter into dialogue with it."

After these prefatory remarks, the Pastoral Constitution began with an introductory reflection on the human situation in the contemporary world, which was followed by two lengthy programmatic sections. The first, "The Church and Man's Vocation," continued the analysis of the introduction, where the Council fathers noted that their concern was for "man considered whole and entire, with body and soul, heart and conscience, mind and will." The second, "Some More Urgent Problems," organized its analysis according to a tripartite scheme of modern society in which politics, culture, and economics were in vigorous interaction, the vibrancy of the culture being the key to the health of both the political and economic sectors. In addition to analyzing specific issues, the Council fathers also highlighted what seemed to them the principal signs of the times: the chief characteristics of modernity to which the late twentieth-century proclamation of the Gospel had to attend.

There is much of enduring value in *Gaudium et Spes*: its sympathetic treatment of the modern human quest for freedom; its dialogical approach to the challenge (and confusions) of modern atheism; its celebration of the genuine achievements of science and democracy; its vision of a Church that proposes, but does not impose; its touching description of conscience as "the most secret core and sanctuary of man . . . [where] he is alone with God, Whose voice echoes in its depths." Above all, the Council fathers grasped the crux of the modern dilemma in their focus on philosophical anthropology—the idea of the human person—as the crucial question of the day. These insights remain entirely pertinent in the twenty-first century to a Church attempting to embody the vision of evangelical possibility laid out in *Gaudet Mater Ecclesia* and deepened in the Council's three great constitutions, *Lumen Gentium*, *Sacrosanctum Concilium*, and *Dei Verbum*.

But read from the perspective of the early twenty-first century, the Pastoral Constitution also seems curiously dated. *Gaudium et Spes* is a photographic still, a snapshot of the "modern world," and the image is true enough for the time in which it was written. But what the Council fathers described as the "modern world" turned out to be a modernity that would soon decompose as a result of internal tensions and contradictions that the Council did not address—a modernity that would produce not obsolescent modern man living under the shadow of global nuclear war, but postmodern humanity: men and women ever more dependent on technology, yet increasingly dubious of their capacity to grasp anything as true; men and women celebrating liberty, but finding less and less satisfaction in license; a human environment in which silence was becoming claustrophobic among the secularized nations, while no small part of the rest of the world was embroiled in religiously based conflict. Which is to say that there were things that *Gaudium et Spes* did *not* see in its portrait of what, fifty years later, is known as "late modernity." And there were other realities of the world after "late modernity" that *Gaudium et Spes* did not anticipate, but that are crucial components of the postmodern circumstance in which the Church must make its evangelical proposal in the twenty-first century. Identifying these is important for understanding the challenges of post-conciliar Catholicism and some of the controversies within it.

G AUDIUM ET SPES recognized that a revolution in human self-understanding had followed Darwin and Freud, just as the discoveries of Einstein and the other great twentieth-century physicists had wrought dramatic changes in our understanding of the cosmos and our place within it. The introductory section of the Pastoral Constitution also acknowledged that, in light of the scientific revolution, humanity had passed through a trap gate, on the far side of which religious conviction must be a matter of personal decision, rather than something inherited from one's ancestors and culture. The Pastoral Constitution did not, however, take the full measure of the effects of the discovery of the DNA double-helix by James Watson and Francis Crick, and the new genetics that would follow. Thus it did not anticipate that biology and the other life sciences would rapidly displace the hard sciences (such as physics) as the source of Promethean threats to the human future—and to man's self-understanding.

Gaudium et Spes depicted a world in which the chief philosophical challenges to the Christian worldview and to the Christian view of the human person were Marxism and existentialism of the Sartrean variety. Yet Marxism was in the ash can of history within a generation of the Pastoral Constitution's promulgation, and Sartrean existentialism is studied in the twenty-first century as a matter of antiquarian interest. Moreover, *Gaudium et Spes* does not seem to have detected that the utilitarianism of Jeremy Bentham and his followers mount a more forceful challenge to the Christian view of the human person (and to the possibility of a truth-centered public moral discourse) than Jean-Paul Sartre ever managed.

Gaudium et Spes welcomed the new roles that women were assuming throughout the world and had important things to say about marriage and the family. But the Pastoral Constitution did not anticipate the harder-edged forms of the new feminism that would break out into mainstream Western culture a few years after Vatican II. Nor does *Gaudium et Spes* seem to have expected the emergence of the two-worker family, in which both parents are wage-earners, and the changes that would mean for family life. Nor did it anticipate the global plague of abortion (a practice closely linked in the West to radical feminism). Nor did it anticipate the gay rights movement, and what would become a worldwide and historically unprecedented struggle over the very definition of marriage.

All of which is to say that *Gaudium et Spes* gave the Church few hints that a new gnosticism, teaching the radical plasticity of human nature, was about to hit the Western world like a cultural tsunami: a gnosticism that, married to the biotechnological revolution produced by the new genetics, would propose remaking the human condition by manufacturing (or retrofitting) human beings. Focused in part on the destructive capabilities of modern weaponry, *Gaudium et Spes* did not anticipate the threat to the human future embodied in "transhumanism" and the "immortality project" of the new genetics and the new biotechnologies, despite the warnings that had been raised by Aldous Huxley thirty-some years before in *Brave New World*. The Pastoral Constitution did acknowledge that "it is in the face of death that the riddle of human existence grows most acute" and suggest that "the prolongation of biological life is unable to satisfy" the deepest desires of the human heart. But the Council fathers do not seem to have anticipated that this "prolongation" might be on the verge of becoming virtually infinite, a technological development with profound consequences for human self-understanding and for society.

Gaudium et Spes sympathetically explored modern man's crisis of religious faith and rightly admitted that the Church's failures must be taken into account when analyzing the roots of modern agnosticism and atheism. But the Pastoral Constitution did not anticipate the demise of sociology's secularization hypothesis: that once-taken-for-granted claim that modernization inevitably leads to secularization, which in the twenty-first century has been empirically falsified in every part of the world except the North Atlantic community and its former colonies in Australasia. *Gaudium et Spes* did not, in other words, imagine a world that is becoming *more* religious and in which religious conviction is having a determinative effect on world politics, not least through jihadism and other radical forms of Islam that are notable by their absence from

Gaudium et Spes (and also from *Nostra Aetate*, the Council's Declaration on the Relation of the Church to Non-Christian Religions).

The Council fathers noted that population growth was putting social, economic, and spiritual pressures on many societies and tried to respond in a pastorally sensitive way. But there is no hint in *Gaudium et Spes* that "overpopulation" would turn out to be a myth, largely propagated by eugenicists and radical environmentalists. Nor is there any suggestion in the Pastoral Constitution that one of the gravest problems of the twenty-first century would be a precipitous drop in fertility, led by a Europe for whose lack of children a new demographic category had to be invented: "lowest low fertility." Thus *Gaudium et Spes* depicted a world in which too-many-people-with-too-few-resources is the norm, and projected that norm into the foreseeable future; it did not anticipate what seems likely to be the mid-twenty-first-century reality, which, in the aggregate, will be one of too few people in many parts of a world of increasing wealth.

Moreover, that wealth will be expanding because of something else that *Gaudium et Spes* did not anticipate: the silicon revolution, the rise of the Internet and other new communications media, and indeed the entire phenomenon of communications-driven "globalization." That the world would soon become, for economic purposes, a single time zone in which virtually everyone is in real-time communication with everyone else is not something a reader of the Pastoral Constitution would have learned. *Gaudium et Spes* also did not anticipate that vast numbers of human beings would lift themselves out of poverty in the late twentieth century, such that by the first decade of the twenty-first century some five-sixths of the world population would be un-poor, or well on the way to being un-poor, while the "bottom billion" would be mired in abject poverty, in considerable part because of something else that *Gaudium et Spes* did not anticipate: the extraordinary corruption and incompetence of postcolonial governments in what was then called the Third World.

In light of the revolutionary upheavals that began in the late eighteenth century and continued for more than 150 years, and mindful of the anticlericalist charge that the Church of 1789 had been essentially a department of the *ancien régime*, the Council fathers in *Gaudium et Spes* recovered a theme from past Church teaching about civil authority and lifted up the legitimate autonomy of the secular, which complemented the Council's teaching on religious freedom in *Dignitatis Humanae*: "The Church, by reasons of her role and competence, is not identified with any political community, nor bound by ties to any political system." But the Pastoral Constitution did not anticipate the emergence of a radical secularism that would seek to enforce a public arena shorn of religious and moral reference points—including reference to what the Council fathers called "the transcendental dimension of the human person," of which the Church is "the sign and the safeguard."

Then there was the Council fathers' call for a new intellectual synthesis focused on the cultivation of wisdom: surely a worthy goal. Yet within a decade and a half of the Pastoral Constitution's adoption, the very idea of "synthesis" in the world of learning would be displaced by self-consciously postmodern theories of the inevitable fragmentation and incoherence of knowledge. Similarly, the Council fathers had some kind things to say about modern art, seemingly innocent of any concern that the avant-garde might soon decay into new forms of decadence.

In its discussion of international affairs, *Gaudium et Spes* suggested that economic inequality would be the primary *casus belli* between nations in the future. Yet since 1965 there have been few, if any, wars caused by economic inequality or the desire to plunder resources. Rather, the world's wars in the decades following *Gaudium et Spes* would be caused by ideological conflict and passion, ancient ethnic, racial, and tribal hatreds, and/or distorted religious conviction—aided and abetted by the failures of the United Nations (in which *Gaudium et Spes* reposed considerable confidence) and the disinclination of the former colonial powers to impose a measure of the peace that St. Augustine called the "tranquillity of order" in the places they once ruled (such as Rwanda and Sudan), or that were once their close neighbors (such as Yugoslavia).

Perhaps most tellingly, *Gaudium et Spes* suggested that an intellectually assertive atheism would continue to pose both a challenge to the Church and an interesting conversation partner about the human future. Yet, in the event, massive religious indifferentism—the phenomenon that theologian David Bentley Hart would dub "metaphysical boredom"—would soon descend over Christianity's European heartland like a thick, choking fog. *Gaudium et Spes* anticipated the possibility of a new, respectful dialogue between belief and unbelief; it did not anticipate that Catholic proposals for such a dialogue would be received with a yawn of indifference in cultures whose deepest civilizational subsoil was once tilled by the Church. The Council fathers argued that "atheism must be accounted among the most serious problems of this age," but the problem would turn out to be much worse. Boredom in both its spiritual and metaphysical forms—a debonair indifference to the question of God, and a stultifying lack of awe and wonder at the very mystery of being—would turn out to be a far more lethal, and far more influential, challenge to the biblical view of the human person than "scientific atheism" or existentialism ever was.

And the net result, in the Western world at least, was not an "obsolescent" modern man of the sort imagined by both a secular analyst like Norman Cousins and the bishops of Vatican II, but postmodern man—metaphysically indifferent, spiritually bored, demographically barren, skeptical about the human capacity to know the truth of anything with certainty, stubbornly relativistic in morals, willing to impose that relativism on others through coercive state power, and determined to live according to the conviction that personal autonomy is the highest expression of the human.

D ID THESE MULTIPLE failures to read accurately the signs of the times suggest a certain naïveté about modernity at Vatican II—a fulsome embrace of what turned out to be a phantom that was on its way to evolving into something quite different? Read from the vantage point of the early twenty-first century, *Gaudium et Spes* does suffer from what seems to have been an acute case of historical myopia. The document's description of the key cultural challenges of "the modern world" sheds light on the situation in the period 1945–1965. But that analysis did not anticipate, much less describe, the end of late modernity and the rise of postmodernity that followed the flashpoint of "1968." On the other hand, the Pastoral Constitution's analysis was both correct for its time and prescient with reference to the future on one absolutely crucial point: in both the late modern world of Vatican II and the postmodern world of today, the anthropological question—the question of the nature and destiny of the human person—was, and would be, fundamental to the human future.

Gaudium et Spes began with the proclamation that the Church that shared the "joy and hope, the grief and anguish" of modern humanity was a "community composed of men . . . who, united in Christ and guided by the Holy Spirit, press onwards toward the kingdom of the Father and are bearers of a message of salvation intended for all men." That Church wished to "cooperate unreservedly with mankind in fostering a sense of brotherhood" commensurate with humanity's eternal destiny, and in so doing to "carry on the work of Christ under the guidance of the Holy Spirit": the Christ who "came into the world to bear witness to the truth, to save and not to judge, to serve and not to be served." The Pastoral Constitution concluded on the same note, affirming that "Christians can yearn for nothing more ardently than to serve the men of this age with an ever-growing generosity and success." For through that service, "men all over the world will awaken to a lively hope (the gift of the Holy Spirit) that they will one day be admitted to the haven of surpassing peace and happiness in their homeland radiant with the glory of the Lord."

The vision was a noble one, for it linked the Church's solidarity with humanity and its service to "those who are poor, or are afflicted in any way," with the Church's fundamental evangelical mission, as underscored by John XXIII in *Gaudet Mater Ecclesia*. Yet *Gaudium et Spes* was received quite differently in different sectors of the world Church over the next decade and a half. In some of those "receptions," principally in Latin America, the evangelical mission tended to evaporate as the work of service, soon enough interpreted to mean radical political activism, came to dominate some Catholic imaginations. In other parts of the world Church, principally Western Europe, the dialogue with late modernity became the occasion for emptying Catholicism of much of its doctrinal and moral ballast.

This was perhaps inevitable after a "Council without keys"—or, to vary the image, a Council without a single interpretative thread by which to weave its sixteen documents together into a coherent and beautiful tapestry. Finding that thread would be the task of the fourth and fifth acts of the drama of Catholicism-and-modernity.

Plurality and Pluralism

I N HIS CATHOLIC reflections on American democracy, the Jesuit theologian John Courtney Murray suggested that there was an important difference, in modernity, between "plurality" and "pluralism," although the two words were often used interchangeably. "Plurality," Murray argued, was modernity's native condition: the condition sociologist Peter Berger described as "the coexistence of different worldviews and value systems within the same society." Plurality was a social fact, given the breakdown of religious and aristocratic authority, the displacement of philosophy by natural science as the paradigm of knowledge, and the tensions between believers and an increasingly secular public culture. Under those conditions, Murray wrote, "pluralism" is a great social accomplishment: for a true "pluralism" involved the transformation of raw plurality into a form of community. Murray defined that community as one in which "creeds" were "intelligibly in conflict," because those different worldviews and value systems had found a mediating grammar by which to turn cacophony into serious argument and deliberation.

Viewed through this lens, the drama of Catholicism-and-modernity comes into clearer focus as a drama about plurality and pluralism and the distinction between the two. In Act One of the drama, the Catholic Church resisted, and indeed rejected, the new facts of plurality, which it judged to be inimical to the proclamation of the Gospel and a decent social order. In Act Two, the Leonine Revolution began to explore the possibility of a conversation between Catholicism and modern plurality, which would involve the development of both the Church's own self-understanding and its proposals for the ordering of modern society. That exploration set in motion a lot of turbulence within the Church, especially in Europe, letting loose energies that John XXIII hoped to focus through the prism of an ecumenical council that would give Catholicism the experience of a new Pentecost. And from that experience, he anticipated, the Church would walk into its third millennium with new evangelical zeal.

Murray's direct influence on Vatican II was limited to his contributions to the debate that eventually produced *Dignitatis*

Humanae and its affirmation of religious freedom as the most basic of civil rights. But there is a sense in which Murray's strategy of transforming plurality into pluralism, or something rather closely resembling it, was a leitmotif of the entire Council—and especially of *Gaudium et Spes*. There, and without using Murray's terminology, the Council nonetheless sought to "solve" the problem of Catholicism-and-modernity through an embrace of "pluralism" understood in Murray's terms: creeds intelligibly in conflict. The Council fathers accepted that plurality—difference—had been written into the script of history. Indeed, plurality seemed to have been written into the script by the scriptwriter, the Creator, so it was fruitless to bang one's head (or miter) against the fact of difference in the vain search for a uniformity of worldview, a monism, imagined to have characterized the premodern world.

The real task, which *Gaudium et Spes* eagerly embraced, was to build the human future by transforming the social fact of plurality or difference into the social (and spiritual) accomplishment of pluralism: an orderly public conversation about the human condition and the common good in all its aspects, made possible by commonly shared intellectual and moral reference points that could be known by reason. Thus, according to Vatican II, the Church would make its proper contribution to humanity's conversation about the human future as one interlocutor among many. Modernity's native condition of plurality and difference would be transformed into a community of conversation by a common commitment to a stable intellectual and moral framework for debate and dialogue.

Yet within a few years after *Gaudium et Spes* was issued and the Council was solemnly closed, late modernity was transformed into postmodernity. And it is precisely that stable framework for public dialogue that postmodernity (which could at best concede "your truth" and "my truth," but nothing properly describable as "the truth") seemed determined to deny. In the Western world, that denial not infrequently took the form of the imposition of a new uniformity by coercive state power: a uniformity in which the skepticism that finally turned late modernity into postmodernity underwrote both nihilism and the imposition of moral relativism in the name of an anorexic notion of freedom as willfulness.

Thus it might be said that, at Vatican II, Catholicism embraced modernity and pluralism just as the pluralism of contrasting (and what might have been mutually enriching) worldviews was on the verge of being deconstructed back into a mere plurality—and moreover, a plurality in which forms of the dominant secular worldview were determined to occupy virtually all the available social space. That, in turn, set the stage for the fourth act of the drama of Catholicism-and-modernity. Before exploring that act, however, it will be useful to sum up the turbulent pontificate of Pope Paul VI while examining three key moments in it with decisive impacts on the Church's future.

The Council Reconsidered

Checking the Drift

DURING VATICAN II's first period, in the fall of 1962, long-simmering tensions in the Church—including those arising from the contest between "Roman" and *ressourcement* theologians and those stemming from the conflict between the Roman Curia and local bishops intent on reasserting their authority in the Church—burst to the surface of Catholic life. So the conclave of June 1963 was a fractious affair. At one point in the voting, an old friend of John XXIII's, Cardinal Gustavo Testa, erupted in the Sistine Chapel, berating fellow-cardinals he thought were defying the recently deceased pontiff's wishes by blocking the election of Cardinal Giovanni Battista Montini, archbishop of Milan. When the dust settled, Montini was finally elected and took the regnal name of Paul VI.

By the standards of the day, Montini seemed to be the perfectly prepared pope. He was the son of a good Catholic family of the upper middle class. He had done courageous pastoral work with Catholic youth organizations under fascism. He was well connected to the leadership of Italy's Christian Democratic Party, among whom he counted several protégés, and he had traveled the world, familiarizing himself with different ecclesiastical situations. After years of service as de facto chief of staff to Pius XII, he had done well in Milan as that city's archbishop. A polyglot of broad culture whose fascinations included modern art, he had serious intellectual interests and was conversant with contemporary trends in philosophy, theology, and literature.

The new pope's choice of name—he was the first "Paul" since the sixteenth century—suggested an intuition that the Church of the future had to recover the missionary zeal of the Apostle of the Gentiles, as John XXIII had indicated in *Gaudet Mater Ecclesia*. But before he could evangelically refashion the Office of Peter by making the pope present to the world Church in its various local expressions, Paul VI had to bring Vatican II to a successful conclusion. He may have been the only man considered seriously *papabile* in the conclave of 1963 who could have done so.

The candidate of those for whom the last years of Pius XII were a viable model for the future, Cardinal Giuseppe Siri of Genoa, might have declined to reconvene the Council at all. The dream candidate of Catholic progressives, Cardinal Giacomo Lercaro of Bologna, would certainly have continued Vatican II, but perhaps without paying much heed to the legitimate concerns of those whom the world press now regularly labeled (and not so subtly deplored) as "conservatives." Paul VI understood his first responsibility to be the completion of the Council that John XXIII had begun: he should give the world Church the opportunity to examine every dimension of its life and thereby bring to fruition in pastoral life and practice the Leonine Revolution and the theological achievements of the twentieth century. And he had to do that while maintaining the unity of a Church that, without deft leadership, might start coming apart at the seams.

In this light, Paul VI's work at Vatican II has to be considered not only a success, but a considerable achievement. All sixteen documents of Vatican II were adopted by overwhelming majorities in what amounted to virtual unanimity among the Council fathers. The Pope, who watched the proceedings on closed-circuit television, intervened rarely; but when he did his interventions helped hold things together and ensure that Vatican II would be a Council that stretched, but did not break, the tradition of the Church. The primary example of such a papal intervention was the *Nota Praevia Explicativa* (*Preliminary Explanatory Note*) that he attached to the Dogmatic Constitution on the Church, *Lumen Gentium*, which clarified the constitution's teaching on the College of Bishops and its relationship to the supreme authority of the Bishop of Rome. When he allowed a vote on the Declaration on Religious Freedom to be postponed from the end of the Council's third period in the fall of 1964 to the beginning of its fourth period a year later, some thought it a supine papal concession to the intransigent defenders of the old altar-and-throne arrangements. But it was in fact a shrewd decision. The extension not only permitted the intransigents to have their say; it allowed for the document to be refined and improved, such that it would pass with only 70 negative votes among over 2,300 cast. And by declaring Mary "Mother of the Church" on November 21, 1964, at the same time as he promulgated *Lumen Gentium*, he satisfied those who had lost the argument over a separate conciliar document on the Blessed Virgin Mary while giving Catholic Marian piety a new ecclesiological depth.

All of this showed a sure hand. That surety of touch was also visible in Pope Paul's early travels: he went on pilgrimage to the Holy Land in January 1964, where, in an unprecedented ecumenical gesture, he met with Ecumenical Patriarch Athenagoras in Jerusalem; he traveled to Bombay in December of that year for an International Eucharistic Congress (thus linking a traditional form of Catholic Eucharistic piety to the liturgical and ecclesiological reforms of the Council); and he went to New York, where he made an eloquent plea for peace at the United Nations in 1965 and celebrated Mass in Yankee Stadium. Gestures such as his simplification of the Papal Court were generally applauded, as was his decision to award the title "Doctor of the Church" to St. Teresa of Avila and St. Catherine of Siena—the first women so honored.

Throughout his fifteen-year pontificate, however, this sensitive man, so intelligent that he could see every side of every issue, was subject to relentless criticism. He defended the Church's classic doctrine on the nature of the Eucharist in the 1965 encyclical *Mysterium Fidei*. But the implementation of liturgical reform was not well managed, leading, on the one hand, to a virtual rejection of the Missal he issued in 1969 by followers of the French archbishop Marcel Lefebvre, and, on the other, to unauthorized liturgical experiments that not infrequently crossed the border into the bizarre. His defense of the Latin-rite tradition of clerical celibacy in a June 1967 encyclical, *Sacerdotalis Caelibatus*, angered some; others were unhappy with the social encyclical he had issued three months earlier, *Populorum Progressio*, which was interpreted in parts of the Latin American Church as a warrant for revolutionary violence in service to justice for the poor (a misinterpretation Paul tried to correct in the 1971 apostolic letter *Octogesima Adveniens*).

The great firestorm of his pontificate broke out in the summer of 1968 and cast a long shadow over the balance of his papacy. John XXIII had removed the discussion of marital chastity and contraception from Vatican II's agenda, assigning it to a special pontifical commission on the subject—a decision Paul VI reaffirmed on his election while expanding the commission's membership. A commission memorandum, leaked to the world press, endorsed a change in the Church's traditional teaching on artificial means of contraception. The public debate over the commission's work and the leaked memo were examples of something that had seen its debut at Vatican I but had become almost ubiquitous at Vatican II: the use of organized lobbies and press pressure to try to shape decision-making at the highest levels of Church authority. And as had become customary during the latter stages of Vatican II, the tendency in the world media was to parse all such debates in terms of good "liberals" or "progressives" versus bad "conservatives" or "traditionalists."

Pope Paul, however, came to understand that there was more at stake in the Catholic debate on contraception than the Church's ethic of human love. He knew that the Church's doctrine can develop, and he was certainly not committed to an ideology of reproduction at all costs, for he deemed planning one's family to be a moral obligation guided by the virtue of prudence. But as he pondered the raucous debate over contraception within the Church and in the global media, he saw that what was really afoot in the contraception debate was the determination of some bishops and theologians to effect a radical shift in Catholic moral theology: the Church would abandon the ancient claim that some things were simply wrong by their very nature in favor of a judgment of "proportion" that involved a calculus of intentions, acts, and consequences set against the overall moral trajectory of one's life. That, the Pope grasped, would empty the Church's moral teaching of ballast, leading to a moral subjectivism that turned conscience into a mere faculty of choice. And under the cultural pressures of late modernity, that would effect within Catholicism the demise of classic, biblically rooted Christian morality, a collapse into relativism already underway in liberal Protestantism.

On July 25, 1968, Paul VI issued the encyclical *Humanae Vitae* (*On Human Life*), which affirmed the obligation of responsible family planning; reiterated the Catholic understanding that births should be regulated by the natural rhythms of fertility, rather than by artificial chemical or mechanical means; and cautioned against the social consequences of a "contraceptive culture." *Humanae Vitae* instantly became the most controversial encyclical in history, and the Pope was vilified, not least within the Church itself. The debate over *Humanae Vitae* continues to rage in the early twenty-first century, even though Pope Paul's affirmation of the positive effects of natural family planning on marriages has been validated by the experience of many couples, even as his warnings about the effects of a contraceptive mentality and culture have been vindicated by Europe's demographic winter of below-replacement-level birth rates and by the world plague of the sexual exploitation and abuse of women.

The *Humanae Vitae* controversy coincided with what seemed to be a comprehensive disciplinary meltdown within the Church. Seminaries, convents, and religious houses of formation emptied. Seminary discipline became extremely lax (with devastating effects in the abuse scandals that would emerge in decades to come). More Catholic priests left the active ministry than at any time since the Reformation. Some clergy took up arms, in Latin America and elsewhere, in the name of various "theologies of liberation." Many bishops in the developed world declined to implement the teaching of *Humanae Vitae* in their dioceses, while others seemed incapable of explaining the Church's sexual ethic. Paul VI declined to apply the whip hand, and in some cases, through his appointment of what were understood to be "pastoral bishops" (whose qualities did not always include a clear understanding of or commitment to the teaching of the Church), he accelerated the disarray.

There were no further Pauline encyclicals after *Humanae Vitae*, and over the last decade of the pontificate, the Pope often seemed withdrawn and disheartened. A final blow came in the spring of 1978, when his old friend Aldo Moro, a leading Christian Democratic politician, was kidnapped by Red Brigade terrorists. Despite Paul's pleas—"on my knees, I beg you, free Aldo Moro"—the Italian statesman was murdered in early May, his bullet-riddled corpse stuffed into the trunk of a car. Presiding at a memorial service in his cathedral, the Basilica of St. John Lateran, an obviously crushed Paul VI literally cried out to heaven, asking God why his prayers for his friend's life had gone unanswered.

Three months later, the Pope himself died at the papal summer residence, Castel Gandolfo.

I N EARLY 1959, Giovanni Battista Montini, an experienced and shrewd ecclesiastic who knew the tensions churning beneath what the world perceived as the stability of the late Pius XII years, may have had his concerns about the "hornet's nest" that that "holy old boy," John XXIII, was stirring up by summoning an ecumenical council. But Pope John's decision to make Montini his first cardinal, his invitation to the archbishop of Milan to live in the Apostolic Palace during the first session of Vatican II, and Montini's role in the Council during the fall of 1962 suggest that the two men shared the vision of evangelically oriented renewal that John XXIII laid out in *Gaudet Mater Ecclesia.* Toward the end of his own troubled pontificate, Montini, as Paul VI, sought to rekindle that vision. Having established the Synod of Bishops at the end of Vatican II's third session, he decided that its fourth meeting, in the fall of 1974, would be on the theme of "Evangelization in the Modern World." It was time, he may have thought, to end the drift and to reorient the Church of the future onto the evangelical path imagined by his predecessor. Doing so would be another means of implementing Vatican II.

The kerygmatic theology of Möhler, Scheeben, and their twentieth-century followers had a measurable effect on the documents of Vatican II. As Avery Dulles, SJ, pointed out in a 1991 lecture, the First Vatican Council had only used the Latin term *evangelium* (gospel) once, and then in reference to one of the four canonical gospels of the New Testament; moreover, Vatican I never spoke of "evangelizing" or "evangelization." For its part, Vatican II spoke of "the Gospel" more than 150 times, summoned the Church to "evangelize" 18 times, and discussed "evangelization" 31 times. In doing so, Vatican II did not speak of teachings that were to be accepted on the authority of a divinely sanctioned Church, full stop; it spoke of a Church proclaiming the Gospel of God's Kingdom come into the world through the person and ministry of Jesus Christ, extended into time by his disciples. Apologetics in the classic sense of logical demonstrations buttressed by biblical and doctrinal proof texts had given way to evangelical preaching and proposal.

The Synod of 1974 had many difficulties, not least the inability of bishops from the comfortable West and from Latin America to appreciate the problems their counterparts behind the Iron Curtain experienced in evangelization: a problem the archbishop of Kraków, Karol Wojtyła, attributed to the difference between those for whom Marxism was a "fascinating abstraction" and those for whom it was an "everyday reality." While there was general agreement that the Church had to recover a sense that mission and evangelization were every Christian's responsibility, there was little consensus beyond that. And there was considerable disagreement on the relationship of evangelization in the Third World to "liberation," the meaning of which was also contested. Cardinal Wojtyła had been named Synod *relator* and charged with developing a final report that the entire Synod could accept, but he was unable to do so. So the Synod of 1974 ended in some discord, and its materials were handed over to a papal commission; the commission then passed things along to Paul VI with the suggestion that he do something. Pope Paul decided to do so. The result was the first post-synodal apostolic exhortation, *Evangelii Nuntiandi* (*Announcing the Gospel*), which was published on December 8, 1975.

Drafted by the Brazilian Dominican Lucas Moreira Neves, *Evangelii Nuntiandi* clearly reflected Paul VI's conviction that the Church of the future had to be a Pauline or missionary enterprise. The document outlined an approach to Catholic self-understanding in which the Church, the Mystical Body of Christ, the first evangelizer, was evangelical in its very essence: mission is what the Church *is*, not simply something the Church does. Moreover, Paul insisted, this evangelical proclamation is not some generic call to human decency; rather, it is a forthright, unapologetic call to encounter the living person of Jesus Christ: "There is no true evangelization if the name, the teaching, the life, the promises, the kingdom, and the mystery of Jesus of Nazareth, the Son of God, are not proclaimed." There could be no imposition here, but neither could there be timidity. What the Church had to proclaim was Jesus Christ and his Gospel.

In discussing how that proclamation and that offer of friendship with Christ could best be done in the late twentieth century, Paul VI struck a characteristic note, deploying in *Evangelii Nuntiandi* a formula he often used in his preaching and teaching: "Modern man listens more willingly to witnesses than to teachers, and if he does listen to teachers, it is because they are witnesses." There could be no distance between what the Church proclaimed and what the Church lived, or between what individual Christian disciples offered to others and the manner in which they conducted their own lives. Proposal and witness were of a piece: a seamless garment of evangelization.

To meet Christ, Paul also insisted, was to meet the Church. To enter the Church was to be incorporated into a community of believers that lived by the sacraments, the fonts of grace that nourished faith, hope, and fraternal charity. And to live in this sacramentally ordered Church in the fullest sense, the evangelized had to become evangelizers: the sacramental life of the Church was both a means of personal sanctification and a platform for mission, witness, and service. Moreover, Paul taught, in becoming evangelists Christians also became transformers and renewers of culture. For the Christian offered the world a true and complete humanism in which the prerogatives of conscience and the demands of truth coincided, as the truth was freely accepted and lived in a reconciled and more deeply humanized world.

On the twenty-fifth anniversary of *Evangelii Nuntiandi*, Neves described the apostolic exhortation as Paul VI's "pastoral testament to the Church." It was, arguably, more than that. It might even be suggested that *Evangelii Nuntiandi* was the prism through which Paul VI urged the Church to read the entirety of Vatican II: as *Gaudet Mater Ecclesia* had been John XXIII's prescription for the Council's work, *Evangelii Nuntiandi* was Paul VI's summary of the Council's achievement and a prescription for living its sixteen documents as a coherent whole. In that sense, the last major teaching document of his magisterium sought to end the post–Vatican II drift in the Church and point Catholicism into a robustly evangelical future.

Although it rarely gets the attention it deserves, *Evangelii Nuntiandi* was a significant turning point in the relationship of Catholicism to modernity. Making its vision an ecclesial reality, however, would be the work of Pope Paul's successors in the fourth and fifth acts of this drama.

Re-Centering on Christ

P OPE PAUL VI had an affection for Poland, first nurtured when he spent time there as a junior Vatican diplomat. His *Ostpolitik*—a policy of attempted accommodation with communist regimes—was not well regarded by the Polish primate, Cardinal Stefan Wyszyński. But the Pope deeply admired Polish popular piety and was keenly disappointed that an agreement could not be reached that would permit him to come to Poland in 1966 for the Polish Church's millennium. (At the Mass concluding the yearlong celebrations, Wyszyński placed a portrait of the absent pope on an empty, rose-draped chair near the altar.) Distressed by clerical defections and other signs of disarray in the post-conciliar Church in the West, Paul VI would look wistfully at photographs of huge Polish crowds, led by their pastors on pilgrimage to the shrine of the Black Madonna in Częstochowa, and say "Ah, Poland. This is only possible in Poland."

Pope Paul also had a high regard for the man he named archbishop of Kraków in December 1963, Karol Wojtyła. On the death of Archbishop Eugeniusz Baziak in 1962, Wojtyła, then a quite junior auxiliary bishop, had been elected apostolic administrator of the archdiocese by the local cathedral chapter; he participated in the first two sessions of Vatican II in that capacity, while Cardinal Wyszyński wrestled with the communist regime over the appointment of Baziak's successor. After all the parties, including the Pope, agreed on Wojtyła as archbishop, the forty-four-year-old philosopher, poet, playwright, and sportsman was even more active at the Council. And in the period between Vatican II's third and fourth sessions, he played a considerable role in developing the final draft of *Gaudium et Spes*, where he worked in close harness with the leading *ressourcement* theologian, Henri de Lubac. Named a cardinal by Paul VI in 1967, Wojtyła led an intense and comprehensive implementation of the Council in Kraków, writing a *vademecum* of the Council documents, *Sources of Renewal*, so that people of all classes and stations of life in his archdiocese could join in discussions of what Vatican II taught and how that teaching should be applied in their challenging circumstances.

In early 1976, Paul VI gave another indication of his esteem for the young Polish cardinal by inviting him to preach the annual Lenten retreat of the Roman Curia (which the Pope attended wearing a penitential hair shirt under his white cassock). It was a daunting assignment: he was being asked to give twenty-two sermons and conferences over five days in a foreign language. Yet Wojtyła's Curial retreat, later published as a book under the title *Sign of Contradiction*, marked another significant moment in the Church's understanding of Vatican II, giving the Council's documents a new, evangelical coherence.

The pivotal text during the retreat was taken from paragraph 22 of *Gaudium et Spes*: "It is only in the mystery of the Word made flesh that the mystery of man truly becomes clear. . . . Christ, who is the new Adam, by revealing the mystery of the Father and his love, also fully reveals man to man himself and makes his exalted vocation known to him." Jesus Christ is the center of the Catholic reality, because he is the center of the drama of creation and redemption—the center of history. In Christ, *Gaudium et Spes* proposed, we see both the face of the merciful Father and the truth about our humanity. In light of Christ's divinity, the truth of our humanity is revealed in all its nobility—we are made by God and for God. The atheistic humanists who imagined the God of the Bible to be the enemy of human maturation and liberation had it precisely backward. Man without the God of the Bible begins to imagine himself as a cosmic accident, and in a quest for power he turns on his neighbors. Encountering the God of the Bible in Jesus Christ, men and women begin to grasp their dignity and their destiny, which is not oblivion, but glory, and are thereby empowered to live in solidarity.

Cardinal Wojtyła wove a host of classical and modern literary and theological sources into his meditations for the leaders of the Church's central bureaucracy: Irenaeus, Augustine, and Thomas Aquinas, Leszek Kołakowski and Paul Ricoeur, Antoine de Saint-Exupéry and John Milton—all were grist for his homiletic mill. Time and again, though, he returned to the centrality of Christ and what Christ had made possible for men and women in the Church: even, perhaps especially, when human beings confront their weakness—"When a man goes down on his knees in the confessional because he has sinned, at that very moment he adds to his own dignity as a man. No matter how heavily his sins weigh upon his conscience, no matter how seriously they have diminished his dignity, the very act of turning again to God is a manifestation of the special dignity of man, his spiritual grandeur . . . the grandeur of the personal meeting of God and man in the inner truth of conscience."

The cardinal's meditations also extended the traditional understanding of Christ as priest, prophet, and king by applying them to a Church in which everyone was being challenged by Vatican II to become a missionary disciple for the sake of converting the modern world. That three-part designation had often been applied to the various ministries of men in holy orders, but in the Council's view, and Wojtyła's, every Christian was priest, prophet, and king. Every Christian was called to live in the truth (the prophetic vocation), for truth is that which "makes man what he is." Every Christian was called to acknowledge and worship God, and in so doing be empowered for mission (the priestly office of the baptized). And every Christian was called to work and to service (the kingly office), for work and service can be forms of the witness that, as *Evangelii Nuntiandi* taught, invites others to meet Christ.

The title, *Sign of Contradiction*, was taken from Luke 2.34 and the ancient prophet Simeon's description of the Christ Child in the Jerusalem temple. Throughout his meditations, in which Wojtyła developed and deepened the themes of Christian humanism that informed his literary, philosophical, and pastoral work, he kept the retreatants' focus on the person of Jesus Christ, who is a "sign of contradiction" to some moderns precisely because he contradicts the claim that faith in the God of the Bible hobbles humanity and precludes the development of an integral humanism. That false concept of the human, Wojtyła believed, was at the root of many of the disasters that had beset political modernity, including the communist project with which he contended as a pastor on a daily basis.

The critique implicit in Wojtyła's message was not only aimed at the darker expressions of political modernity, however. Throughout the 1976 Curial retreat, he seemed to be suggesting to the senior leaders of the central organism of Catholic governance that the great promise of the Council—its evangelical promise—was being impeded by the internal quarreling about the Church that had dominated the Catholic landscape since Vatican II. It was time to refocus on Christ. It was time to put Christ, his Gospel, and its witness to the dignity of the human person back at the center of the Catholic discussion. It was time to hear the Great Commission again—and then to go and make disciples of all nations.

Communio *and the Rebirth of Theological Pluralism*

ALTHOUGH THE DRAMA of Catholicism-and-modernity is often described in terms of a battle between modernizers and traditionalists, it is more accurate to think of it as a three-way contest among those committed to resisting modernity in all its forms; those seeking an accommodation with modernity because they believed modernity had made classic Christian truth claims and practices implausible if not false; and those seeking to convert modernity by placing its noblest aspirations on a firmer, Christ-centered foundation.

The fault lines among these positions were evident throughout Vatican II and led to one of the most significant ruptures of the post-conciliar years. That split, which was not without its rhetorical sharp edges, was not between the pro-reform conciliar theologians and the rejectionist camp of Archbishop Marcel Lefebvre and his traditionalist followers, but *within* the group of theologians who had set the intellectual table for the Council and who had the greatest influence on Vatican II's work. It was not, in other words, a war between diametrically opposed theological camps, of the sort that had resulted in *Humani Generis*. It was a civil war *within* the reformist camp.

The occasion for difference to become division and then chasm involved the establishment of a new theological journal. Its very name, *Concilium*, telegraphed its intent: it was to be a journal of and by the reformist conciliar theologians who had come under Holy Office scrutiny in the 1950s but were being vindicated as *periti*, theological advisers, at Vatican II. The first coeditors of the new journal were two of the most prominent theological reformists of the era: the German Jesuit Karl Rahner, and the Flemish Dominican Edward Schillebeeckx. Rahner and Schillebeeckx were eager to engage their fellow reformist *periti* in the *Concilium* project, and among those they recruited was the French Jesuit Henri de Lubac, the most venerable of the reformers and a man who had suffered considerably during the theological chill of the late Pius XII years. So in November 1963, toward the end of the Council's second period, de Lubac accepted Rahner's invitation to participate in *Concilium*. Less than a year later, in October 1964, de Lubac wrote Rahner expressing concerns about the direction the new journal might take.

Like other ecclesiastical meetings, Vatican II had an important "Off Broadway" dimension. Lectures, seminars, and discussions among bishops, theologians, and other interested parties were held outside the Council *aula* in St. Peter's Basilica, and what happened Off Broadway could make a significant impact within the Council debates themselves. One of the most important venues for these extramural discussions was the Dutch Documentation Center, where Father Schillebeeckx gave a lecture floating the idea that the world had always been "Christian" in some sense and that divine revelation had made that tacit Christianity explicit.

As he recorded in his Council journal, de Lubac thought any such notion was "a betrayal of the Gospel" and told Rahner that, if this were to be the line *Concilium* would follow, he could not be identified with the new journal. Rahner (who would later pen an influential and highly controversial essay on "Anonymous Christians") assured his Jesuit confrere that Schillebeeckx was speaking for himself only, and that his was only one view among the many that *Concilium* would entertain.

De Lubac was temporarily reassured. But seven months later, on May 24, 1965 (i.e., during the period between Vatican II's third and fourth sessions), he wrote Rahner again, stating that the first five issues of the new journal had not relieved his concerns, that he believed *Concilium* had become a "propaganda tool in the service of an extremist school" pretending it was "in line with the Council," and that he was, therefore, resigning quietly from the journal's editorial committee. It was the first skirmish in what would become a theological War of the Conciliar Succession in the post–Vatican II years.

D E LUBAC WAS not the only Council theologian who believed that other theologians, during and after Vatican II, were going so far in their embrace of intellectual modernity that they were emptying Catholicism of its doctrinal content and betraying John XXIII's evangelical intention for the Council. Their opponents, of course, denied this charge and claimed they were the true heirs of the "spirit" of Vatican II, which they often defined by reference to a selective set of quotations from *Gaudet Mater Ecclesia.*

In 1969, de Lubac, the French Oratorian Louis Bouyer, the Chilean Jorge Medina Estévez, and the German Joseph Ratzinger agreed to meet during the first session in Rome of the International Theological Commission, an advisory body to the Congregation for the Doctrine of the Faith, as Paul VI had renamed the old Holy Office. At a meeting arranged and led by the Swiss theologian Hans Urs von Balthasar, they discussed the possibility of a new theological journal that would challenge the intellectual hegemony enjoyed by *Concilium* and the theologians associated with it. They chose the name *Communio*, Ratzinger later recalled, because the Latin word for "communion" connoted a "harmonious coexistence of unity and difference" that stood in contrast to the ideologically straitened perspective of *Concilium*. The name *Communio* would also challenge the appropriation of the term "communion" by Catholic progressives who were using it to deemphasize the vertical or transcendent dimension of the Church in favor of a horizontal, populist Church that functioned more like a political party than a community of disciples in mission.

The "communion" of the Church, these new theological dissidents insisted, had to be understood in reference to the Holy Trinity, a dynamic communion of self-giving love and receptivity. Absent that tether, the *communio* of the Church would be understood in merely mundane or sociological terms, and the Church would become a voluntary organization with religious interests. That Trinitarian communion—God's own life—was made known to humanity through Jesus Christ, so the authentic renewal of theology in and for the Church, and for the conversion of the world, had to be Christocentric as well as Trinitarian. That meant, in turn, that the Bible had a privileged place in Catholic theological reflection and in the renewal of Catholic pastoral practice. For in the scriptural Word of God the Church continued to ponder the full mystery of the incarnate Word of God, Jesus Christ. And to be "engrossed in God's speech," Ratzinger later noted, was to be missionary: reaching out to an increasingly pagan developed world that nonetheless manifested a thirst for the divine, even if it tried to quench that thirst by drinking from the wells of many false gods.

Perhaps above all, the *Communio* theologians would "read" Vatican II through the prism of the entire Catholic tradition—including Vatican I—and would thereby challenge the sometimes tacit and sometimes explicit notion among the *Concilium* theologians that Vatican II marked a rupture with the past. To undertake that kind of reading of Vatican II meant engaging in an open conversation, not one based on certain ideological admission tickets. The conversation had to be international, so that cultures mutually enriched each other. And the conversation had to be a creative enterprise, not one that simply repeated formulas from the past as if Catholic tradition had been frozen for all time in a syllabus of propositions.

Over the post-conciliar years, the polemics between the *Concilium* and *Communio* theologians sometimes displayed the nasty *odium theologicum* that had marred intra-theological debates in the past since at least the First Council of Nicaea in 325 (during which St. Nicholas of Myra, who would eventually become "Old St. Nick," or Santa Claus, was said to have taken a punch at the theologian Arius, whom he deemed a heretic). This ferocity was not altogether surprising: the *Concilium*-oriented thinkers had achieved a great deal of power over Catholic intellectual life, enjoyed exercising it, and resented a challenge from those who had once been allies, while the *Communio* theologians chafed at the hegemony of their former compatriots. By the twenty-first century, however, *Communio* was being published in fifteen languages, and perhaps even some of the *Concilium* theologians recognized how much the journal they resented had contributed to the diversification of methods and perspectives within Catholic theology—precisely what all reformist theologians had demanded when they were under Roman scrutiny in the 1950s.

Moreover, and more importantly for this drama, the *Communio* challenge helped bring about the next two acts in the drama of Catholicism-and-modernity by embodying the possibility of a third option for the Church's third millennium: neither a Catholic surrender to modernity nor a flat-out rejection of modernity, but the *conversion* of modernity, beginning with a critique of modernity from within modern intellectual premises.

Which brings us to Act Four.

Catholicism Critiques
Modernity from Within

Distinctively Modern Men

IRRESPECTIVE OF HOW its other achievements are measured, the Second Vatican Council ensured that the next act in the drama of Catholicism-and-modernity would revolve around the question, "*What kind* of modernity?"

Events played their role in forcing that question to the fore, not least the great cultural rupture in Europe known, simply, as "1968." By this moment in our drama, however, the Catholic Church was fully a protagonist in the contest over modernity's future. It no longer engaged the debate about modernity in reaction to the tides of history. Thanks to the previous two acts in the drama, the Church now entered the conversation with its own, distinctly Catholic understanding of the modern project, its possibilities and its discontents. And in this fourth act, the papal magisterium was fully involved in the debate over the future of the modern world in ways that would have surprised many of the principal ecclesiastical actors in Act One, including Popes Gregory XVI and Pius IX: the authoritative voice of the Church would speak not as a supra-worldly authority pronouncing *dicta*, but as a conversation partner making proposals.

The two key figures in Act Four of the drama, Karol Wojtyła and Joseph Ratzinger—Popes John Paul II and Benedict XVI—were considerable figures at the Second Vatican Council.

Although he was one of the Church's youngest bishops at the Council's opening, Wojtyła played an increasingly active role as Vatican II unfolded, particularly in shaping the final draft of the Pastoral Constitution on the Church in the

Modern World. After a pause in 1966 for the celebrations of Poland's Christian millennium, Wojtyła, named cardinal in 1967, led one of the most comprehensive implementations of Vatican II conducted in any diocese in the world: both clergy and laity in Kraków participated in a nine-year-long synodal process to plan the Council's implementation in the archdiocese, a process preceded by several years of preparation in which the people of Kraków, led by their archbishop, studied the documents of Vatican II and prayed for the Holy Spirit's guidance in understanding them—another attempt to live the experience of Vatican II as a new Pentecost.

Ratzinger, only thirty-four when John XXIII delivered *Gaudet Mater Ecclesia,* was something of a theological *wunderkind* at the Council. As *peritus* to Cardinal Joseph Frings of Cologne, he shaped Frings's decisive intervention in Vatican II's first days, which helped the assembly wrest control of the proceedings from the Roman Curia. Active during and between the Council's four periods, Ratzinger made major contributions to the drafting and development of *Dei Verbum* (the Dogmatic Constitution on Divine Revelation) and *Lumen Gentium* (the Dogmatic Constitution on the Church) while helping develop three other documents: the Decree on the Church's Missionary Activity (*Ad Gentes*), the Declaration on Religious Freedom (*Dignitatis Humanae*), and *Gaudium et Spes.* During the Council's final year, he was also one of the reformist conciliar theologians who became concerned that the development of Catholic thought and practice they had advocated was coming unstuck from the Church's authoritative tradition.

Wojtyła and Ratzinger exchanged books for some years before meeting in person during the first conclave of 1978, which, after the death of Paul VI, elected Cardinal Albino Luciani of Venice as Pope John Paul I. Trying to find some fresh air after they had been locked into the Apostolic Palace during an especially purgatorial Roman summer, the fifty-eight-year-old archbishop of Kraków and the fifty-year-old, newly appointed archbishop of Munich and Freising took an evening's walk in the Cortile San Damaso and discovered that they shared an appraisal of the Catholic Church's current situation: the Council had been a good and necessary thing, but its implementation had gone awry; a course correction was required if the evangelical purposes that had led John XXIII to summon Vatican II were to be realized.

A month later, when Wojtyła unexpectedly found himself pope after the thirty-three-day papacy of John Paul I, he immediately thought of bringing Ratzinger to Rome to participate in that course correction. The Bavarian begged off, saying it was too soon to leave Munich. But when John Paul raised the question again in late 1981, offering to make Ratzinger prefect of the Congregation for the Doctrine of the Faith, Ratzinger accepted. Three times during the ensuing decades, Ratzinger asked permission to resign and pick up the threads of his scholarly life in Germany; three times John Paul asked him to stay on; and three times Ratzinger agreed to put his own plans aside—a deference that ultimately led to his own election as pope.

They worked in close harness for the twenty-three years in which Ratzinger was John Paul II's chief theological adviser, and their pontificates should be understood as a continuous, thirty-five-year-long effort to give Vatican II its authoritative interpretation. Yet they were something of an odd couple: a Pole and a German; a philosopher whose baseline convictions came from the realism of Thomas Aquinas, and a theologian who grew up with an intellectual aversion to scholasticism; a poet/playwright, and a musician; a mystically inclined outdoorsman who craved company, and a shy bookworm; a great public personality, and a man of somewhat eremitic temperament.

Yet for all their differences, they were both permanently marked by their experience of the Second World War. Wojtyła the conscripted manual laborer and underground seminarian, and Ratzinger the draftee who walked away from the crumbling Wehrmacht and briefly found himself an American POW, took away from that nightmare a profound sense of the fragility of modern public life; both learned in very personal ways what happened when the moral and cultural foundations of the free society collapsed. In the cauldron of war, they also found heroes who shaped their understanding of the Catholic priesthood and its contemporary significance.

For Wojtyła, the hero was Maximilian Kolbe, the Polish Franciscan who died in the starvation bunker at Auschwitz after offering himself as a substitute for a condemned prisoner with a wife and children. For Ratzinger, the hero was the Jesuit Alfred Delp, whose pastoral ministry and preaching under the Third Reich was a model of the intellectually engaged priest who sought new ways of bringing Catholic truth alive under the gravest conditions. (Father Delp was executed for his participation in the Kreisau Circle, an anti-Hitler group the Gestapo associated with Claus von Stauffenberg and an abortive attempt at tyrannicide in July 1944.)

Videos of Pope John Paul II's inaugural Mass on October 22, 1978, show the normally reserved Cardinal Joseph Ratzinger with an enormous smile on his face as he embraces the newly elected pontiff, whose candidacy he had vigorously supported. That tableau suggests that, during the two conclaves of 1978, Wojtyła and Ratzinger formed a spiritual and intellectual bond rooted in two shared characteristics that would prove decisive for their collaboration and their pontificates. They were both fiercely loyal to the authoritative Catholic tradition, which they understood to be a living, developing reality rooted in settled and permanent truths. And they were both deeply familiar with contemporary ideas, some of which they thought could help explicate those settled truths in ways that would be persuasive in the late modern world.

That last assertion requires a bit of unpacking, as it challenges certain stereotypes that must be corrected in order to understand just what John Paul II and Benedict XVI did in this drama of Catholicism-and-modernity.

THEOLOGICAL CRITICISM OF John Paul II, not least that mounted by German-speaking theologians, was often battened on the claim that Karol Wojtyła's was a premodern mind.

But "premodern" is not an adequate category through which to understand the intellectual development of a man who, in the late 1940s, was clearly dissatisfied with aspects of the syllogistic philosophy and theology in which he had been trained, to the point where he deliberately chose to study the experimental phenomenology of Max Scheler for his second doctoral thesis. Nor does "premodern" seem an apt description of a philosopher who participated for over a decade in a thoroughly modern attempt to rebuild the foundations of ethics, not from the cosmological top down (as in classic thought), but from the anthropological bottom up, through a deep reflection on real-world moral decision-making. Nor does it seem appropriate to call "premodern" one of the most intellectually engaged bishops in Europe in the years just before and after Vatican II: a man who deliberately sought the company of philosophers, theologians, historians, scientists, and artists from a wide range of intellectual perspectives; a man who, as both pastor and scholar, displayed a warm sympathy for those caught in the modern crisis of unbelief; a man who was an avid reader of contemporary philosophy and literature for more than a half-century; a man whose own poems and plays employed a radically modern literary method.

Then there is the record of John Paul II's pontificate. Would a pope with a "premodern" mind have written the first papal encyclical on Christian anthropology, making the renovation of Christian humanism one of the leitmotifs of his pontificate? It seems unlikely. Would a "premodern" pope have defended the universality of human rights before the United Nations in 1979 and 1995, while transforming the Catholic Church into perhaps the world's foremost institutional promoter of the democratic project? It seems unlikely. Would a "premodern" pope have underscored the importance of the method of freedom in an encyclical on Christian mission, writing that "the Church proposes; she imposes nothing"? Would a pope who lived intellectually in the premodern world have given the Church an empirically sensitive social magisterium in which there is no hint of nostalgia for the world of the *ancien régime*? Would a "premodern" pope have written an international bestseller in which he described philosophy's "turn to the subject" as irreversible, or an encyclical that acutely analyzed the challenging conditions in which human reason found itself three centuries after that epic turn? It all seems very unlikely.

Nor does it seem likely that a "premodern" pope would have visited the Great Synagogue of Rome and the Umayyad Grand Mosque in Damascus, called world religious leaders together twice for days of prayer in Assisi, and (against considerable opposition within his own bureaucracy) established full diplomatic relations between the Holy See and the State of Israel. A "premodern" pope would not have made the Catholic Church honestly confront the Galileo case and its corrosive effects on the dialogue between the Church and science. A "premodern" pope would not have hosted seminars including agnostic and atheistic philosophers, historians, and scientists at Castel Gandolfo. A "premodern" pope would most certainly not have described sexual love within the bond of marital fidelity as an icon, or image, of the interior life of God, the Holy Trinity. And no "premodern" pope would ever have told the leadership of the Roman Curia that the Church of discipleship formed in the image of a woman, Mary, had a certain theological priority over the Church of authority and jurisdiction formed in the image of a man, Peter.

As for Joseph Ratzinger, he rebelled against the logic-chopping theology of his seminary days and, as a scholar and university professor, took up the distinctly modern Catholic theological option of a "return to the sources"—the Bible and the Fathers of the Church—as the best means of renewing twentieth-century Catholic theology. Ratzinger's bold interpretation of St. Bonaventure's thought in the first draft of his habilitation thesis (the second doctoral dissertation that would qualify him as a university professor) almost cost him his academic career. That searing experience further convinced him that if mid-twentieth-century Catholic theology were to avoid decaying into aridity, it had to break new ground. His commitment to theological renewal found expression in an international bestseller, *Introduction to Christianity*—which, in another of this drama's ironies, grew from a course Ratzinger taught at Tübingen in place of the man who had brought him to that university, Hans Küng, post-conciliar Catholicism's most mediagenic theological dissident. Throughout his academic career and during his years as prefect of the Congregation for the Doctrine of the Faith, Ratzinger was a creative, innovative theologian, concerned with the contemporary problem of belief and convinced that Christian community provided an alternative to an increasingly fragmented and atomized human environment.

THE CATHOLIC ENGAGEMENT with modernity in the first act of this drama—the years of Gregory XVI and Pius IX—was a critique from *without*: the Church, as embodied by the papal magisterium, stood outside the modern project and criticized both its intellectual and cultural roots and the social, political, and economic arrangements that grew from those roots.

In the second act of the drama, Catholicism tentatively explored various forms of engagement with modernity—but once again from outside, as it were. There were occasional probes toward a Catholic renovation of modernity. In Europe, these probes revolved around intellectually engaged lay movements trying to devise alternatives to secular liberalism and Marxism. In the United States, Catholics lived modernity without all that much theoretical reflection on what they were doing, the exceptions being the prolific author and controversialist Orestes Brownson (America's first Catholic "public intellectual") and the founder of the Paulist Fathers, Isaac Hecker. But for a Catholicism that, in the late nineteenth and early twentieth centuries, remained thoroughly Eurocentric, modernity was still something foreign, something "other." And there was no little European Catholic nostalgia for a return to the premodern world of the putatively stable and coherent Middle Ages.

In our drama's third act, Catholicism, as embodied by the work of an ecumenical Council, embraced modernity, most fulsomely in Vatican II's Pastoral Constitution on the Church in the Modern World. Some called that embrace long overdue; others found it too enthusiastic. But during the Second Vatican Council and in its immediate aftermath, the Catholic critique of modernity from outside the modern project found itself on the far margins of Catholic intellectual and pastoral life.

A decade after the Council, however, the templates began to shift again. At the end of his tumultuous pontificate, Paul VI had made a valiant effort, in *Evangelii Nuntiandi*, to call the Church back to John XXIII's project of converting the modern world with a fresh presentation of Catholic truth. That Pauline effort would be carried forward by John Paul II and Benedict XVI, two distinctively modern men who revered Paul VI. They would do so on the understanding that converting the modern world necessarily involved a critique of certain aspects of late modernity—a critique, this time, from *within*.

Fault Lines in Late Modernity

B Y 1978, WHEN Karol Wojtyła was elected Bishop of Rome—the first Slavic pope in history and the first non-Italian pontiff in 455 years—various fault lines within the modern project had opened into fissures, creating considerable tectonic instability in society, culture, and politics as well as in the dramas of individual human lives.

Having long abandoned metaphysics (i.e., thinking about truth) for epistemology (i.e., thinking about thinking), the modern intellectual project had begun to decompose a step further, into thinking-about-thinking-about-thinking. That meant getting caught in what Wojciech Chudy, a younger colleague of Wojtyła's at the Catholic University of Lublin, called "the trap of reflection": an intellectual playpen of self-absorption with little tether to the challenges late modernity posed to living freedom well.

Thanks in large part to the sexual revolution that reached hurricane-level force in the 1960s, the modern social project had begun to deconstruct such previously assumed givens as the nature of marriage and the family. In the later years of John Paul II's papacy, this shift would lead to the dismantling of the very idea of innate sexual differentiation and complementarity (now deemed a "cultural construct") and to hitherto unimaginable conflicts over the very ideas of "man" and "woman."

The worlds of late modern culture—in music, the plastic arts, literature, theater, and film—were drifting further and further away from the comprehension of any but the critics, who encouraged ever more assertive probes into the avant-garde. The fine arts had thus become increasingly disconnected from most people, even as popular culture became ever more vulgar.

Modernity had long been characterized by a certain Promethean tendency to remake the human condition. By 1978, new knowledge and new technologies had given human beings unprecedented control over their options at either end of the life spectrum (and at many points along that line). Yet late modernity had not evolved ethically as rapidly as it had scientifically and technologically. So the only publicly available moral calculus for coping with these new capacities to create, alter, or end human life was the utilitarian one, with moral questions often being reduced to "Does it work?" and "Who benefits?" In the late decades of the twentieth century, debates over these new capacities in the world's most developed societies had created a new phenomenon: deep and often bitter political divisions based not on status or wealth, but on one's position in what came to be known as the culture wars.

For a man who had spent his entire adult life living under, and contending with, totalitarian regimes, Karol Wojtyła had an acute sense of the discontents that were gathering force on the other side of the Iron Curtain, as well as within his native Poland and its neighboring captive nations. In a letter to Henri de Lubac some years after Vatican II, Wojtyła suggested that, no matter which side of the Berlin Wall one was on, the modern project, in both its democratic/capitalist and communist forms, was heading for a crisis because of inadequate concepts of the human person. Because of Marx's economically reductive concept of the human, a false anthropology was built into communism from the beginning. In Wojtyła's view, however, false anthropologies were also bedeviling the seemingly prosperous and stable West. On both sides of the Cold War divide, the "evil of our times," he wrote to de Lubac, "consists in the first place in a degradation, indeed in a pulverization, of the fundamental uniqueness of each human person." What should the Church do about that disintegration? It should not engage in "sterile polemics," he wrote, but should propose a "kind of 'racapitulation' of the inviolable mystery of the person."

The pontificate of John Paul II can be read as a comprehensive effort to address this anthropological crisis of modernity in all its forms. A synopsis of John Paul's project to rescue late modernity can be found in his 1994 book, *Crossing the Threshold of Hope*, in which he discussed in a lengthy personal interview the dilemmas and possibilities of living a fulfilled human life under the unprecedented social and cultural circumstances of late modernity. His vast papal magisterium—which fills some twenty-two linear feet of library shelf space—displays that rescue project in full. A few examples here will help give some sense of the scope of this papal critique of modernity from within, as well as of John Paul II's proposals for rebuilding the moral and cultural foundations of the modern aspirations to freedom, equality, solidarity, and dignity.

J OHN PAUL'S 1979 inaugural encyclical, *Redemptor Hominis* (*The Redeemer of Man*), was the first authoritative papal exposition of Christian anthropology: a deliberate counterproposal to those late modern ideas of humanity that identified human aspiration with the pleasure principle and human choosing with mere willfulness, thereby reducing men and women to the sum total of their immediate desires. The Pope, by contrast, described human nature and human aspiration as a vocation to love: a vocation embodied in, and thus confirmed by, the life, death, and resurrection of Jesus Christ. The Church's role in late modernity, John Paul suggested, was to lift up the vocation to love and speak the truth in charity about the modern quest for freedom. That quest would find its fulfillment in living the truths about human flourishing that could be known by all people of goodwill. (Along with other dissident intellectuals contesting communist tyranny, John Paul II would use that theme of "living in the truth" to help animate the human rights resistance in East-Central Europe in the 1980s, giving the Revolution of 1989 and the nonviolent collapse of communism its distinct moral character.)

Beginning with the Industrial Revolution and continuing at an ever-accelerating pace in postindustrial high-tech

economies, modernity and late modernity had radically transformed the nature of work. In that process, work, and workers, had too often become commodified and dehumanized. In
his third encyclical, *Laborem Exercens* (*On Human Work*),
John Paul II sought to restore to work its humanistic and spiritual dimensions. There, the first pope in centuries who had
been a manual laborer taught that the essence of truly human
work is not making more, and the object of truly human work
cannot be simply getting more: through their work, men and
women *become* more. Work, rightly understood, is humanity's participation in God's ongoing creation of the world. By
sharing in that creative process, those who work (in whatever
capacity) live out the capacity for responsibility that is one
marker of human dignity.

Finding a tether for the moral life, and thus creating an
ethical framework for disciplining and directing public debate in democracies, had become increasingly difficult in a
late modern cultural and intellectual environment uncom-
fortable with what it deemed "absolutes": a culture in which
there might be "your truth" and "my truth," but nothing either party recognized as "the truth." Yet that, John Paul saw,
could make for serious difficulties in the free society. How,
in particular, were late modern societies to defend the idea
of human equality—a bedrock of the modern political project—in a world in which human inequality (of wealth, phys-
ical capacity, intellect, or beauty) was encountered daily?
How could free societies live plurality and difference without coming apart at the seams, or descending into cultural
civil war? In his 1993 encyclical on the moral life, *Veritatis
Splendor* (*The Splendor of Truth*), John Paul proposed that
the most secure foundation for asserting equality in a world
of manifest inequality is the common obligation of all—no
matter what their talents, beauty, status, or wealth—to avoid
acts that are intrinsically wrong. The proper template for
living difference in equanimity is to be found in everyone's

equal responsibility before the moral law that can be known by reason.

Modernity had long struggled with the relationship between religious faith and human reason. By 1978, when John Paul II was elected, influential voices in the late modern cultural and political worlds seemed determined to confine faith, regarded as a mere lifestyle choice, to a private sphere. In the 1998 encyclical *Fides et Ratio* (*Faith and Reason*), John Paul sought to build a bridge over this widening chasm, writing powerfully of faith purified by reason and reason opened up to the transcendent by faith, and insisting that faith and reason "are like two wings on which the human spirit rises to the contemplation of truth." For all its Promethean assertiveness, modern intellectual life was far too modest in its aspirations, he argued. It was long past time for late modern humanity to take up once again the Big Questions: Why is there a world, a universe, at all? What is good? What is evil? What is true happiness, and what is mere delusion? Is there anything human beings can look forward to beyond the grave? Too much of late modern intellectual and cultural life seemed to have become cynical and jaded, aiming low rather than high. It was time, John Paul urged, for late modernity to recover that sense of awe and wonder at the sheer mystery, the unmerited gratuitousness of being, which ancient philosophers knew was essential to a truly human life.

A ND THEN THERE was sex. Late modernity prided itself on its liberation from what Freud and others regarded as the repressive sexual taboos of the past. And yet, was the net result of that liberation a true enhancement of human happiness? How was it that sexual liberation had been accompanied by increasing difficulties in forming and sustaining relationships of love and fidelity? Was a sexual free-fire zone a truly humane environment?

As a university chaplain, Karol Wojtyła dealt with these questions at ground level in counseling and spiritual direction—and then offered others what he had learned in a path-breaking book on sexual ethics, *Love and Responsibility*. Now, as pope, he proposed what came to be known as his "Theology of the Body," arguably the boldest of his many attempts to heal fissures that were breaking the modern project—and the people of late modernity—into atomized fragments.

Developed over five years of general audience addresses and later published as a book, the Theology of the Body was a response to the sexual revolution in all its expressions. In the first part of his exposition, John Paul reread the creation stories in Genesis 1–3 through modern literary and philosophical lenses and insisted that the body is not a machine the self happens to inhabit. The body is an integral part of the full human person and the visible expression of the spiritual dimension of man and woman. Thus the body, and its capacity to offer and receive love, discloses truths about the God who breathed the spark of life into Adam and Eve. Treating the body as a machine, even a machine ordered to pleasure, is dehumanizing.

Unpacking Christ's caution against lustful hearts in Matthew 5.27–28, John Paul retrieved and developed the idea of sexual love as self-donation and receptivity, not domination or use of the other. Use of the other as merely an instrument of pleasure dehumanizes both user and used. Desire for the other that includes desire for the good of the other is at the center of a passion that is truly human and informs a sexual love in which the other becomes the beloved.

Then, in the third section of his *Theology of the Body*, the Pope made his boldest proposal for reconceiving human sexuality and laid down his greatest challenge to the dehumanization caused by deconstructing sexual love into another contact sport. The God whom Christians confess in the Creed is a Trinitarian community of self-giving love and receptivity. The primordial intuition humans get of that divine reality is through the mutual gift and reception of man and woman in a committed, permanent, and fruitful relationship, a giving and receiving of which sexual love is a privileged expression. Thus sexual love within the bond of marriage, he taught, is an icon of the interior life of God.

Thus John Paul II said to post-Freudian, post-pill modernity, "When it comes to valuing sexual love, the Catholic Church will see you and raise you."

The Free and Virtuous Society

A DECADE AFTER HIS death, Pope John Paul II's impact on the public life of his time was remembered by historians primarily in terms of his pivotal role in the collapse of European communism, which began with his epic first pilgrimage to Poland in June 1979 and continued with his subsequent defense of Solidarity and other human rights movements behind the Iron Curtain. Those were no mean accomplishments, and it is unlikely that, without John Paul II, the Revolution of 1989 would have happened when it did and how it did. Yet a strong case can be made that John Paul's public impact will be remembered in the next century because of his social doctrine. That body of thought—his critique of political modernity from within, and his proposals for renewing and developing the modern political project—built upon the foundations laid by Pope Leo XIII in *Rerum Novarum* and Pope Pius XI in *Quadragesimo Anno*.

With Leo, John Paul taught that all right thinking about political community begins with the inalienable dignity and value of the individual human person. To begin with the tribe, or with the social or economic class, or with the racial, ethnic, religious, or gender group, is to begin at the wrong place, and that inevitably leads to one form or another of authoritarian repression. In the Leonine tradition, John Paul regarded what we call "human rights" as something built into the human person. Civil and political rights are inalienable and inherent liberties whose proper exercise the just state should protect and foster; they are not concessions from, or benefits distributed by, the state. And with Leo, John Paul closely linked that dignitarian starting point for politics and that personalist concept of rights to the principle of the common good: the rights enjoyed by persons because of their inalienable human dignity are closely linked to duties and responsibilities, and should be exercised in such a way as to benefit all of society.

With Pius XI, John Paul's vision of the free society under the conditions of modernity was richly textured and multilayered. In a society capable of living freedom nobly, the state and the individual are not the only actors of consequence. There are social institutions, beginning with the family, that enjoy a moral priority over the state, and the just state will recognize that. There are also a variety of economic, cultural, and social associations, freely entered into, that stand "between" the individual and the state. The totalitarian project failed precisely because it did not acknowledge these fundamental human associations and the mediating institutions of civil society. Indeed, it tried to control and even eradicate them, and in doing so violated Pius XI's principle of subsidiarity. Like Pius XI, John Paul understood that concentrations of power in the hands of a single individual (the *Führerprinzip*), vanguard (the Leninist model), or party ("illiberal democracy") could not be a solution to the challenges of a post–*ancien régime* world. These had led to civilizational disaster both before and after World War II and could do so again. Civil society was essential to the proper functioning of a modern political order.

The answer to the dilemmas of political modernity was not, however, to be found in a return to the old regimes. As John Paul taught in his most developed social encyclical,

Centesimus Annus, those answers would come from renewing and strengthening the moral and cultural foundations supporting the institutions of freedom that had evolved in modernity. Such a renewal would be based on the truths that could be known by reason about the dignity and value of every human life—and those truths could provide the template by which dissonance could be turned into real dialogue in the public square of the post–Cold War world, with plurality transformed into true civic pluralism.

In *Centesimus Annus*, John Paul II followed a pattern established by Vatican II in *Gaudium et Spes* and laid out a multi-sectoral Catholic vision of the free and virtuous society of the late modern and postmodern eras. The free societies of the twenty-first century and third millennium, he proposed, would involve the dynamic, ongoing interaction of three component parts: a democratic polity (in which rights-bearing citizens participate in governance); a free economy (in which the state is not the chief economic actor, even as it regulates economic life); and a vibrant public moral culture (expressing itself primarily through the natural communities and free associations of civil society). The last—the public moral culture—was the key to the rest. Free politics and free economics, John Paul understood, let loose tremendous human energies. A sturdy, vibrant, truth-based public moral culture was essential to disciplining and guiding those energies so that the net result of free politics and free economics was genuine human flourishing: not human degradation, and not social chaos.

Thus, for John Paul II, functionalist theories of democratic politics and libertarian economic models were defective, because they imagined that democracy and the market were machines that, properly designed, could run by themselves. They could not. It takes a certain kind of people to make democracy and the market function so that the net result is both social cohesion and individual human flourishing. So the free society of the future depended on moral as well as material development. To keep freedom from decaying into license and the free society from deconstructing into chaos, late modernity needed a critical mass of men and women possessed of certain habits of the heart and mind that would enable them to direct democracy and the market in light of the common good. It was the task of the public moral culture to form those habits of heart and mind, or virtues, and it was the task of the Church to help form that culture. The Church served the late modern political world as a former of character, a teacher, and a conversation partner in public debate, not as a political actor among other political actors.

Living the virtues that allowed free polities and free economies to promote human flourishing and social solidarity also meant understanding freedom in a richer, nobler way than had become common in the late twentieth century, when "freedom" was often reduced to a mantra of individual "choice" untethered from truth, goodness, or the common good. Freedom, John Paul II insisted, is not a free-floating faculty of will that can legitimately attach itself to anything: that is a childish, even inhuman, notion of freedom that reduces liberty to license. A truly human freedom is one in which we freely choose what can rationally be known to be good, and do so as a matter of habit. Freedom as willfulness is like a child banging on a piano; the freedom that makes for mature individuals and coherent societies is like an artist who has mastered the disciplines that allow him or her to make real music on the piano: freedom for excellence. Freedom as license is like a child babbling, whereas freedom for excellence is like a maturing human being learning vocabulary and grammar so that he or she can really communicate with others. Freedom as willfulness, John Paul II believed, was a corrosive eating away at political modernity's commitments to equality and solidarity. Freedom lived for excellence, by people who have internalized the disciplines of self-mastery and the habits of virtue, makes democratic self-governance and properly functioning markets possible.

Where do the habits of mind and heart that make it possible to live freedom well get formed? According to John Paul II's proposal for the free and virtuous society of the twenty-first century, those habits—virtues—are first formed in civil society, not by the state. They are formed primordially in the family, which John Paul dubbed the first school of freedom: the community in which little tyrants, small children for whom willfulness is everything, begin to grow into mature men and women who can live in community with those who are different, who can debate the common good with passion but without rancor—who can, in other words, be democratic citizens.

The free, voluntary associations of civil society are also crucial players in the drama of political modernity, according to John Paul II. Voluntary organizations—business and labor associations as well as cultural and social groups built around various interest and concerns—are the sinews and muscles that allow the skeleton of the political community, its constitutional form and legal institutions, to function as a living, healthy body: the "body politic." Late modernity's political aspiration to freedom will only be fulfilled, John Paul suggested, if our understanding of political and economic modernity widens and deepens—if that understanding goes beyond the individual and the state to include the many forms of human community that shape the character and develop the capacities of the men and women who have to make the machinery of democracy and the free economy work.

I N THE YEARS immediately following the 1991 publication of *Centesimus Annus*, John Paul II developed his internal critique of the modernity project in several teaching documents that addressed specific issues in post–Cold War public life. As noted before, he offered an imaginative solution to the theoretical problem of the ground of democratic equality in the 1993 encyclical *Veritatis Splendor* (*The Splendor of*

Truth), suggesting that the most secure foundation for asserting equality in social and political life is the equal responsibility of all before the demands of the moral law we can know by reason. In the 1995 encyclical *Evangelium Vitae* (*The Gospel of Life*), he argued forcefully against the widespread practice in the developed world of enshrining wrongs (such as the willful taking of innocent human life) as "rights." This bad habit, he asserted, involved a profound moral incoherence that would eventually lead to political disarray and new forms of authoritarianism. In that same context, he also argued that creeping utilitarianism—the categorization of human beings as "useful" or "not useful"—was another philosophical cancer destroying the vital organs of the modern political project. A utilitarian calculus of public life would inevitably lead to dangerous, even lethal, assertions of the will to power; it had done so in the Third Reich, where those deemed "unworthy of life" because of their otherness or uselessness were simply eliminated. Innate dignity, not utility, was the true measure of the human, and thus the true measure of political modernity was its capacity to instantiate that dignity in law and public policy.

In the 2003 apostolic letter *Ecclesia in Europa* (*The Church in Europe*), John Paul II wrote a kind of report card on the social, cultural, and political condition of the late modern West a dozen years after the Cold War. The immediate focus was Europe, but his critique-from-within applied throughout the West. Addressing the United Nations in 1995, John Paul had expressed the fervent wish that the "tears of [the twentieth] century" and the victory of freedom in the Cold War would lead to "a new springtime of the human spirit." Yet in 2003 the West seemed caught in a self-made trap of "grave uncertainties at the levels of culture, anthropology, ethics, and spirituality." This distemper had led to a strange loss of faith in the future precisely at the moment when the political integration of Europe had taken a considerable step forward through the expansion of the European Union to include the countries of the former Warsaw Pact.

John Paul also saw a late modern West in which too many had squandered their spiritual and cultural patrimony, too many were experiencing an "inner emptiness," and too many felt disconnected and lonely—all of which he attributed to "a kind of practical agnosticism and religious indifference," a self-absorption that shortened the horizon of human aspiration to immediate gratification. A world in which the transcendent was silent, he believed, had profound public consequences: "Forgetfulness of God has led to the abandonment of man." One stream of the modern political project had deemed the God of the Bible the enemy of human maturation and freedom. But without faith in the God of the Bible, faith in reason was breaking down, and so was rationality in public life.

It was time for Europe, and the rest of the West, to leave the sandbox of infantile God-bashing and recognize the fuller truth of its history: that it was from "the biblical conception of man [that the West] drew the best of its humanistic culture, found inspiration for its artistic and intellectual creations, created systems of law, and, not least, advanced the dignity of the person as the subject of inalienable rights."

Two centuries earlier, Pope Pius VII had tried to deepen the aspirations of one form of political modernity by modifying one of its mottos to read, "Liberty, equality, and peace in Our Lord Jesus Christ." John Paul II's variant on his predecessor's proposal might be summarized as "Liberty, equality, and solidarity." Solidarity for John Paul was more than the philosophical concept he had analyzed as a scholar, as it was more than the name of a trade union and social movement that had helped bring down the Iron Curtain. Solidarity was, and is, a virtue, a habit of mind and heart that allowed the men and women of the late modern world to perceive in the "other" a companion and partner in a great, common enterprise, not just an "other" bound by the same laws. If the only thing that citizens of a late modern democracy knew about each other was that they had the legal capacity to take each other to law when "rights" (or "your truth" and "my truth") came into conflict, then the modern political project was in serious trouble. During the 1980s, through their banned union and movement of national renewal, Poland's dissidents had proclaimed that "there is no freedom without Solidarity." John Paul II extended that intuition by insisting that there can be no democracy without solidarity, the virtue.

How would the men and women of twenty-first-century late modernity discover a new solidarity that would re-enliven their democracies? They might, John Paul II suggested, consider the vision of human dignity and destiny embodied in Jesus Christ and proposed by the Church in a social doctrine that now included solidarity as its fourth foundational principle, building on the triad of personalism, the common good, and subsidiarity.

Professor Ratzinger's September Lectures

ON APRIL 18, 2005, Cardinal Joseph Ratzinger, the Dean of the College of Cardinals, preached the homily at the Mass *Pro Eligendo Romano Pontifice*, "for the election of the Roman Pontiff." It was the penultimate public act before the cardinals took their conclave oaths in the Sistine Chapel, after which they would be sequestered inside the Vatican to elect the successor to Pope John Paul II—and Ratzinger wanted to make a point. He reached back to John XXIII and

Gaudet Mater Ecclesia, speaking eloquently of the "holy restlessness" that should characterize the elders of the Church—a "restlessness to bring everyone the gift of faith," so that the world might be "changed from a valley of tears to the garden of God." But then he identified one of the primary causes of the tears of the early twenty-first century: the danger of what he termed a "dictatorship of relativism," in which coercive state power was used to impose moral relativism on all of society in the name of the autonomous individual and his or her desires.

A mediagenic, if not very well informed, American commentator on Catholic affairs said the next day that the use of that provocative phrase, "dictatorship of relativism," was a clear indication that Ratzinger knew he wasn't going to be elected pope and wanted to leave the stage with a final, reactionary trumpet blast. Unfortunately for that commentator's reputation for sagacity, Ratzinger was in fact elected pope that very day, taking the regnal name of Benedict XVI after a very short conclave. Which suggests that the Bavarian theologian was certainly not, in his homily, making a farewell address. Rather, he was proposing a theme for the future: the Church of the twenty-first century and the third millennium would continue to challenge modernity from within, calling it to live up to its highest aspirations by strengthening its moral and cultural foundations, which were beginning to crumble.

Like his immediate predecessor, although in a shorter span of time, Benedict XVI addressed many of the fissures in the modern social, cultural, economic, and political project through his papal teaching. As had been the case during his years as a university professor, he was especially concerned with the problem of belief in the late modern world, and strove in several encyclicals to underscore that at the center of the Christian proclamation is the God who is love, who calls humanity to build a civilization of love, and whose commandments are intended to foster the growth of love in individuals and societies. That was Ratzinger's summary of the kerygmatic theology that had so decisively influenced Vatican II.

Throughout his academic life and during his time as prefect of the Congregation for the Doctrine of the Faith, Joseph Ratzinger had also been keenly attentive to the quandaries of late modernity. That attentiveness carried over into his pontificate, where, in a series of notable lectures from 2006 to 2011, each in the month of September, he deepened the Catholic critique of political modernity from within while making important suggestions about the work of renewal that was necessary if the modern project was to succeed.

THE FIRST OF these lectures, given at his old university in Regensburg on September 12, 2006, caused a media firestorm because of its reference to a robust dialogue between a Byzantine emperor and a Persian scholar. It was, however, far more noteworthy for the proposals Pope Benedict made about the developments necessary in the Islamic world if what Samuel Huntington had called Islam's "bloody borders" were going to be pacified so that Islam and "the rest" could coexist peacefully.

There were two great issues confronting the Islamic world in the twenty-first century, Benedict XVI suggested. Could Islam, from within its own religious, philosophical, and legal resources, create warrants for religious tolerance (if not religious freedom in full), including the legal inviolability of conscientious decisions to change one's religion? And could Islam, again from within those same Islamic sources, find a way to legitimate the distinction (if not the complete separation) of religious and political authority in the Muslim-majority states of the future? Benedict admitted that it had taken the Catholic Church some time and no little effort to find Catholic warrants for affirming religious freedom and the institutional separation of Church and state. But it had done so, not least at Vatican II in the Dogmatic Constitution on the Church, the Pastoral Constitution on the Church in the Modern World, and the Declaration on Religious Freedom. And it had done so not by surrendering to modernity, but by making the encounter with modernity the occasion to retrieve and develop elements of its own self-understanding that had gotten lost through the contingencies of history. Might there be some analogy in the various Islamic traditions to this Catholic experience of reaching back into one's own religious and intellectual patrimony in order to recover lost ideas that could be sources of renewal in late modernity?

It was absurd, Benedict implied, to expect that the answer to "Islam and the rest" was the transformation of over a billion Muslims into secular liberals: that simply wasn't going to happen. So if answers to the dilemmas of Islam and pluralistic late modernity were to emerge, they would have to be found through a process of retrieval and renewal within Islam itself. That process, Benedict proposed, should be the focus of interreligious dialogue between Catholics and Muslims for the foreseeable future.

At Regensburg, Benedict also addressed the intellectual difficulties late modernity experienced in creating a true dialogue of cultures. One reason for those difficulties, he proposed, was the late modern tendency to reduce all knowledge to the empirically verifiable, in a philosophical form of materialism that radically constrained the reach of human inquiry. A related problem was the tone-deafness of late modern understandings of reason to the claims of religious experience. Still another was the false notion of the God of the Bible and the identification of the divine with sheer willfulness (a problem that modernity, which got the idea from Duns Scotus and William of Ockham, shared with many currents in Islam). Once more reaching back into the patristic history of Christian thought that he knew so well, Benedict reminded his listeners that, through its own creative encounter with classical antiquity, and especially

Greek philosophy, the Church had come to understand that the God of the Bible was a God of reason, who had imprinted the divine rationality onto the world, thus giving philosophy a secure ground and making science possible. That same God of reason could not command the unreasonable, such as the radical dehumanization of "the other" and the murder of innocents, for to do so would be self-contradictory. Thus faith in the God of the Bible was one possible path to late modernity's recovery of a robust concept of the dignity of the human person, which implied a rejection of coercion and violence in matters of conscience.

At Regensburg, and in his other September Lectures over the next five years, Benedict XVI emphasized that the civilization of the West was the result of the fruitful encounter of Athens, Jerusalem, and Rome: Greek faith in reason's ability to get to truths built into the world; Jewish convictions about the dignity of the human person and about life as purposeful pilgrimage into the future; Roman assertion of the superiority of the rule of law to the rule of brute force. Renovating and strengthening the modern project, he concluded, required a fresh encounter with all three of the West's civilizational building blocks.

Two years later, in a lecture on September 12, 2008, at the Collège des Bernardins in Paris, Benedict XVI further developed his internal critique of certain aspects of late modernity while broadening his proposals for a renewal of the modernity project. In the striking setting of a thirteenth-century Cistercian monastery transformed into a twenty-first-century cultural and conference center, the Pope suggested that the monastic vocation—*quaerere Deum,* "to seek God"—was of considerable cultural consequence, not only centuries ago, but now.

As Benedict put his case, God can only be sought because God can be known, and God can be known because God has revealed himself in the People of Israel and in Jesus Christ. That self-revelation continues in time through the study of the

Scriptures, the written record of divine revelation. *Lectio divina*, the prayerful contemplation of the Bible, was a major part of monastic life when the Collège des Bernardins was built, so the monastery had classrooms and a library as well as the chapel. That study of God's revealed Word had had profound consequences in the West, for it informed and infused a culture of the word: a culture of conversation and learning; a culture of intelligibility and intellectual curiosity. The intense study of the Bible, Benedict proposed, had developed important intellectual skills within Western civilization, including the disciplines of textual translation and interpretation. Those skills had then spilled over from monastic life to shape the unique culture of the West, the first culture in human history to evince an insatiable curiosity about other cultures.

The careful study of the Bible, he also noted, leads inexorably to the conviction that there are truths in the human condition that cannot be reduced to empirical measurement— including the deepest truths of the human condition, such as the truths about love, loyalty, fidelity, suffering, and purpose in history. So the Collège des Bernardins, in its medieval origins and in its contemporary role as a place of human encounter, represented a refutation of the materialism and radical empiricism prevalent in late modernity. Late modern positivism, Benedict argued, was "the capitulation of reason." To succumb to the temptation of positivism, he argued, would be "the renunciation of [reason's] highest possibilities." And the twentieth century should have taught modernity what happened when reason gave way to systematic irrationality and falsehood.

Late modernity might want to consider another option. It might consider the recovery of one key element in the civilization of the West, embodied in the Collège des Bernardins and its originating commitment, *quaerere Deum*: "What gave Europe's culture its foundation—the search for God and the readiness to listen to Him—remains today the basis of any genuine culture."

THE THIRD OF the Ratzingerian September Lectures took place on September 17, 2010, in another evocative venue: Westminster Hall, the oldest part of the Palace of Westminster, home to the "Mother of Parliaments" and site of the trial and condemnation of Sir Thomas More in 1535. Benedict XVI, the German-born pope who thanked the British people for having won the Battle of Britain in 1940, used the occasion to reflect with his audience, composed of what the locals call "the great and the good," on the relationship of ethics to politics. Reminding his listeners of William Wilberforce's parliamentary struggle to end the slave trade—a decades-long effort motivated by Christian conviction—Benedict suggested that legal positivism, or indeed any notion of law detached from ethics, inevitably led to the abrogation of human rights, to repression, and ultimately to tyranny. Faith and reason had to work together to solidify the moral foundations of late modern democracies so that the Weimar experience in interwar Germany did not repeat itself in the twenty-first century.

That proposal then led the Pope into a discussion of religiously informed moral conviction in public life. In Britain as elsewhere in the West, loud voices were demanding that religious conviction be quarantined within the sphere of personal or private life—an expansion of the French concept of *laïcité* beyond the borders of habitually anticlerical France. There were even those who argued, Benedict noted, "that the public celebration of festivals such as Christmas should be discouraged, in the questionable belief that [this] might somehow offend those of other religions or none." These were "worrying signs of a failure to appreciate . . . freedom of religion [and] the legitimate role of religion in the public square." And they were worrisome because they were undemocratic. For if the rights of believers to express their faith publicly and to bring religiously informed moral judgments into public life were denied, citizens of a democracy were being denied the right to bring the deepest sources of their moral judgments to bear in their civic lives.

To bring religiously informed moral conviction into the public square, however, was a matter of appealing to the natural moral law, not to theological principles that could only be fully grasped by believers. The Church was not in the business of designing public policy, "which would lie altogether outside the competence of religion." The Church's role was to be a voice of clarification in public debates, working to ensure that true moral reason was not confused with mere pragmatic calculation, and reminding late modern politics that, throughout the tradition of the West, politics had always been understood to engage questions of "ought," and specifically the question, "How ought we live together?" The natural moral law that can be known by reason, Benedict suggested, might provide a grammar allowing the divergent voices in the public square to understand each other and wrestle with each other's claims. Keeping that grammar alive in public life was the primary task of the Church. In that sense, he proposed, "Religion . . . is not a problem for legislators to solve, but a vital contributor to the national conversation."

The last of Benedict XVI's September Lectures, delivered in Berlin at the Bundestag on September 22, 2011, developed and sharpened themes from the Westminster Hall address. The native son laid before his countrymen Augustine's telling question in *The City of God*: "Without justice—what else is the State but a great band of robbers?" Ratzinger did not spare himself or his fellow Germans a modern history lesson. Germany knew, lethally, what happened when power was divorced from right—when politics became a Nietzschean exercise in the will to power rather than the pursuit of the common good guided by ethical principle. Citing the biblical example of King Solomon, who had asked God to grant him a "listening heart," Benedict told the legislators of a united, post–Cold War

Germany that they might well consider the same plea: "What would we wish for? I think that, even today, there is ultimately nothing we could wish for but a listening heart—the capacity to discern between good and evil, and thus to establish true law, to serve justice and peace."

In the Bundestag, Benedict XVI returned to the theme of Jerusalem, Athens, and Rome—biblical revelation, faith in reason, and confidence in law—as the three pillars of the West, not only in the past but in the late modern (and increasingly postmodern) present. What happened, he asked, when Jerusalem was eliminated from the conversation—which meant eliminating the idea that the God of creation had imprinted the divine reason on the world, such that the world was intelligible? It seems that faith in reason itself—the Athenian factor in the equation—begins to weaken: Was that not the situation of a late modernity in which faith in reason had so atrophied that the best that could be conceded was that there was "your truth" and "my truth"? If that's all there is, however, then convictions about the superiority of law to brute force would soon weaken. Why? Because if there is only "your truth" and "my truth," and neither party recognizes anything as *the* truth, then there is no criterion or horizon of judgment by which to settle the argument. In that circumstance, someone is going to settle the argument by an imposition of power. And if the imposing "someone" is the state, then we are back to the dictatorship of relativism of which Joseph Ratzinger warned on April 18, 2005.

The West had been brutally alerted to the danger of irrational religion on September 11, 2001, and in the many acts of jihadist terrorist terrorism that followed. Ratzinger had long warned that faith unpurified by reason threatened to become superstition, or worse; he now raised a caution against secular fundamentalism, which often expressed itself in notions of law detached from moral truth—the law is what it says it is, period. That legal positivism, Benedict XVI reminded the

German legislators, had played a deadly role in their own history: "We Germans know from our own experience that [Augustine's warnings about a state without justice] are no empty specter. We have seen how power became divorced from right, how power opposed right and crushed it, so that the State became an instrument for destroying right—a highly organized band of robbers, capable of threatening the whole world and driving it to the edge of the abyss."

Then the Pope pointed a way into the future that drew a humanistic lesson from Germany's twenty-first-century obsession with the natural environment:

> The importance of ecology is no longer disputed. We must listen to the language of nature and we must answer accordingly. Yet I would like to underline a point that seems to me to be neglected, today as in the past: there is also an ecology of man. Man too has a nature that he must respect and that he cannot manipulate at will. Man is not merely self-creating freedom. Man does not create himself. He is intellect and will, but he is also nature, and his will is rightly ordered if he respects his nature, listens to it and accepts himself for who he is, as one who did not create himself. In this way, and in no other, is true human freedom fulfilled.

The natural world about which Germany's Green Party was so concerned included the world of human self-understanding and aspiration. If the men and women of the twenty-first century rediscovered the moral truths embedded in the world, they and their children and grandchildren could avoid the catastrophes suffered by their parents and grandparents: lethal political catastrophes caused by defective concepts of the human person, human community, and human destiny. It was possible to live freedom as something grander than an expression of personal willfulness. Nietzsche was wrong; there was more to more modernity than will; and the rediscovery of that "more"—of a reason informed by faith—could lead to a rediscovery of the deep truths about political modernity's great aspiration: freedom.

Three Crucial Points

AS ARTICULATED BY Popes John Paul II and Benedict XVI, the gist of the internal Catholic critique of modernity in the fourth act of this drama, and the Church's proposals for a revitalized modern project, can be summarized under three headings.

Culture First. Picking up themes from early modern political theory that had been influenced by the mechanistic imagination of Newtonian science, late modernity tended to think of the political and economic institutions of freedom—the democratic state and the market-based economy—as machines capable of running by themselves. Get the design right, put the proper key into the ignition, and the machine would function properly. John Paul II and Benedict XVI thought the Great Depression, and the Weimar experience of a democracy self-destructing into Nazi tyranny, ought to have disabused modernity of that misunderstanding. For it takes a certain breed of "mechanics," a certain kind of people living certain virtues, to make the machinery of democracy and the free economy work so that the outcome is individual and societal flourishing.

Democracy and the market, in other words, are dependent upon a vital, life-affirming public moral culture: one that inculcates a commitment to the common good in future citizens, fosters civic friendship, and lifts up the virtue of solidarity. Moreover, that vibrant public moral culture has to teach a nobler concept of rights than is summarized under the late modern mantra of "choice." For the key question—the question that reflects the dignity of the human person as more than a bundle of desires—is always, "Choose *what*?" Rights untethered to responsibilities, like freedom disconnected from moral truth and uninterested in the good, become mere trump cards in a politics of power.

John Paul II and Benedict XVI reminded the late modern world that the aspirations of political modernity were once greater than that. Modern man wanted to look up, as a free human being, and lead his life against a larger horizon of imagination and purpose. Late modern humanity had increasingly given itself over to looking down, or looking around, rather than looking up. The revitalization of public moral culture was essential in recovering and living the noble aspirations with which the modern project had begun.

Reason Reaffirmed. It is surely one of the great ironies in this drama of ironies that, in the late twentieth and early twenty-first centuries, the Catholic Church should have emerged as the world's chief institutional defender of the prerogatives of reason in human affairs. One stream of modernity—first embodied by Voltaire, then in the nineteenth century by the atheistic humanism analyzed by Henri de Lubac, and later in Sartrean existentialism—considered Catholicism the chief institutional obstacle to the triumph of reason. Then the heirs of Voltaire, Auguste Comte, Ludwig Feuerbach, Karl Marx, and Friedrich Nietzsche lost their own faith in reason, some through a long sojourn in the epistemological "trap of reflection," others through the experience of the twentieth-century world wars, or through strange postmodern notions that rationality was itself a cultural construct. It would surely have come as a surprise to Voltaire that a Polish pope would pen an encyclical more celebratory of the capacities of human reason than anything on offer in the late twentieth century in the philosophy faculties of the Sorbonne or Harvard. Yet there it is: another irony in the fire.

The Catholic defense of reason mounted by John Paul II and Benedict XVI in their internal critique of late modernity—a critique, to repeat, that sought modernity's renewal, not its overthrow—was particularly sharp in its insistence on the rational availability, so to speak, of moral truth. Karol Wojtyła's philosophical project at the Catholic University of Lublin from the mid-1950s through the late 1970s aimed at nothing less than putting ethics on a firm, reality-grounded basis, after morality had retreated into the realm of the subjective in the centuries after David Hume detached fact from value and Immanuel Kant tried mightily, but unsuccessfully, to reestablish a secure basis for the moral life. Wojtyła's experience of the Second World War confirmed for him what he had first learned from the scholastic metaphysics and ethics that formed the bedrock of his philosophical work: unless moral truth was tethered to objective reality—unless modernity could learn again to discover moral truths in a disciplined reflection on the world and the human condition—the modern project was going to find itself in the gravest of difficulties. Wojtyła understood that this recovery of the objective truth of the moral order would have to be done differently than in the Middle Ages; it could not begin with cosmology, but had to start with the philosophical study of the human person. In that study, he was convinced, modernity could rediscover the truth that moral norms are not subjective ephemera, and that living by those reality-based norms makes human happiness and flourishing, and social solidarity, possible.

In the Catholic internal critique of modernity, the defense of the prerogatives and capacities of reason is also a defense of political modernity's most cherished creation, democracy. The imperative of democratic self-governance had first been proposed in terms of self-evident truths of a moral character. The defense of twenty-first-century democracy, against its own self-destruction under the dictatorship of relativism, or against the assault upon it by violent global forces with a different idea of what was reasonable and right, required re-tethering reason, including moral reason, to reality. Given the early modern assault on Catholic morality as the by-product of an ecclesiastical authoritarianism inimical to freedom, here was another irony: the Church in defense of the human capacity to know, to grasp, and to do the good by means of reason—and thus the Church in defense of the democratic future.

Freedom for Excellence. John Paul II and Benedict XVI were both indebted to the Belgian Dominican Servais Pinckaers, whose modern rereading of the moral theory of St. Thomas Aquinas put beatitude at the center of the moral life, gave virtue ethics a fresh tether to both the Bible and philosophy, and described moral laws as pathways to human flourishing and virtuous living. The modernity project was in deep trouble, these two popes knew, if "freedom" is simply willfulness. For willfulness is an attribute of the immature, and it takes mature citizens to make freedom work in a democracy so that the common good is enhanced. The alternative to freedom-as-willfulness—which Pinckaers dubbed "the freedom of indifference"—was what the Belgian theologian called "freedom for excellence": freedom understood as the moral habit of choosing the good habitually; freedom as a virtue, not just a slogan for self-assertion.

Critiquing modernity from within, John Paul and Benedict constantly called the late modern world to this freedom for excellence. They did so by lifting up the human capacity to know and choose the good, by offering the Church's ministry of reconciliation when efforts to live the good fail (as they so often do, and for everyone), and by challenging the late modern world to lift its sights when considering its capacities. Freedom for excellence, they argued, was humanism in full. Living freedom for excellence would redeem the promise of social, cultural, and political modernity to be a liberator of the human spirit.

The Catholic critique of modernity from within, and the Catholic proposal for living freedom well, had now been defined. But this fourth act remained to be incorporated into the fifth act of the ongoing drama of Catholicism-and-modernity, which is the next phase of this story. Understanding that fifth act requires another step back to ponder Vatican II and its immediate aftermath.

A Communion of Disciples in Mission

The Council Without Keys

HISTORIANS OFTEN REMARK that the Second Vatican Council, the twenty-first such gathering in two millennia of Catholic history, was unique in that it was not summoned to deal with a crisis. That is true enough, but it's not the whole truth of the matter.

The great dogmatic councils of the first millennium were certainly responses to crises. Nicaea I, in 325, was called to settle deep divisions in the Church caused by the Alexandrian theologian Arius, who denied the standard account of the divinity of Christ and taught that "there was a time when the Son was not." In 431, the Council of Ephesus had to resolve a Church-dividing crisis caused by Nestorius, archbishop of Constantinople, who refused to use the title "Mother of God" in reference to the Virgin Mary—which seemed another way of denying the full divinity of Christ. The Council of Chalcedon in 451 was the result of yet another Christological controversy: "monophysitism," which, as the Greek name suggests, denied the full humanity of Jesus of Nazareth by claiming that Christ had only one nature, a divine one, for which his humanity was a kind of mask or disguise. The Second Council of Nicaea in 787 tried to end the Church-dividing iconoclast controversy by affirming the veneration of icons as "images of the Image": the incarnate Son of God was the Image of the Father, so created things, like Christ's humanity, could make divine realities present; thus icons were images making present spiritual realities, including God, Christ, Mary, and the saints.

Then there was the sixteenth-century Council of Trent, which met over three periods and eighteen years to craft a comprehensive response to one of the greatest crises in Church history, the fracture of Western Christianity in the various Protestant Reformations. Vatican I also fits this pattern, insofar as Pius IX believed that modernity was creating a crisis of belief, and thus a potential cataclysm, for both Church and society.

These councils-called-in-crisis also provided keys to their proper interpretation. And over time, those keys became part of what John XXIII called in *Gaudet Mater Ecclesia* "the sacred deposit of Christian doctrine": the bedrock of Catholic orthodoxy. Those interpretive keys came in several forms.

The key to what Nicaea I meant was the Creed it composed—which many Christians recite every Sunday—with its affirmation that the Son is "consubstantial with the Father" in the Holy Trinity. The keys to the great Christological councils of the fifth century are found in their dogmatic definitions. The identification of Mary as *Theotokos* (God-Bearer, or Mother of God) at Ephesus, and Chalcedon's dogmatic formula of the two natures (human and divine) in the one divine person of Jesus Christ, are the keys to understanding what the bishops at Ephesus and Chalcedon intended. These councils, and some of the others that met over the centuries, also provided interpretive keys by condemning heresies. Still others gave the Church authoritative keys to their interpretation by writing canons into Church law. Trent offered the Church numerous types of interpretive keys, including condemnations and canons, but perhaps its most effective and influential key was the *Roman Catechism* it commissioned, which St. Charles Borromeo, the reforming archbishop of Milan, played a pivotal role in editing. Vatican I, for its part, gave the Church the keys to its proper interpretation by solemnly affirming the reality of divine revelation and defining the infallibility, under certain circumstances, of the Bishop of Rome.

VATICAN II CONDEMNED no heresies, defined no dogmas, and wrote no canons into the law of the Church; nor did it give the Church a new Creed or a new catechism. Thus the striking difference distinguishing Vatican II from its twenty predecessors was not only that it was called at a time of seeming calm and stability in the Church's life, rather than a time of crisis, but that it lacked any of the interpretive keys other ecumenical councils had provided.

The sixteen documents of Vatican II were the Council's work product, and it was generally understood by informed Catholics that those documents were of varying ecclesiastical and theological heft. The two Dogmatic Constitutions (*Lumen Gentium*, on the Church, and *Dei Verbum*, on Divine Revelation), the Constitution on the Sacred Liturgy, and the Pastoral Constitution on the Church in the Modern World were the Council's four heavyweights (with *Lumen Gentium* and *Dei Verbum* being the weightiest of the heavies). Then there were the Council's decrees (on bishops, priests and their training, communications, the Eastern Catholic Churches, ecumenism, the renewal of consecrated life, missions, and the laity). And, finally, there were the Council's declarations (on Catholic education, non-Christian religions, and religious freedom).

In the two decades following the Council, however, little effort was expended on understanding these sixteen texts as a coherent whole. And that lack of coherence, due in part to a lack of Council-provided "keys," had an unhappy result. What John XXIII had envisioned in *Gaudet Mater Ecclesia* as a Pentecostal experience energizing the Church for the task of converting the world led to something quite different: decades of internal struggle over the Council's proper interpretation.

The sixteen documents of Vatican II can be likened to differently colored and variously cut pieces of cloth. A connecting thread was required to weave those patches of cloth into a cohesive tapestry. Six years into his pontificate and twenty years after the Council was solemnly closed, Pope John Paul

II decided to find the thread by calling a special meeting of the Synod of Bishops, which would consider what had gone right and what had gone not-so-right in the implementation of the Council. There was no question in John Paul's mind that Vatican II had been God's gift to the Church. The challenge was to understand the nature of that gift, so that it might be shared throughout the Church and then proclaimed to the world. And if, as a result, the Church began to move beyond the dog-and-cat fights that had marred the post–Vatican II period, so much the better.

It was a bold initiative that produced another hinge-moment in this drama.

The Extraordinary Synod of 1985

IN THE ARGOT of the Vatican, Synods are deemed "extraordinary" if they fall outside the typically triennial schedule of "ordinary" Synod meetings. Synod-1985 was extraordinary in that sense. It was also "extraordinary" in the ordinary sense of the word: it was an extraordinary moment in that it was instrumental in shaping Act Five in the drama of Catholicism-and-modernity.

Most biographies of Pope John Paul II give short shrift to the Extraordinary Synod of 1985, and its exceptional character has only come into focus in retrospect. When it met from November 24 to December 8, 1985, the Synod was often taken to be yet another skirmish in the ongoing ecclesiastical civil war between post-conciliar "progressives" and post-conciliar "conservatives." The banner of the latter had been nailed to the mast by Cardinal Joseph Ratzinger's pre-Synod book *The Ratzinger Report*, a lengthy interview with the Italian journalist Vittorio Messori that was a sharp critique of post-conciliar

Catholic thought and life. As for the "progressives," one of their paladins at Synod-1985 spoke for many of his cast of mind when he said, as the Synod began its work, "Why does there have to be a change? What's wrong with the way things have been going?" Three decades later, Synod-1985 is typically remembered for the *Catechism of the Catholic Church* that it mandated; the publication of the *Catechism* in 1992, under the authority of an apostolic constitution in which John Paul II described it as a fruit of Vatican II, helped put ballast back into Catholic religious education around the world.

The internecine Roman battles of November and December 1985 had their fascinations, not least because it was the "progressives" who were now the party of the status quo and the "conservatives" who argued for deeper reform. And the Synod-mandated *Catechism* was certainly an influential accomplishment. By digging deeper into the substance of the Synod's *Relatio Finalis* (*Final Report*), however, the Extraordinary Synod of 1985 comes into clearer focus as a crucial moment in which the Church reclaimed the evangelical vision of John XXIII's *Gaudet Mater Ecclesia* and began to move into the evangelical future imagined by Paul VI in *Evangelii Nuntiandi.*

THE POST-CONCILIAR BATTLES within Catholicism were often fought over questions of who's-in-charge. At bottom, however, these were conflicts over the very nature of the Church. Synod-1985 laid down several key markers for Catholic self-understanding at the close of the twentieth century.

The Church could not be understood in merely sociological, and certainly not political, terms, the Synod fathers insisted. The Church was and is a "mystery," a living, dynamic, ongoing encounter between God and humanity. That quality of mystery cannot be reduced to mundane categories without the Church losing its essence. Any efforts to suggest that the world sets the agenda for the Church (as the World Council of Churches had claimed), or that the essence of the Church is to be found in political activism, misconstrued and distorted the teaching of Vatican II.

As for the Council itself, Synod-1985 demanded that it be read in its entirety, with the four conciliar constitutions setting the framework and providing interpretive keys for the decrees and declarations. Nor was it appropriate to set the "spirit" of the Council over against the letter of its texts, according to the *Relatio Finalis*. The reformist spirit animating Vatican II ought to enliven the reading of its documents, but its documents were, and are, the Council in a privileged way; no proper interpretation of those texts can prescind from them in the name of enthusiasms justified as expressions of "the spirit of Vatican II." Further, the Synod fathers stated, Vatican II ought to be read as part of the living history and tradition of the Church. The Council did not mark some pristine new starting point for Catholic belief and practice, untethered from what had gone before. Thus Vatican II could not be set against Vatican I, or Trent, or any other ecumenical council. Vatican II was to be understood and received as a Spirit-led development of all that had come before it. The Council was not, in the language that Thomas Kuhn had introduced to the history of science, a "paradigm shift." The Catholic Church did doctrinal development, always in continuity with the deposit of faith; the Church didn't do paradigm shifts.

Gaudet Mater Ecclesia's injunction to the Church to read the "signs of the times" was, the Synod agreed, a perennial obligation of the Church. The Synod fathers of 1985 were also honest enough to admit that the signs of their times were not identical to the signs of the times in 1962–1965. Various forms of secularism had become aggressive, and while the Synod fathers reaffirmed with Vatican II that the worlds of politics, economics, society, and culture had their own "legitimate autonomy," that was not to be confused with ideologically driven efforts to deny the spiritual character, inalienable dignity, and transcendent destiny of the human person. Nor were political systems based on a reduction of the human condition to material measures an expression of the world's legitimate autonomy. The human person was far more than an accident of cosmic biochemical or mundane economic processes, Synod-1985 insisted; to think of human beings as mere playthings of material forces was to degrade the human person and set a public course toward tyranny. Like Vatican II, Synod-1985 wished for a genuine dialogue with secularists, of either an agnostic or an atheistic cast of mind. Twenty years after Vatican II, though, it was unclear whether there were any serious interlocutors for the Church in that conversation. For where the secular world was not overtly hostile to religious believers, it tended to be suffocating in a terrible spiritual ennui.

S ECULAR HOSTILITY AND secular boredom notwithstanding, the Synod fathers of 1985 also discerned signs of a new interest in, or at least openness to, the sacred. This openness to the mystery of being and life was an important opportunity for evangelization. And evangelization, Synod-1985 insisted, was what the Catholic Church was *for*: the "primary mission of the Church is to preach and to witness to the good and joyful news of the election, the mercy, and the charity of God that manifest themselves in salvation history"—in the story of the People of Israel, and, above all, in Jesus Christ. The Synod fathers spoke in no triumphalist tones here. Rather, they took a note from St. Paul and immediately went on to affirm that "the Church makes herself more credible if she speaks less of herself and ever more preaches Christ crucified." That meant, among other things, that there could be no friction-free encounter between the Church and late modernity, as some might have imagined after Vatican II. The Gospel always was, and always will be, a challenge.

The challenge the Gospel posed to a sometimes jaded late modernity was an invitation to reckon with some amazing and good news. For in meeting Jesus Christ, crucified and risen, the men and women of late modernity, and indeed people of all times, were being offered something astonishing: friendship with the Son of God, and thus "a participation in the life of God" himself. And here, the Synod fathers taught, was the essence of Christian conversion. Catholicism begins not with rules or even certain practices, but with friendship with Jesus Christ. At a moment when so many were experiencing a spiritual crisis that reflected a sense of helplessness before the tides of history and the power of technology, friendship with Christ—discipleship—offered late modern humanity the possibility of the greatness that modernity had long promised but had so often failed to deliver.

To be a friend of the Lord Jesus Christ was not another, if more elevated, form of individualism, and it was certainly not a matter of anyone's autonomy. Thus the Synod of 1985 also stressed that the "intimate conversion of heart" involved in knowing and embracing Jesus Christ inserted the believer into the community of Christ's other friends, the Church. Relations within that community were like none other, for that community was unique. It had the characteristics of a voluntary association, in that no one was compelled to join it, but to reduce it to that sociological category was to empty it of its essential meaning. It had a public life, but it was not a political party. It had an economic life, but it was not a business or trade union. It had some of the characteristics of a family, but the Church was not biologically generated.

In trying to find a word to capture the unique reality of the Church, the Synod of 1985 settled on the Latin term *communio*, which somewhat inadequately comes into English as "communion." The term thus requires some explication.

The bonds within the *communio* of the Church are even deeper than the bonds of family, for they are bonds forged by grace: by the divine life poured into the Church by the Holy Spirit at the first Christian Pentecost, and ever after. Thus perhaps the best analogy for the character of relationships within the *communio* of the Church is the relationship of living cells within the same body—in this case, what Pius XII called the Mystical Body of Christ. And this concept of *communio*, according to Synod-1985's *Final Report*, was "the central, fundamental idea in the documents of the Council." It was the thread that wove the sixteen documents of the Council together into a coherent and beautiful tapestry.

The Synod fathers insisted that this *communio* transcended national boundaries by its very nature. Catholicism is not a federation of national churches, but a universal community that transcends the vagaries of borders, which are historically contingent (think of Alsace, Lorraine, the Tyrol—or Arizona). In this quality of universality, as in its preaching of a Gospel addressed to everyone without regard to race, ethnicity, socioeconomic status, or sex, the Church makes present, as a kind of sacrament, the unity of the human race. And in doing so, the Church is a place of "reconciliation . . . [and] peace" here and now, while also pointing toward humanity's ultimate destiny, which is not oblivion in the entropy of a burnt-out solar system, but communion—that word again—with God in what Scripture calls the New Jerusalem (Revelation 21.2). The *communio* of the Church thus has an eschatological or Kingdom character, not just a present and a past. And a proper understanding of the mystery of the Church means keeping all those temporal and transtemporal dimensions of its reality in mind.

Within the Church, according to the Synod of 1985, everyone shares a vocation to holiness by virtue of their baptism (the sacramental marker of their friendship with Jesus Christ). Everyone in the Church is called to holiness, and that call demands that all be evangelists. Some are evangelists by witness; others by proclamation; still others by argument or patient persuasion. But everyone in the Church receives a missionary vocation at baptism, and if both the spirit and the letter of Vatican II are to come fully alive in the Catholic Church, every Catholic must live that missionary vocation in his or her particular state of life.

The *communio* of the friends of Jesus Christ does not exist for itself alone: it exists to offer others the gifts of grace and faith it was given. Thus to be true to itself and to Vatican II, the Church must not close itself in on itself, wasting energies on internal quarrels. "Missionary openness for the complete salvation of the world," the Synod fathers wrote, ought to be the hallmark of the Church of Vatican II, as it had once been the hallmark of the Church of the New Testament.

Thus the Synod of 1985 helped prepare the way for the fifth act in the drama of Catholicism-and-modernity. By finding the thread that bound the Council's texts together—by describing the Church as a *communion* of *disciples* in *mission*—the Synod accelerated the process by which the next phase of the drama would be one of Catholicism converting modernity. And within that fifth act, the fourth act would continue. For as the Church offered the postmodern world friendship with Jesus Christ and incorporation into the *communio* of the friends of the Son of God, it would also challenge the world with a social doctrine that just might provide a more secure foundation for twenty-first-century modernity's political, economic, and social aspirations.

Reliving the Easter Effect

IN ADDITION TO the Synod of 1985, one other moment captured the essence of the transition to Act Five in the drama of Catholicism-and-modernity: Pope John Paul II's pilgrimage to the Holy Land in March 2000.

By the calculations governing the actions of most world figures, that journey was a rather crazy idea. The Pope, soon to turn eighty, was feeling the debilitating effects of the Parkinson's disease that had struck him years before. The region was replete with political landmines. John Paul had more than one hundred other public events on his calendar during the Great Jubilee of 2000. So why go to the Holy Land?

There were several reasons. He was satisfying the desire of his own Christian pilgrim's heart to pray in the places where his Lord had walked, taught, healed, and prayed. He wanted to remind the world that there was more to the turn into that talismanic year "2000" than the threat of Y2K computer malfunctions. He wanted to dramatize his efforts at reconciling Catholicism and Judaism by paying his respects at the Yad Vashem Holocaust Memorial and praying at the Western Wall. He may even have hoped he could set an example that would eventually improve relations between the squabbling tribes of the Middle East.

But above all, one imagines, he wanted to embody in a dramatic and personal act of witness the Church's turn into what he had begun to call the New Evangelization.

In going on pilgrimage to the chief sites of salvation history, John Paul II was putting the entire Catholic Church on his back and making the people of the Church, through him, see and hear and touch a crucial truth that both Church and world needed to remember as the third millennium opened: Christianity is not a fairy tale, a pious fiction, or a form of religious myth. Rather, Christianity began at a certain moment in history, in places where you can still go, when the lives of quite marginal people were radically transformed by their encounter with the man they first knew as the itinerant Rabbi Jesus from Nazareth—and whom they later met, after what had seemed utter catastrophe, as the resurrected Lord Jesus Christ. In that knowing—in the experience of Easter completed by Pentecost—these marginal folk from the far eastern edges of what they thought of as civilization were so transformed that they formed a *communio* that went out and launched a revolution. And over the next two and a half centuries, that revolution converted much of the Mediterranean world.

Thus, to be a communion of disciples in mission, a communion that begins with personal friendship with Jesus Christ, was the essence of the Church from its very beginning. As it had begun, so it must continue.

John Paul II had begun thinking about the Great Jubilee of 2000 shortly after his election. That jubilee was never, for him, mere commemoration. It was an occasion to complete the Pentecostal experience of Vatican II, so that the Church would enter the twenty-first century and the third millennium radically committed to the conversion of the late modern world, the postmodern world, and whatever worlds were coming next. Thus it was time, at the end of the Great Jubilee, to open the fifth act in the drama of Catholicism-and-modernity.

Catholicism
Converting Modernity

Into the Deep

POPE JOHN PAUL II often said that the celebration he named "The Great Jubilee of 2000" was the interpretive key to his entire pontificate. That he also saw it as a potentially decisive, even epochal turning point for the Catholic Church was suggested by the fact that the jubilee year lasted two weeks longer than a calendar year.

The Great Jubilee opened at Christmas Midnight Mass at St. Peter's on December 24–25, 1999, when John Paul II knelt at, then walked through, the basilica's open Holy Door, which represented the breadth of God's mercy. The jubilee continued throughout 2000 and extended into the first week of 2001. On January 6, 2001—the Solemnity of the Epiphany, when the Church liturgically celebrates the first public manifestations of the incarnate Son of God—the two bronze panels of the Holy Door of St. Peter's were solemnly closed, and John Paul issued the apostolic letter *Novo Millennio Ineunte* (*Entering the New Millennium*), marking the conclusion of the Great Jubilee and lifting the curtain on the fifth act of the drama of Catholicism-and-modernity.

Throughout that letter, which gave more precise definition to Catholicism's grand strategy in the twenty-first century and the third millennium of Christian history, the Pope repeated a biblical antiphon drawn from the fifth chapter of St. Luke's gospel. There, several Galilean fishermen have spent a long night on the Lake of Gennesaret, fruitlessly plying their trade. Jesus walks into the scene and borrows Simon's boat as a kind of floating stage from which to address the crowd gathering on the seashore. After teaching the people about the inbreaking of the Kingdom of God, he tells Simon to "put out into the deep" for a catch. Simon grumbles that they hadn't caught anything all night, but, since Jesus says to set out into the deep, he'll do just that. The haul of fish is so immense that another boat has to help them bring it to shore. Simon, who will later be known as Peter, leaves everything to follow Jesus, along with his brother Andrew and their partners in the other boat, James and John.

The Latin phrase for "put out into the deep," *Duc in altum*, reverberated throughout *Novo Millennio Ineunte*. Repeated five times, it was John Paul II's metaphor for the fifth act of the drama of Catholicism-and-modernity: the Church must leave the shallow, comfortable waters of institutional maintenance and set out into the roiling, turbulent "deep" of the late modern and increasingly postmodern world. To do what? To make a great catch—to *convert* the twenty-first-century world to Christ and to help strengthen the moral and cultural foundations of modernity's noblest aspirations and achievements.

THIS GRAND STRATEGIC change—from ecclesiastical institutional maintenance to robust evangelism and critical civic engagement—was made possible in the twenty-first century by a chain of developments reaching back to the late eighteenth century. So a brief review of the drama's plot thus far will help bring the fifth act into sharper focus.

The first act in the drama of Catholicism-and-modernity, which ran from the French Revolution through the pontificate of Pope Pius IX, was the apogee of the Counter-Reformation. As animated by the reformist Council of Trent, Counter-Reformation Catholicism was not simply defensive, common misconceptions notwithstanding. In its first decades, Counter-Reformation Catholicism was full of missionary zeal, as names like Francis Xavier (the "Apostle of the Indies"), François de

Laval (founding bishop of Québec in New France), and Bartolomé de las Casas (defender of the human rights of native peoples in the Western Hemisphere) suggest. Confronted by aggressive ideological and political challengers in the eighteenth and nineteenth centuries, however, the Catholic Church became, in the main, a defensive bastion focused on the imperative of institutional maintenance—not unreasonably in some cases, given the assault by various anticlerical regimes on classic Christian culture and Catholic educational and charitable institutions. In its encounter with emergent political modernity, Catholicism was also burdened by the fact of the Papal States, which linked the papacy (and the Church) to autocracy as a method of governance. However devastating it seemed to Pius IX at the time, though, the demise of the Papal States in 1870 cleared the stage of an obstacle impeding the development of a serious Catholic engagement with political modernity.

In the second act of the drama, which opened with the election of Pope Leo XIII in 1878 and ran through the pontificate of Pope Pius XII, the Catholic Church began to probe the possibility of a conversation with cultural, social, economic, and political modernity, conducted on the basis of philosophical first principles that could be known by reason. The Leonine Revolution began with the encyclical *Aeterni Patris* in 1879, was further developed by Leo's great encyclicals on the state, liberty, law, and social doctrine, and continued in fits and starts for the next eighty years; the controversies over its boundaries, and even over its advisability, were continual and sometimes quite sharp-edged. In the fourth decade of this second act, a predominantly European Catholic Church found its people embroiled in the First World War: an exercise in mass slaughter in which the products of modern science and technology gave lethal expression to some of the worst ideas of intellectual and cultural modernity, including Social Darwinism, eugenically fueled theories of racial and ethnic conflict, and xenophobic nationalism. In the aftermath of that disaster,

Catholicism was next confronted by the totalitarian project in its communist, fascist, and German national-socialist forms—each of which posed a sharp challenge to the very existence of the Church. Throughout its struggles with these extreme manifestations of political modernity, and despite internal opposition from churchmen wedded to what they imagined as the stability and certainties of the past, the dynamism of the Leonine Revolution was sustained within the Church. Thus a path beyond the defensiveness of the later Counter-Reformation period and its institutional-maintenance Catholicism began to open up.

With the election of Pope John XXIII in 1958 and his address opening the Second Vatican Council, the curtain was raised on the third act of the drama of Catholicism-and-modernity. Judging from the proposals received by the Vatican commission charged with preparing the Council's agenda, which solicited discussion topics from the entire world episcopate, many of the bishops who gathered in Rome in October 1962 expected Vatican II's work to fine-tune Counter-Reformation Catholicism. But other bishops and their theological advisers, more alert to the dynamics created by the Leonine Revolution, had other ideas. And as he made clear in *Gaudet Mater Ecclesia*, so did John XXIII. Leo XIII's *Aeterni Patris* had opened the possibility of a Catholic engagement with intellectual and cultural modernity, and the Leonine social and political encyclicals had created conditions for the possibility of a Catholic engagement with political modernity. In his opening address to Vatican II, John XXIII signaled that another pope elected as an elderly placeholder was proposing another bold, grand strategic initiative: the Catholic Church would reclaim its evangelical patrimony through the conciliar experience of a new Pentecost, which would lead it to engage modernity more fully in order to convert it. The terms of that engagement were sharply debated throughout the four sessions of Vatican II, but by the time Pope Paul VI solemnly closed the Council on

December 8, 1965, the curtain had come down on Counter-Reformation Catholicism.

The character of the Catholicism of the future remained contested, however. A minority element in the Church, determined to resist modernity in all its expressions, clung to what it understood as settled and unchangeable forms of Catholic thought and ecclesial life, although many of those conceptions and practices were time-bound and historically contingent. A not inconsiderable part of the world Church engaged in a decades-long experiment in the exuberant, often uncritical embrace of modernity, but in so doing seemed to forget the evangelical summons of *Gaudet Mater Ecclesia*. Some even suggested that Christian mission was no longer an imperative, since the world was already implicitly Christian and conversion to Jesus Christ was simply one among many ways of making explicit what was already present in a maturing humanity.

Then, in the latter years of the pontificate of Paul VI, a dual-edged counterproposal came into play. According to that alternative understanding of the Catholic future, the Church should critically engage cultural, economic, social, and political modernity as a full participant and partner in the public debate about the great questions of meaning and value that would decide the human future. And it should do so in two ways: through evangelism, which responded to modernity's quest for meaning, and on the basis of its social doctrine, which might provide a more secure foundation for modernity's aspirations to liberty, equality, prosperity, and solidarity. The reformist critique of social, political, cultural, and economic modernity from within modern intellectual premises was the fourth act in the drama of Catholicism-and-modernity; it came to its first mature expression in the pontificates of John Paul II and Benedict XVI, both in their teaching and in the living parts of the world Church they inspired.

Concurrently, the pontificates of John Paul and Benedict embodied the other dimension of the post-conciliar reformist counterproposal: the recovery of the evangelical, missionary imperative found in John XXIII's opening address to Vatican II. So the fifth act of this drama would incorporate the fourth, the Catholic critique of modernity from within, while living a robust, evangelical commitment to *convert* the late modern and postmodern worlds to friendship with Jesus Christ. In that encounter with the incarnate Son of God, John Paul and Benedict believed, modernity would find the most satisfactory answers to its twenty-first-century dilemmas, which included an enervating skepticism about the possibility of any human grasp on the truth, including moral truth, and a concomitant loss of a sense of the meaning and value of life.

I N *NOVO MILLENNIO INEUNTE*, John Paul II stressed that living a thoroughly evangelical Catholicism in the twenty-first century would require Catholics, especially in the developed world, to think of themselves and their religious obligations in a radically different way.

In the era of Counter-Reformation Catholicism, Catholics typically thought of "missionaries" as brave men and women who left their Christian homelands for exotic and sometimes dangerous places, offering those who had never heard of Jesus Christ the possibility of friendship with him and incorporation into his Mystical Body, the Church. That type of missionary activity, John Paul understood, remained an urgent part of the Church's twenty-first-century task. But given the realities of late modernity and postmodernity, and the rise of "post-Christian" societies throughout the North Atlantic world, new concepts of who was a "missionary" and what constituted "mission territory" were urgently needed.

As John Paul said in his homily at the Mass that concluded the Great Jubilee of 2000, the Catholic Church must "start out afresh on a new stage of the journey on which we become proclaimers and heralds." That was how Catholicism would "become in history a true epiphany of the merciful and glorious face of Christ the Lord." To be that and do that, the Pope wrote in *Novo Millennio Ineunte*, the entire Church, not just a small subset of Catholics dubbed "missionaries," had to put out into the deep in order "to take up the evangelizing mission with fresh enthusiasm."

That, he believed, was the summons issued by the Second Vatican Council. It was to recall that summons and make it the Church's grand strategy for the third millennium that he had proclaimed the Great Jubilee of 2000. Vatican II had spoken eloquently of Catholicism as a "pilgrim Church." On pilgrimage, John Paul wrote, "there is no time for looking back." Rather, the Church should always look forward, always ready to answer the question the apostle Peter's stunned listeners had asked on the first Christian Pentecost: "What must we do?" (Acts 2.37). The answer to that query must first be given by Christians who have met Christ and embraced the friendship he offers, so that they can offer that same encounter and friendship to others.

Every Catholic, in other words, was called to be a missionary disciple in the third millennium. And to be that, John Paul wrote in *Novo Millennio Ineunte*, was to be holy. Holiness—mirroring God's love and mercy in the world—was not something for a few extraordinary people. No, John Paul wrote, holiness is the "standard of ordinary Christian life." Holiness is nurtured in prayer, and the Church ought to become ever more a school of prayer—prayer that energizes Catholics for mission and evangelization. Mission, the Pope insisted, "cannot be left to a group of 'specialists' but must involve the responsibility of all the members of the People of God."

As Pope Paul VI taught in *Evangelii Nuntiandi*, the Church's proclamation of the Gospel was first given concrete expression by the quality of the Church's own life. By living its life as a "communion of love," the Church of the twenty-first century embodied the definition of its essence offered by Vatican

II: as a communion of love, "the Church would appear as a 'sacrament,' as the sign and instrument of intimate union with God and of the unity of the human race." At the same time, and even as it engaged in dialogue with other world religions and with twenty-first-century skeptics, agnostics, and atheists, the Catholicism of the third millennium must always live out its constituting conviction: that, in meeting Jesus Christ, crucified and risen, the men and women of the late modern and postmodern worlds would be empowered to "live the life of the Trinity" here and now. And with Christ, they would be empowered to "transform history until its fulfillment in the heavenly Jerusalem."

This evangelical commitment to conversion and transformation, John Paul concluded, had always been at the heart of the Church. And it is "our program for the Third Millennium."

Evangelical Catholicism

THE PONTIFICATE OF John Paul II was a coherent whole in which his authoritative interpretation of the Second Vatican Council, his reform of the Church, and his action on the world political stage were mutually reinforcing dimensions of a single pastoral project. If the 1991 encyclical *Centesimus Annus* and the 1998 encyclical *Fides et Ratio* set the terms of the Catholic Church's twenty-first-century engagement with intellectual, cultural, political, and economic modernity, the 1990 encyclical *Redemptoris Missio* (*The Mission of the Redeemer*) was the magna carta of the mission-driven Church of the future that John Paul II proclaimed in *Novo Millennio Ineunte*. It was also the most important explication of the ecclesiastical grand strategy and global project the Pope constantly promoted in the last fifteen years of his papacy, which he dubbed the "New Evangelization."

Redemptoris Missio was formally signed and dated on December 7, 1990, in order to commemorate the twenty-fifth anniversary of Vatican II's Decree on the Church's Missionary Activity, *Ad Gentes* (*To the Nations*). Like John XXIII's opening address to the Council, *Ad Gentes* sought to reignite a sense of evangelical excitement in the Catholic Church. In the ensuing quarter-century, however, there had been intense debates within Catholicism over whether the Church should even have a mission "to the nations"—the traditional phrase for evangelizing those who had never heard of Jesus Christ and his Gospel. Some theologians described previous efforts at evangelization as exercises in cultural imperialism, arguing that the Church should go to other cultures to learn from them, not to offer its own faith. Still others saw no point in Catholic evangelism; in their view, Jesus Christ was but one of many avatars of a divine will-to-redeem that appeared in different forms in different cultural settings. Jesus might be the "redeemer for Christians," but that role was filled in other cultures by other great religious figures. In light of these speculations, it was little wonder that Catholic missionary orders shrank in the years after Vatican II, despite John XXIII's intention for the Council and the teaching of *Ad Gentes*. At the same time, the post-conciliar struggles in the Church over the proper interpretation of Vatican II were draining it of evangelical energy.

John Paul II believed that fidelity to Christ's command to "go and teach all nations" (Matthew 28.19), fidelity to John XXIII's vision for Vatican II and fidelity to the Council's teaching all required that he weigh into this debate and set a course correction. He did so by changing the terms of the argument, which had centered for twenty years on what kind of mission the Church should deploy. That, he taught, was the wrong question. The Church did not just have a mission, as if "mission" were one of a number of things the Catholic Church did. The Church, he insisted, *is* a mission.

"The Church is missionary by her very nature," John Paul wrote. In its pivotal document *Lumen Gentium*, the Dogmatic Constitution on the Church, the fathers of Vatican II had spoken of a "universal call to holiness." That summons to holiness included a summons to mission, and the summons was issued to everyone. Friendship with Jesus Christ, the essence of Catholic faith, demands to be shared. As Christ himself had said in Matthew 10.8, his friends and disciples had freely received, so they must freely give, offering others the gift they had been given. In doing so, John Paul taught, they would discover the paradox of faith: defying all mathematical logic, faith increases the more it is offered and given to others. Thus a Christian's willingness to share the Gospel of Christ with others is one crucial measure of the depth of that Christian's commitment to Christ and to the truth Christ offers.

Evangelization—the offer of the Gospel and of friendship with Christ—takes many forms, *Redemptoris Missio* taught, and the answer to the question, "Who is to be evangelized?" is straightforward and comprehensive: everyone. There is the pastoral care of the already-catechized members of the Church, deepening their faith and empowering them for mission. There is the re-evangelization of those who have fallen away from the Christian community and its practice of the faith. And there is the classic "mission *ad gentes*" to those who have never known Christ. All of this is "evangelization": which, to repeat, is not one facet among others of the Church's life, but Catholicism's very reason for existence.

In discussing the various fields of missionary activity in the twenty-first century, *Redemptoris Missio* laid considerable stress on the evangelization of culture. The media, the feminist movement, environmental organizations, the world of science, academic life in its various forms—all these, John Paul II taught, were the "modern equivalents of the Areopagus," the Athenian hill on which St. Paul tried to persuade his listeners that the "unknown god" to whom they had dedicated an altar was the God he proclaimed and worshiped, the God who had raised Jesus from the dead and thus made him the Lord of history. In each of those arenas, the Pope suggested, the men and women of late modernity were struggling with that "pulverization of the human" he had pondered with Henri de Lubac in 1969. Because of that struggle, each of those fields of culture was implicitly "waiting for a compelling proclamation of Jesus Christ as the answer to humanity's most urgent questions."

In evangelizing the worlds of culture, as in evangelizing the worlds of political and economic life, the Church's method must be that of freedom. "*The Church proposes; she imposes nothing,*" John Paul wrote with characteristically italicized emphasis. "She respects individuals and cultures, and she honors the sanctuary of conscience." At the same time, the Church evangelizes in the conviction that it has been given the truth about humanity and its destiny in Jesus Christ and is solemnly obliged to propose that truth to everyone. And the beginning of evangelization will often be a matter of example: people who have seen love in action, especially in service to those who have been harshly "pulverized" by modernity, will be more willing to consider the Christian proclamation that God is love.

Evangelization should also take place in everyday life, according to *Redemptoris Missio*. If everyone in the Church is called in Baptism to be a missionary disciple, then owning one's baptism and giving expression to the grace received in the first sacrament means that every place is "mission territory." One kitchen's table is mission territory. So is one's neighborhood, one's workplace, and one's life as a consumer and a citizen. John Paul II's vision of the Evangelical Catholicism of the future was truly catholic, in the sense of universal: everyone a missionary; every human environment a mission field; all mission, all the time.

THROUGHOUT THE LAST fifteen years of his pontificate, John Paul II returned time and again to the theme of the New Evangelization he had put squarely at the center of the world Church's agenda in *Redemptoris Missio*. In doing so, he confirmed a dramatic transition in Catholic self-understanding while describing a distinctive program for the future. In the first two acts of the drama of Catholicism-and-modernity, the Catholic Church thought of itself in juridical terms as the *societas perfecta*, a "perfect society" set over against the world, to which it primarily related as a critic and judge. With his proclamation of the Church of the New Evangelization, John Paul II summed up the transition that John XXIII envisioned in *Gaudet Mater Ecclesia*, that Vatican II described in detail in *Lumen Gentium*, that Paul VI again proposed in *Evangelii Nuntiandi*, and that the Extraordinary Synod of 1985 lifted up: the transition from the Church as a *societas perfecta* against modernity to the Church as a communion of disciples in mission, engaging modernity in order to convert modernity.

In light of that, the temptation to think of *Redemptoris Missio* and *Centesimus Annus* as quite different encyclicals—the former addressing "internal" Church matters and the latter making proposals to "the world"—should be stoutly resisted. Viewed through the historiographic lens of the drama of Catholicism-and-modernity, the two encyclicals complement each other as they give definition to the fifth act of the drama, which incorporates the great themes of the fourth act. In striking contrast to the didactic approach taken to modernity in the drama's first act, both *Redemptoris Missio* and *Centesimus Annus* define a Church that proposes truths on the basis of reason and revelation—a Church that imposes nothing on anyone, and that sees in modernity's aspirations to freedom, equality, and solidarity echoes or traces of Christian convictions about the dignity of the divinely created human person. *Redemptoris Missio* reminds the Church of the core evangelical content of its proclamation, and explains why making that proclamation—of Jesus Christ, the Risen Lord in whom God's Kingdom emerges in history—is the Church's first responsibility to "the world." *Centesimus Annus* spells out the Catholic proposal to political and economic modernity while reminding the Church that its first mission in society is the formation of a vibrant public moral culture, a culture capable of disciplining and directing the energies generated by free politics and free economics so that they serve the common good. Together, the two encyclicals envision a Catholicism for the twenty-first century and the third millennium that is both evangelically robust and fully engaged in the public debate over humanity's future. The two, as Vatican II and John Paul II insisted, go together.

This dramatic transition in Catholic self-understanding was surely influenced by the Church's encounter with modernity, notwithstanding the fact that the first century of that encounter was one of anathemas hurled by both parties. And no doubt there was an ironic quality to that line of influence: in a historical drama that began with modernity considering Catholicism an alien pathogen to be destroyed for the health of the body politic, and the Catholic Church sharply contesting modernity on all fronts, the Church reclaimed the foundational truth about its own evangelical and missionary essence and developed a sophisticated social doctrine. Yet the vision of an evangelizing and publicly engaged Catholicism expressed in *Redemptoris Missio* and *Centesimus Annus* did not evolve simply in reaction to the challenge of modernity. Rather, the publicly engaged and evangelically assertive Catholicism of the fifth act of this drama was gestated within a Church that had become a protagonist in the drama of modernity in its own right.

Redemptoris Missio stands in a line of development that can be traced back to Johann Adam Möhler and Matthias Scheeben, whose biblical and patristic studies were crucial in encouraging a Catholic self-understanding in which the juridical or structural dimensions of the Church's life were at the service of the Church's liturgical and spiritual life and its evangelical mission. Those insights from kerygmatic theology then played an important role in the theological renaissance of the twentieth century and the recovery of some of the deepest sources of the Church's self-understanding, which was the precondition to the Second Vatican Council and the idea of the Church the Council taught in *Lumen Gentium*.

Centesimus Annus brought to a fine point of analysis and prescription the distinctively Catholic approach to social, economic, and political modernity that Wilhelm Emmanuel von Ketteler and Pope Leo XIII had pioneered in the nineteenth century. And while it is true that both Ketteler and Leo were responding to the challenges posed by modernity, their response was shaped by deeply rooted Catholic understandings of the nature of the human person, of what it means to be a human society, and of what the members of that society owe each other; indeed, Thomas Aquinas had worked out those understandings conceptually in the thirteenth century, drawing on themes from the Bible.

The emergence of Evangelical Catholicism in this fifth act vividly illustrates the claim that, in the drama of Catholicism-and-modernity, modernity was not, and is not, the sole protagonist, against which Catholicism is always reacting. The relationship between Catholicism and modernity has been far more complex than that. It is also far more interesting, because the Catholicism envisioned in *Centesimus Annus* and *Redemptoris Missio* positioned the Church to offer late modernity and postmodernity a path beyond its early twenty-first-century dilemmas and discontents. What was once decried as the loathsome horror that had to be crushed in the name of freedom—*Écrasez l'infâme!*—now had a proposal to make—a proposal that the late modern world badly needed to hear if it was to avoid imploding as a result of false ideas of freedom based on anorexic understandings of the human person.

Reimagining the Modern Story

THE DEVELOPMENT OF the Catholic Church's thinking about modernity that began in the Leonine Revolution, that underwent further development at the Second Vatican Council, and that reached its maturation in the internal line of critique proposed by Pope John Paul II and Pope Benedict XVI positioned Catholicism in the third millennium as a genuinely public Church: a Church engaged in the debate over the future of public life as a conversation partner, speaking a language that other participants in the conversation could understand. There is virtually nothing, for example, in John Paul II's *Centesimus Annus* and *Ecclesia in Europa*, or in Benedict XVI's September Lectures, that cannot be engaged by anyone willing to work through a serious argument. To put it another way, John Paul II and Benedict XVI did not require distinctively Catholic theological admission tickets from those who wished to engage them in conversation about the future of twenty-first-century social, cultural, political, or economic life.

This concept of a *public* Church stood in contrast to several other options that had appeared throughout the drama of Catholicism-and-modernity.

The public Church envisioned by John Paul II and Benedict XVI was not an *established* Church that sought to put state power behind its truth claims. Various forms of ecclesiastical establishment continued to exist in world Catholicism in the twenty-first century, particularly in Europe, and usually in terms of state payment of clergy salaries, state support for Catholic education and charitable institutions, and state subsidies to maintain the cultural patrimony in the Church's care. But in none of these cases was the Catholic Church claiming, as a matter of divine right, a unique and privileged role as the state's favored religious community.

Nor was the public Church that John Paul II and Benedict XVI described a *privatized* Church, withdrawn from the public square by its own decision, by the application of coercive state power, or by both. Throughout this drama, various attempts by secularist forces to push Catholicism out of public life and dismiss it as a mere lifestyle choice of no public consequence were all successfully resisted. So were those forces within the Church that counseled a full-scale retreat from public life into Catholic bunkers and enclaves until the nightmare of modernity had ended.

During the first half of the twentieth century, a kind of halfway-house strategy—the creation of distinctively Catholic trade unions, newspapers and magazines, schools, youth organizations, and political parties—had some success in developing Catholic self-understanding amidst the challenges of modernity while making modest contributions to the public debate. But in most European countries, those halfway-house institutions were destroyed during the Second World War, and the Church's own evolving sense of its mission in modernity made their resuscitation unlikely in the second half of the twentieth century.

The alternative to ecclesiastical establishment, the Catholic Church came to understand during the second, third, and fourth acts in the drama of Catholicism-and-modernity, was neither a privatized Church nor a ghettoized Church but a *public* Church: what John Paul II called in *Redemptoris Missio* a *proposing* Church, of the kind embodied in Benedict XVI's September Lectures.

As John Paul II taught explicitly in *Centesimus Annus*, this proposing Church would work in public primarily through the free associations of civil society, rather than as a partisan political actor. The proposing, public Catholicism of the twenty-first century would make arguments; it would not seek to craft policies, although the arguments it made would suggest that some policies were more compatible than others with freedom lived nobly, in solidarity, and for the common good. The proposing, public, evangelical Church of this fifth act would also work at a deeper level of public life—the level of cultural self-awareness and self-understanding as embodied in civilizational narratives, or storylines. At this level, and given the nature of twenty-first-century modernity's discontents and dilemmas, Catholicism's most important public role may well be to help the postmodern world reimagine the story of modernity, drawing on the Church's long tradition of reflection on human dignity, society, and human destiny.

F OR BETTER AND for worse, civilizations and political cultures live narratively, not just politically and economically. Perhaps the most telling, and chilling, modern example is Weimar Germany, where a story of national betrayal—the "stab in the back" of November 1918—so gripped the public imagination that a democracy under pressure set in motion its own destruction by a genocidal maniac. The international aggressiveness of twenty-first-century China, to take another case, is reinforced by an ancient civilizational narrative of cultural superiority and by a modern national narrative of the pre–Mao Zedong "century of humiliation." In shaping national and civilizational destinies, it is not just gross national product and military capacity that matter. Stories count. Indeed, over the long haul, both GNP and military capacity are influenced by narrativized self-concepts.

The conventional telling of modernity's story came into disturbing focus in 2003, during the debate over the constitutional treaty that would govern the newly expanding European Union. The treaty itself was a massive document of several hundred pages, but the sharpest debate came over whether a single word should be included in the treaty's preamble: "Christianity." As originally proposed, the preamble claimed that twenty-first-century Europe's commitments to civility, tolerance, human rights, democracy, and the rule of law were rooted in Europe's classical Greco-Roman heritage, the Enlightenment, and modern thought—an absurdly truncated view of history, for it suggested that nothing of consequence to twenty-first-century Europe's noblest aspirations had happened between Marcus Aurelius (d. AD 180) and Descartes (b. AD 1596), which was a long time for nothing to have happened.

As John Paul II pointed out in a series of addresses to general audiences in the summer of 2003, the deliberate omission of biblical religion from that preambular catalogue of decisive influences on contemporary Europe was historically false and dangerous for Europe's future. Why? Because such a deliberate act of historical amnesia—erasing from the story of Europe and its public cultural memory the contributions of Judaism and Christianity—was being undertaken in service to a project inimical to sustaining democracy and the legal protection of human rights over the long haul: the elimination of transcendent moral reference points from the European public square. That the Pope was not exaggerating about the confusions in play here was inadvertently demonstrated by the most famous op-ed essay written during the Euro-constitutional debate, in which German philosopher Jürgen Habermas and Jacques Derrida, the French theorist of deconstruction and postmodernism, argued that the new Europe must be "neutral between worldviews." But that claim, of course, involved the imposition of a worldview: moral relativism based on deep epistemological skepticism.

After a 2004 debate in Munich with Cardinal Joseph Ratzinger, Habermas would admit that his "neutrality" concept of *laïcité* (what Richard John Neuhaus would have called a "naked public square") may have been too stringent and his notion of pluralism too incoherent to sustain democracy. And, as finally agreed to, the European Constitutional Treaty's preamble—its declaration of moral purpose—began with an anodyne reference to the continent's "cultural, religious, and humanist inheritance" as the source of its commitment to the "inviolable and inalienable rights of the human person, freedom, democracy, equality, and the rule of law." But as Benedict XVI noted in his September 2012 address to the German Bundestag, the relationship of Jerusalem, Athens, and Rome to political modernity remained contested. Throughout European high culture, some continued to insist that the roots of twenty-first-century democracy lay in soil no deeper than the rationalist Enlightenment, while others (including postmodern critics of Enlightenment rationalism) were having difficulty giving any account of the democratic project other than that it seemed to work better—a claim challenged in the opening decades of the twenty-first century by China, jihadist Islam, and new forms of European authoritarianism.

In the first decades of the new century, sharp criticism of democratic dysfunction was heard all over the West: governments incapable of reaching decisions; profligate spending and borrowing; a public discourse increasingly dominated by the shrillest. Yet an argument can be made that the gravest problem of political modernity in the twenty-first century is that it is having trouble giving an account of what it believes to be its greatest achievements: the protection in culture and law of basic human rights, understood as inalienable attributes of persons by reason of their humanity; freedom as the method of politics, expressing itself in democracy; the rule of law. Twenty-first-century modernity's shallow story about itself and its origins seemed incapable of animating political communities that could meet the challenges of the moment. John Paul II suggested that the beginning of an answer to this serious political-cultural dilemma might be found in widening the narrative lens and restoring biblical religion to its proper place in the story of the modern freedom project. For, as he proposed in *Ecclesia in Europa*, that story did not begin in 1789. It began much earlier, with the idea of the human person found in the Bible.

W HAT DID BIBLICAL religion bequeath to the civilization of the West, from which political modernity sprung?

Perhaps most fundamentally, the Bible gave Western civilization the idea that time is directional and unilinear, not cyclical or random. History is not a repetitive cycle; nor is it simply one damn thing after another. From the story of Israel's Exodus from Egypt, which is a foundational metaphor not only for the Western concept of freedom but also for the Western concept of time and history, the West learned that history is adventure and pilgrimage—that history is going somewhere.

The prophets of Israel laid another foundation stone of the West, and of political modernity, when they railed against injustice and insisted that justice is owed to all, not only to the members of one's family, clan, tribe, or nation. Christianity would develop that moral insight into human equality by stressing that the individual, not the family, is the focal point of hope for a human future beyond the grave; that individual human beings can grasp the truth of things; and that because of everyone's capacity to know the truth and to choose to live by the truth, all men and women are morally equal—and ought to be equal before the law. No doubt that notion took centuries to mature. Its deepest and sturdiest roots lay in St. Paul's teaching about the moral unity of humanity (which itself drew on themes in the prophet Isaiah), not in the French Declaration of the Rights of Man and of the Citizen.

Then there was Christ's injunction in Mark 12.17 and its gospel parallels that, while Caesar is owed his due, there are things of God's that are not Caesar's. Which means that Caesar is not God: Caesar is not omnipotent and cannot legitimately claim a monopoly on authority. Desacralizing politics and limiting the range of public authority's remit were essential in building the institutions of political modernity, including limited government. The roots of those distinctively Western ideas lay, once again, in biblical religion.

The witness of the Christian martyrs and their veneration, a development of the celebration of the Jewish martyrs of the Maccabean revolt, redefined heroism for Western civilization, and ultimately for modernity. Prior to the martyrs, heroes were successful men like Homer's Odysseus: clever, resourceful aristocrats turned into quasi-divine figures. And in classical antiquity, the "heroic" almost never included women. Christian martyrdom, by embodying the conscientious conviction of ordinary people, changed all of that, redefining and democratizing heroism—another deep root of the West's concept of the individual as well as of modernity's emphasis on human equality.

Open-minded historians of culture have credited St. Benedict and his monks with saving the classical heritage and thus one deep source of Western civilization during the so-called Dark Ages, when monks in scriptoria carefully copied the great texts of the classical world and preserved them for future generations. But perhaps a postmodern West grappling with its too-thin and too-shallow story could also recognize that monasticism injected the idea of voluntary free associations into the West (no one was forced to join a monastery), even as monasticism experimented with democracy and created new models of authority (abbots were elected by a free vote of all monks). In addition, monasticism gave new meaning to labor through Benedict's insistence that the truly human life was one of *ora et labora*: prayer and work.

And what about the first true autobiography ever written, Augustine's *Confessions*? Here, one might argue, and not in Descartes's *cogito* or Rousseau's self-absorption, was the source of the West's unique emphases on self-examination and interiority as essential qualities of the human—emphases that were the deep taproots of political modernity's insistence on the rights of conscience and the crucial importance of consent (typically registered through representation) in a just political order.

As for political modernity's distinction between spiritual and political authority, did the institutional separation of Church and state prescribed by the First Amendment to the U.S. Constitution really owe everything to John Locke? Or did that crucial distinction not draw on a tradition that reaches back to the thirteenth-century Investiture Controversy, in which the popes successfully battled with the Holy Roman Emperors over the authority to appoint bishops, and to Pope Gelasius I's insistence in the fifth century that princely power and sacerdotal power were distinct?

One of modernity's most cherished institutions is the university, and the twenty-first-century university prides itself on protecting academic freedom (even as it struggles to do so against new forms of intolerance). Where did the university as the West knows it begin? It began with religiously established centers of higher learning in Italy, Bohemia, England, Spain, Poland, and France in the Early and High Middle Ages. There, the tradition of academic freedom amidst robust debate was born in the practice of the *quaestio disputata*, a public forum in which a professor had to defend a thesis against all comers, including lowly students.

As for one of political modernity's most cherished moral achievements, the abolition of the once universal practice of chattel slavery, twenty-first-century human rights activists may remember the heroic labors of William Wilberforce in nineteenth-century Great Britain. But what was the source of Wilberforce's conviction and dogged determination if not the Christian notion that all human beings were capable of conscientious reflection and decision—a notion that, over time, broke down the cultural barriers between those who were free and those who were slaves by eradicating what had long seemed a fixed moral boundary between two different castes?

The list could be extended, but perhaps the point has been made. How can one give an account of modernity's emphasis on the integrity of persons as bearers of inalienable rights, or its insistence on the distinction and institutional separation of spiritual and political authority, or its conception of the rights of conscience, its commitment to the principle of consent in governance, its understanding of legal equality, or its rejection of autocracy, without including the contributions of biblical religion to the cultural ecology from which those commitments and practices derived? To do so—and many try—is to tell a superficial, shallow story. It is also a deliberate, self-inflicted wound—a self-mutilating act of cultural lobotomization that accounts in no small part for the twenty-first-century West's inability to explain and defend itself in other than pragmatic and utilitarian terms. Such a truncated, willfully foreshortened telling of the story of modernity is an act of cultural disloyalty, a falsification of history. And falsifications of history always lead to bad ends.

I N THE FIFTH act of the drama of Catholicism-and-modernity, the public Catholicism of the twenty-first century, which incorporates lessons of the fourth act, ought to help the late modern and postmodern world deepen its understanding of its own story, by reminding modernity that there is more to freedom than the mantra of "choice," just as there is more to the human person than a cluster of desires. That deepening ought to be philosophical, as Benedict XVI's September Lectures suggested by bringing Augustine back into the twenty-first-century conversation about public life. It ought to be theological, as John Paul II proposed in *Ecclesia in Europa*, reflecting on the desolation of a civilization that, without

God, had no means of seeking forgiveness for its failures. And that deepening should be historical. The roots of the noble aspirations proclaimed in the preamble to the European Constitutional Treaty (or in the Universal Declaration of Human Rights, or in the American Declaration of Independence) lie in richer and deeper soil than one or another variant of Enlightenment thought. Finding nourishment for the future in that deeper soil is a cultural imperative—and a necessary work of reconstructing modernity's political foundations. The Catholic Church should be in a distinctive position to help modernity reimagine its story, not least because its own ironic, yet ultimately enriching, experience of the modern world helped Catholicism recover forgotten elements of its own past and make them into sources of renewal.

The Franciscan Stall

THERE HAVE BEEN moments in the drama of Catholicism-and-modernity when the Leonine dynamic that led to the recovery and development of an evangelically vibrant Catholicism with a distinctive public role seemed to stall. The pontificate of Pius X could be considered such a pause, although that papacy also drove the action forward in important ways. The latter years of Pope Pius XII might be considered another such pause, even though Pius XII's first decade was crucial in advancing the Leonine Revolution theologically and preparing the ground for the Second Vatican Council. From the vantage point of the early twenty-first century, the two decades of confusion that followed Vatican II appear to have been years when the Church spun its wheels, unable to get the traction necessary to live out the vision of Catholicism converting modernity that John XXIII laid out in *Gaudet Mater Ecclesia*.

The challenging, puzzling, and, to some minds, deconstructive pontificate of Pope Francis may be another one of those moments of pause.

At his election on March 13, 2013, Jorge Mario Bergoglio, the first Latin American and first Jesuit pope, seemed well positioned to continue developing the evangelically vibrant and publicly engaged Catholicism that had been proposed as the authentic interpretation of Vatican II by his two predecessors, John Paul II and Benedict XVI. As the cardinal archbishop of Buenos Aires, Bergoglio was a leader at the Fifth General Conference of the Bishops of Latin America and the Caribbean, held in the Brazilian city of Aparecida in 2007. There, the bishops had concluded that the institutional-maintenance Catholicism of the past—a faith passed on by cultural, ethnic, and national habit—had no future in the most densely Catholic continent on the planet. Rather, the Gospel had to be proposed anew, and at the center of that proposal must be the offer of personal friendship with Jesus Christ. The general assembly's final report, the Aparecida Document, was as vibrant an expression of Evangelical Catholicism as had been written in the wake of John Paul II's summons to the New Evangelization—and Cardinal Bergoglio had been one of its principal authors.

Eight months after his election, Pope Francis issued the apostolic exhortation *Evangelii Gaudium*, which seemed to apply the analysis of the Aparecida Document to the entire world Church. Catholicism, Francis wrote, had to live from the "joy of evangelizing," and it could only do so if it rediscovered the "eternal newness" of the Gospel. The Church of the twenty-first century must be a Church "permanently in mission," a Church in which everyone is a "missionary disciple." Those disciples would be formed, Francis continued, by a recovery and renewal of the great traditions of "keryg-matic and mystagogical catechesis": Christian formation in sermons, homilies, and education programs centered on the Gospel and the sacraments. Through those privileged places of encounter with Christ, the Church's people learn to see the world through biblical and sacramental lenses, experiencing the extraordinary that lies on the far side of the ordinary and perceiving the salvific figure in the carpet of human history.

A biblical optic on reality would also help the missionary disciples of the twenty-first century address the wounds of the late modern and postmodern world. A biblical understanding of the human person would cure the astigmatism of a new cul-tural gnosticism that teaches the utter plasticity of the human condition, in which nothing is given and everything is sub-ject to human willfulness. A biblical lens on the twenty-first-century world would also enable a Church permanently in mission to perceive the aridity of the spiritual desert in which so many now live and to respond to it through acts of charity, compassion, and solidarity—acts of witness that would open desiccated souls to the possibility of being revived by faith.

At the center of all of this, Francis insisted, is Jesus Christ. The Church does not preach itself or offer itself. The Church offers the gift it has been given, personal friendship with the Son of God, and through him, entry into the life of grace that is the eternal reality of God.

Evangelii Gaudium had its distinctive "Franciscan" notes, as would have been expected. Taken as a whole, however, it was a ringing summons to the kind of evangelizing Cathol-icism, fully engaged as a conversation partner in the public debate over the human future, that had been proposed by John Paul II and Benedict XVI. At its publication, continuity between the pontificate of Francis and the pontificates of his two predecessors, and the dynamic development of Evangeli-cal Catholicism, seemed assured.

THAT SENSE OF continuity amidst development was then strained, sometimes severely, as Francis's papacy unfolded and puzzlement over the Pope's intention and method deepened—especially in those parts of the world Church that had come alive by embracing the teaching of John Paul II and Benedict XVI as the template for getting on with the New Evangelization. In short order, puzzlement gave way to controversy, and it seemed to more than a few Catholics that the twenty-first century had reverted to the confusions of the immediate post–Vatican II period: the difference being that, in those days, the Church was led by a pope who often seemed incapable of contending with the confusion, while Pope Francis seemed to be encouraging it.

Amidst the controversies unleashed in the new pontificate, two issues in particular posed serious obstacles to the New Evangelization and to the Church's capacity to help reconstruct the foundations of modern public life.

The first of these came to light during the meetings of the world Synod of Bishops called by Francis in 2014 and 2015, ostensibly to address the problems of the family in the late modern and postmodern world. On the surface, the most heated debates in those meetings involved a question of sacramental discipline: Could the Church legitimately admit to Holy Communion men and women living in marriages that had not been blessed by the Church? Given the widespread incidence of divorce in the West, this was an issue with serious pastoral implications. As the debate unfolded, however, it became clear that those promoting a change in the Church's traditional discipline—which held that those living in marriages not blessed by the Church ought not present themselves for Holy Communion at Mass, because they were not in full communion with the Church—were also pressing another point. They were proposing, even insisting, that history judges divine revelation, such that contemporary circumstances permit, and may even require, the Church to modify or radically change what had long seemed to be clear instructions from Christ himself on the nature of marriage, and from St. Paul on worthiness to receive Holy Communion.

This theological historicism—the notion that history is everything and that in the flow of history there are no fixed reference points determinative for the present and future—had been a grave problem for nineteenth- and twentieth-century liberal Protestantism and had contributed to the virtual disappearance of doctrinal and moral boundaries from many Protestant communities throughout the West. Its emergence in the Catholic Church was particularly odd, however, in that it contradicted the clear teaching of the Second Vatican Council on the reality and binding nature of divine revelation. With the Dogmatic Constitution on Divine Revelation, *Dei Verbum*, the Council fathers of Vatican II sought to restore the Bible to a central place in the thought, religious practice, and spiritual imagination of Catholics. In promoting that biblical renewal, they affirmed that the Church should learn everything it can from modern methods of understanding ancient texts. But such textual analysis ought to take place, according to *Dei Verbum*, within the conviction that revelation is a reality. God had indeed spoken to humanity through deeds and words, and ultimately in the person of the Son of God, and this revelation is always the standard by which Christians assess, judge, and respond to every moment in history—and to the patterns of life typical of those moments.

The new (or perhaps not-so-new) historicism that underwrote the claims of some at the Synods of 2014 and 2015, and that seemed at work in Pope Francis's apostolic exhortation concluding the work of those Synods, *Amoris Laetitia* (*The Joy of Love*), effectively denied what Vatican II affirmed. For it denies that the Church is bound to what Jesus plainly said about the indissolubility of marriage in the synoptic gospels, and to what St. Paul plainly said about worthiness to receive

Holy Communion in his first letter to the Corinthians—and does so on the grounds that contemporary experience has given us a deeper insight into what Christian fidelity means. A deconstructive historicism of that sort is not a development of the teaching of Vatican II. It is a contradiction of the teaching of Vatican II.

The second large issue roiling the world Church during the papacy of Pope Francis was closely related to this theological question of the reality of revelation: the emergence of a new, twenty-first-century Gallicanism that imagined Catholicism as a federation of national Churches rather than a universal Church with distinctive local expressions.

In yet another irony in the drama of Catholicism-and-modernity, the Gallican or nationalist conception of the Church, long associated in name and historical fact with controversies centered in France, acquired a decidedly Teutonic flavor in Francis's pontificate. Within five years of the Argentine pope's election, what had been tacit for some time became explicit: the Catholic Church in Germany, in German-speaking Austria, and in the German-speaking parts of Switzerland was living a different ecclesial reality than much of the rest of the world Church and saw nothing wrong with that de facto state of schism; indeed, it eagerly sought to export its skepticism about settled Catholic truths throughout the world. The majority of German-speaking bishops seemed committed to the history-redefines-revelation position that their representatives had taken at the Synods of 2014 and 2015. And the pastoral practices they encouraged—including offering Holy Communion as a matter of course (rather than emergency) to those in marriages not blessed by the Church, as well as to the Protestant spouses of Catholics—seemed to underscore that commitment.

This Gallican deconstruction of the unity of Catholic self-understanding and pastoral practice was also a theme at the Synod of 2018. Officially intended to be a global reflection on the Church's mission to evangelize young adults, the Synod's managers, presumably with the Pope's encouragement, inserted into the draft of its final document a lengthy reflection on "synodality" that seemed, again, to hint at a Catholicism in which what was deemed true in Poland was not deemed true in Germany, and in which pastoral practices regarded as obstacles to evangelization in Africa were thought essential to the Church's future in parts of Western Europe.

How any of this confusion over the very foundations of Catholic faith was supposed to contribute to the Catholicism Pope Francis had proclaimed—a Church of "missionary disciples" who are "permanently in mission"—was not clear. Moreover, the historicist and Gallican confusions were furthest advanced in those parts of the Catholic world that had seen a catastrophic decline in Catholic practice. It should have been no surprise, then, that some of the strongest opposition at the Synods of 2014 and 2015 to the deconstructive notion that history can modify the plain truths of revelation, and to proposals to change classic Catholic sacramental practice, came from vibrant and rapidly growing parts of the world Church that were living the New Evangelization as an expression of what Pope Francis had called in *Evangelii Gaudium* the "eternal newness of the Gospel." Thus African bishops at those two Synods vigorously defended the classic, revelation-based understanding of permanent, monogamous marriage, which had come to their cultures as a liberating proposal—especially for women. Those same bishops, joined by North Atlantic bishops with impressive records in implementing the New Evangelization, stoutly resisted attempts at Synod-2018 to have the Church make further concessions to gender theory, gay rights theory, and transgenderism.

The figures within this particular ecclesiastical carpet were not all that difficult to discern. Catholicism in the twenty-first century experienced growth and vitality where the Gospel was embraced in full and where the teaching of the *Catechism of the Catholic Church* was regarded as a stable template for missionary discipleship, not a compendium of ideals impossible to achieve. The growing parts of the Church recognized that living Catholicism in full is a challenge, and that every missionary disciple often fails to live what he or she professes. But the living, growing parts of the Church were also those that declined to lower the bar of expectation in the face of failure; that sought reconciliation and forgiveness after failure; and that got up after experiencing the divine mercy in order to try again, with the help of God's grace, to live missionary discipleship joyfully. Conversely, the moribund or dying parts of the world Church were those that continued to try to make the new historicism and the new Gallicanism work, in another attempt to instantiate the do-it-yourself version of post–Vatican II Catholicism that was dubbed Catholic Lite. Yet there was no evidence, in any part of the world Church, that Catholic Lite could give birth to the Church of Christ-centered disciples permanently in mission for which Pope Francis had called. Rather, Catholic Lite was the Catholicism of once-vibrant parts of the Church that were not bearing evangelical fruit in the twenty-first century: the German-speaking Catholic world; Belgium; too much of France and the Netherlands; Ireland; Québec; and too much of Italy, Spain, and Portugal.

The empirical evidence was not subject to serious dispute: the Catholicism that joyfully sought to live the *Catechism* in full was living, compelling, and had a chance to be the culture-transforming Catholicism that could convert twenty-first-century modernity both to friendship with Jesus Christ and a nobler concept of freedom in public life; Catholic Lite was a failure. Yet in the puzzling Franciscan pontificate, the Pope, rather than seeing his Petrine Office as a reference point for stability, seemed to encourage those whose deconstructive arguments had manifestly failed to create the Church of missionary discipleship he himself had described with such passion and beauty in *Evangelii Gaudium*.

And then there emerged an even graver, more sordid challenge to the Church's capacity to be a communion of disciples in mission and a forceful conversation partner in public life.

From Bitter Irony to Purification

B IBLICAL RELIGION TAUGHT Western civilization that history is ultimately linear. As the multiple ironies in the drama of Catholicism-and-modernity attest, however, there are no givens within history—and history's ironic turns can be deeply disturbing and agonizingly painful.

In the fifth act of the drama of Catholicism-and-modernity, a bitter irony came into the white-hot glare of public attention: just as the living parts of the Catholic Church were beginning to put the New Evangelization into practice while offering important proposals for the renewal of public life, it was revealed that Catholic clergy of all ranks had sexually abused the young and that the Church's leaders at all levels had too often failed to address these grave sins and crimes by brother-priests and brother-bishops with decisive and timely action.

Of all the modern assaults on Catholicism in this drama, this was arguably the most lethal, because it was a self-inflicted wound.

The intellectual assault on Catholicism from Enlightenment rationalism and postmodern skepticism posed a serious challenge that cost the Church the allegiance of many intellectuals. That assault was successfully met, however, by the renovation of Catholic philosophy and theology, which offered a more compelling account of the human condition than much that was on offer in Western high culture and intellectual life in the late twentieth and early twenty-first centuries.

The political assault on Catholicism—which began with the French Revolution and continued through enlightened despotism, the German Kulturkampf, the Italian Risorgimento, the anticlerical French Third Republic, and the mid-twentieth-century totalitarianisms—took an enormous toll, not least in the lives of millions of modern martyrs. But that assault, too, was finally met. And in one of the ironies pondered here, it became the occasion for the Catholic Church to detach itself from the stifling embrace of state power and develop a social doctrine that spoke to many of twenty-first-century democracy's most pressing issues.

The abuse crises were different. Yes, the post-1960s breakdown of clerical discipline that resulted in grave sins and crimes reflected in part the sexual revolution's assault on all traditional norms of good behavior, and in that sense might be regarded by some as another assault on the Church from without. At the bottom of the bottom line, however, the abuse crisis in the Catholic Church could not be blamed on "the world." The deepest, most diseased root of the abuse crisis was internal. For this was a crisis of fidelity, in which the wickedness of those assumed to be among the Church's leaders betrayed and trampled upon the truths the Church was privileged to bear as a gift from its Lord. That the abusers' sins and crimes left Catholicism vulnerable to the charge of hypocrisy, and not only from its cultured despisers, compounded the impact.

From the available empirical evidence, the sexual abuse of the young was a worldwide plague in late modernity and postmodernity, and sociological studies did not suggest that abuse was any more prevalent in the Catholic Church than in other institutions. Some studies suggested that, in the United States, sexual abuse of young people was far more prevalent in public schools than in the Catholic Church, and there seemed little doubt that most sexual abuse took place, horrifically, within families. Yet the sexual abuse crisis within the Church, which was intensified throughout the early twenty-first century by evidence of feckless Church leaders engaging in cover-ups, struck hard at a Church that was beginning to understand that evangelism begins with witness, not argument. And it was, and is, difficult to imagine a more severe counter-witness to the truth of Christ than the manipulative sexual abuse of innocent young people by those claiming to speak in Christ's name.

The geographic breadth of the abuse scandals confirmed that grave breakdowns of clerical discipline and major defaults in episcopal leadership had done damage to virtually the entire Church. Abuse scandals and episcopal failures came to light in the United States, Canada, Austria, Ireland, Great Britain, Belgium, Italy, Germany, Chile, the Dominican Republic, Guam, Honduras, India, Norway, and Poland—and were inadequately addressed by the Vatican, particularly under Pope Francis. In the United States, academic studies, as well as a Pennsylvania grand jury report, indicated that the incidence of clerical sexual abuse of the young spiked dramatically in the 1970s and 1980s—the period of doctrinal confusion and disciplinary laxity that followed the Second Vatican Council— and that the great majority of the abused were adolescent and young-adult males. The incidence of abuse dropped significantly in the 1990s as John Paul II's reform of the priesthood began to take hold, and new practices adopted by the bishops of the United States in 2002 led to a steep drop in these sins and crimes, to the point where it could be empirically demonstrated that the Catholic Church was one of the safest environments for young people in America.

But when it was revealed in 2018 that the former archbishop of Washington, Theodore McCarrick, was credibly alleged to have been a serial sexual predator, specializing in the abuse of seminarians under his authority, and that bishops throughout the country had failed to act decisively in dealing with abuse cases prior to 2002 (and occasionally afterward), the crisis reignited in the United States—just after Pope Francis had dealt clumsily with charges of sexual abuse by the Chilean clergy, including a bishop, which eventually compelled a public papal apology. Dramatic charges about sexual misconduct in the Vatican also broke out in the Italian press.

Sexual predation has as many causes as there are individual predators. In the American context, however, and quite possibly in Europe as well, it did not seem accidental that the incidents of clerical sexual abuse saw a major spike during the period of confusion, controversy, and disarray in the Church that reached its nadir in the widespread dissent, by both priests and bishops, from the teaching of Pope Paul VI's 1968 encyclical, *Humanae Vitae*. Priests who had convinced themselves that they did not have to believe or teach what the Church definitively taught to be true were especially vulnerable to their passions in the cultural free-fire zone of the sexual revolution; having convinced themselves that intellectual duplicity was acceptable, they were all the more vulnerable to moral duplicity and behavioral decadence. Infidelity came at a very high cost: the victims were frequently vulnerable innocents who had believed these men lived what they putatively professed.

The malfeasance (and worse) of bishops in handling cases of sexual abuse by their priests also reflected the internal turbulence of the post-conciliar Church. Bishops, who governed according to the institutional-maintenance model of late Counter-Reformation Catholicism, were less likely to lead a thoroughgoing reform of their clergy than those who had grasped the imperative of leading an evangelically dynamic Church. Institutional-maintenance bishops were also more inclined to employ a method of leadership that stressed keeping the basic Catholic machinery of parish, school, and diocese ticking as smoothly as possible—by compromises with truth and discipline, if necessary. Bishops who misconstrued

Vatican II's teaching on the collegiality of bishops as a warrant for the creation of an episcopal caste were incapable of seeing that calling their brother bishops to account through fraternal correction was an imperative—especially because the failure to forthrightly address sexual abuse by priests was doing the gravest imaginable damage to the evangelical mission of the Church.

The Roman response to the clerical sexual abuse crisis that reemerged in 2018 suggested that, at all levels of the Vatican, institutional-maintenance and status-quo thinking continued to prevail over the imperatives of the New Evangelization. This institutional inertia was compounded by an ingrained tendency in the Roman Curia, first displayed in 2002, to blame the crisis on an aggressive media. The new Roman tack in 2018 was to suggest that sexually abusive clergy and malfeasant bishops incapable of disciplining either wayward priests or their brother-bishops were manifestations of a "clericalism" that had to be expunged from the Church. This was a piece of the truth masking a deeper and more disturbing reality, one that the highest authorities of the universal Church seemed unwilling to face.

No serious student of Catholic affairs doubted that "clericalism," meaning a malevolent distortion of the powerful influence priests enjoy by virtue of their office, was a factor in the clerical sexual abuse of young people especially vulnerable to that influence. And if by "clericalism" was meant some bishops acting as if they were members of a privileged caste taking care of their own, rather than as shepherds protecting the flocks entrusted to their care, then it was certainly a factor in Chile, Ireland, Germany, the United Kingdom, and Poland, as well as in the McCarrick case (and others) in the United States. The diagnosis of "clericalism" as the root malady in the crisis was too often used, however, to avoid the hard, empirically demonstrable fact that the overwhelming majority of the cases in the United States (and, it seems, elsewhere)—some

80 percent on most data-based reckonings—involved sexually dysfunctional clergy preying on young men. Here, then, was a devastating instance of the sexual revolution's impact on Catholic fidelity and discipline. The failure to recognize and address it was the Church's failure, not the culture's, however. And that failure caused grave damage to the people of the Church while seriously eroding Catholicism's credibility in proposing its ethic of human love.

The abuse crisis dominated commentary on the Catholic Church at the end of the second decade of the twenty-first century. Meanwhile, the puzzling pontificate of Pope Francis became even more ominous for those committed to an evangelically vibrant and publicly engaged Catholicism. That the Pope, contrary to the vision he had laid out in *Evangelii Gaudium*, seemed to countenance, and even encourage, the new theological historicism and the new Gallicanism—the manifestations of the failed project of Catholic Lite—created real difficulties for evangelism and public witness. Those difficulties were immeasurably compounded by the loss of Vatican and papal credibility due to the sexual abuse crisis.

THIS MOST BITTER of ironies made unmistakably clear that the fifth act of the continuing drama of Catholicism-and-modernity must be an era of ongoing purification and deep Catholic reform. That reform would have to be led by both clergy and laity animated by the vision of evangelically assertive Catholicism born of Vatican II—and Vatican II as authoritatively interpreted by John Paul II and Benedict XVI. It could not be led by either the Church's traditionalist or progressivist camps, neither of which seemed capable of coming to grips with the abuse crisis.

The traditionalist claim that such wickedness was the result of the Second Vatican Council was weakened by the fact that some of the worst clerical sexual abuse took place prior to the Council, in traditionalist bastions like Ireland and Québec; a similar pattern of sexual misconduct and institutionalized cover-up could be traced in pre-conciliar Boston, the epicenter of the 2002 crisis in the United States. As for progressivist Catholicism, its seeming determination to tolerate, even embrace, the many expressions of the sexual revolution made it virtually impossible for those who still defended their rejection of *Humanae Vitae* to acknowledge the role that doctrinal dissent and confusion, and Catholic Lite more generally, had played in the abuse crisis in the 1970s and 1980s, as sexually dysfunctional clergy preyed (in the main) on young men. By contrast, it was those parts of the world Church that had embraced Evangelical Catholicism in full, and were living the teaching of the *Catechism of the Catholic Church* and the Theology of the Body, that were less vulnerable to the crisis and most engaged in developing proposals for authentic Catholic reform, thereby showing a path beyond the crisis.

Viewed through the prism of the centuries-long drama explored here, the abuse crisis comes into focus as a moment of necessary purification. To be the Church of the New Evangelization, and the Church that offers modernity a remedy for its ills, the Church must purify itself, not least of the detritus of doctrinal and moral dissent. And the Church must live—and be seen to live—what it proclaims. The countercultural truths of Catholic teaching on the ethics of human love, and the challenge the Church's social doctrine poses to postmodern understandings of freedom as willfulness, are difficult enough to proclaim; they cannot be proclaimed with any credibility by a Church that fails to discipline itself, whose clergy and laity live freedom-as-willfulness, and whose leaders' failures lay it open to charges of hypocrisy.

Deep Catholic reform necessarily involves every Catholic. John Paul II described chastity as the integrity of love, and that understanding must be embodied by all the people of the Church, lay men and women as well as clergy. But the abuse crisis has also demonstrated that there was a particular need for deep and evangelically oriented Catholic reform in the priesthood and the episcopate. No one who does not believe what the Catholic Church believes to be true, and who has not demonstrated that conviction by his life and his experience as a missionary disciple, should be admitted to a seminary, much less ordained a priest. No priest who has not shown himself a successful evangelist, deepening the faith of the people entrusted to his care and bringing others into the communion of disciples that is the Church, should be called to the episcopate.

At the end of the second decade of the twenty-first century, no one could know how this most bitter irony would play itself out in the drama of Catholicism-and-modernity. In the most extreme scenario, legal action, instigated by individuals and the state and resulting in the Church's financial ruin, would play a role similar to that of Nebuchadnezzar in the Old Testament when he razed the Temple—which in this case would mean the large-scale deconstruction of the Catholic institutions built during the drama of Catholicism's encounter with modernity. But even in that worst case, the path forward for Catholicism would be the path defined during the fourth and fifth acts of this drama: the path of missionary discipleship and public witness to the truths that make it possible to live freedom nobly.

The Culture-Converting
Counterculture

I NCORPORATING ITS FOURTH act, the fifth act of the drama of Catholicism-and-modernity will continue to be played out amidst ecclesiastical and cultural turbulence, some of which will be quite severe.

Throughout this drama, and even in those moments when the Church's own grave human failings became massive obstacles to its witness and teaching, the Catholic Church has been the bearer of a message that is of critical importance to the realization of the modern project's highest aspirations. That important message can be summed up in the term "human ecology." The term as such was introduced to Catholic social doctrine by John Paul II and stressed by Benedict XVI, but the idea has been implicit since Leo XIII: it is insufficient to attend solely to the machinery of economic and political modernity; attention must be paid to culture, to the truths (including the moral truths) by which modern men and women live, if the machinery of modernity is to lead to genuine human flourishing. After a twentieth century that had become an abattoir because of false and wicked ideas about the truth of things, it might have been hoped that the appropriate ecological lesson would have been learned. Moreover, the "twentieth century"— considered as an epoch on which the curtain rose with World War I and fell with the collapse of the Soviet Union in 1991— ended on a different, more hopeful, note, with the defeat of totalitarian power by a revolution based on what Czech human rights activist Vaclav Havel called "living in the truth." In the twenty-first century, however, that lesson remains contested.

Thanks to what it learned from its engagement with modernity, Catholicism has recommitted itself to missionary discipleship and permanent evangelization: to proposing to the world what it believes to be liberating truths about salvation and the ultimate destiny of human beings, which include truths about how we ought to live together in society. At a moment of deep cultural confusion and political tension throughout the West, when some are questioning whether modernity is worth saving, and others are defining the modern project in terms of a profound rupture with any concept of "givens" in personal and public life, Catholicism's task is to be a culture-converting counterculture that offers skeptics a path beyond doubt, relativists a path beyond the naked will to power, and nihilists a path beyond emptiness. The core of that offer is friendship with Jesus Christ, whom the Catholic Church proclaims to be the answer to the question that is every human life. The offer also includes proposing truths essential to the rescue of the modern project from its own self-demolition: truths whose reality and veracity can be engaged by all people of goodwill.

What are the truths that will make it possible for modernity to realize its noblest aspirations and longings?

Among the most important is the truth that every human being has an inherent dignity and value, not ascribed by government but hard-wired or built in.

Then there is the truth that reflection on the built-in dignity and inalienable value of every human life discloses certain moral obligations and responsibilities, including the obligation to defend innocent life, the obligation to contribute to the common good, and the obligation to live in solidarity with others, especially those who find living their obligations and responsibilities difficult.

And there is a further and deeper truth about the moral nature of the human person. For citizens of a democracy to think of themselves and others, for constitutional and legal purposes, as nothing more than twitching bundles of commensurable and morally inconsequential desires is not an act of tolerance but an exercise in self-abasement, even self-degradation, that reduces human beings to an infantilism that cannot indefinitely sustain the modern aspiration to democratic self-governance.

The truth that the good life cannot be measured solely, or even primarily, in financial terms must also be proclaimed and reclaimed. The aspiration to prosperity and abundance that is characteristic of modernity is not the problem; the problem lies in the reduction of "the abundant life" to indices of financial status. The human person is more than his or her salary, investment portfolio, or net financial worth, and the twenty-first-century world needs to be reminded of that.

Finally, there is the truth that a vulgar culture appealing to the basest of our instincts, be that high culture or popular culture, damages the human ecology necessary to make political and economic modernity work. For a degraded and debased culture is likely to produce a vulgarized political culture in which base instincts dominate, as Berlin during the Weimar Republic ought to have demonstrated.

THERE HAVE BEEN many ironies in the drama of Catholicism-and-modernity over the past two centuries or more. No doubt some will find it not merely ironic, but ridiculous, to suggest that the Catholic Church is a safe deposit box of certain truths about the human condition that are essential for the survival and flourishing of civility and tolerance, self-governance and the rule of law, prosperity and solidarity, liberty and equal justice for all. In the first two decades of the twenty-first century, the failures, sins, and crimes of the Church's own priests and bishops loomed large as obstacles to the effective proclamation of those truths. Indeed, an argument could be made that corruption and scandal in the twenty-first-century Church reflected a Catholicism not so much converting modernity as imitating it. For the wickedness evident among churchmen in the United States, Canada, Ireland, Great Britain, and elsewhere often reflected late modern and postmodern confusions (and worse) about what makes for happiness, beatitude, and genuine human flourishing— including, most particularly, the many false promises of the sexual revolution. There can be no doubt that serious, deep-reaching reform, particularly of the Catholic priesthood and the Catholic episcopate, is essential if the Church of the future is to live its commitment to being a culture-converting counterculture in a transformative way.

The fact remains, however, that the noblest aims and moral commitments of the modern project were not self-generating in a world begun anew by Voltaire and Rousseau. Nor is their successful pursuit in the twenty-first century and beyond going to be possible in a public culture dominated by skepticism, relativism, spiritual boredom, and vulgar decadence. Modernity's finest aspirations grew from cultural soil long tilled by the Catholic Church. After the many twists and turns of the Catholic encounter with modernity, Catholicism embraced those aspirations and now seeks to serve the world by setting them on a firmer foundation for the future. If crossing the fiery brook of modernity was the prerequisite for the Catholic Church to rediscover both its own evangelical character and the essential contribution it can make to saving the modern project from incoherence, well, that is just another irony in the fire.

Some might even call it a providential irony, for both modernity and the Church.

Acknowledgments

I first began learning from that great sociologist, Peter Berger, when I read *A Rumor of Angels: Modern Society and the Rediscovery of the Supernatural* and *Invitation to Sociology: A Humanistic Perspective* in college. Peter later became a friend and colleague in several enterprises, and there was never an encounter with him that didn't teach me something—and make me laugh. In April 2015, Peter hosted an international symposium at Boston University, *The Two Pluralisms— Toward a Paradigm for Modernity and Religion*, and invited me to prepare a paper on Catholicism and modernity. The paper's challenge to the conventional wisdom on that subject provoked a lively discussion and planted the seed of an idea that there might be a book here—an intuition confirmed when the same revisionist proposal I made to scholars in Boston received a positive response from a general audience in New York at the 2017 Magnificat Foundation Lecture. So my first word of thanks must be to the late Peter L. Berger, whose death in 2017 was a great loss to scholarship, even as it left a large void in the many lives Peter touched with his wisdom, his wit, and his Old World charm.

Russell Hittinger knows more about nineteenth-century Catholic history in general, and Leo XIII in particular, than anyone else I know. Our conversations and collaboration over the past quarter-century have left a deep and permanent impress on my thinking, which should be obvious here. Father Jay Scott Newman of St. Mary's Catholic Church in Greenville, South Carolina, is my longtime tutor in all things evangelically Catholic.

I am grateful to the rector and faculty of the Pontifical Theological Faculty of St. Bonaventure in Rome, the Seraphicum, for the invitation to deliver the 2008 lecture in which I developed my critique of *Gaudium et Spes*, Vatican II's Pastoral Constitution on the Church in the Modern World.

Natalie Robertson, Mark Shanoudy, and Stephen White of the Ethics and Public Policy Center helped in preparing the manuscript and in keeping my office running efficiently. Like all my EPPC colleagues, I am deeply grateful to Ed Whelan for his leadership of our lively, productive, and collegial institution, as I am to the benefactors who make my work possible. As of 2019, EPPC has been my professional home for thirty years, and I cannot imagine a better one.

Thanks, too, to my family, and especially my wife, Joan, for their love and support.

This is the fifth book I have done with Lara Heimert since she took up the reins at Basic Books. She and her colleagues, especially Michelle Welsh-Horst and Katherine Streckfus, are the best.

Don J. Briel, who died far too soon, on February 15, 2018, was one of the most important Catholic educators of the post–Vatican II period. He was also a close and cherished friend with whom I discussed this book's analysis, in general and in its component parts, on more occasions than I can remember. His death was a grievous blow to authentic Catholic reform, but I am confident that his present station in the Communion of Saints affords him the opportunity to intercede for those of us who mourn him—and for the great cause of a culture-converting Catholicism to which he gave his life. The dedication of this book is a small token of respect to the memory of a great man.

G.W.

North Bethesda—Kraków—Allumette Island
February–November 2018

Sources

Throughout this work of historiographic revisionism, I have relied for factual material on the scholarship of many distinguished historians. Sources consulted for all five acts of the drama, and its entr'actes, include J. N. D. Kelly, *The Oxford Dictionary of Popes* (Oxford: Oxford University Press, 1986); Eamon Duffy, *Saints and Sinners: A History of the Popes* (New Haven, CT: Yale University Press, 1997); Bruno Steimer and Michael G. Parker, eds., *Dictionary of Popes and the Papacy* (New York: Crossroad, 2001); and Karim Schelkens, John A. Dick, and Jürgen Mettepenningen, *Aggiornamento? Catholicism from Gregory XVI to Benedict XVI* (Leiden: Brill, 2013).

Act One:
Catholicism Against Modernity

For an overview of the period and for specific incidents in the drama I have relied on two books by Roger Aubert, Johannes Beckmann, Patrick J. Corish, and Rudolf Lill: *The Church Between Revolution and Restoration* (New York: Crossroad, 1981), which is the seventh volume of *History of the Church*, edited by Hubert Jedin and John Dolan, and *The Church in the Age of Liberalism*, the eighth volume.

Other works consulted include Frank J. Coppa, ed., *Controversial Concordats: The Vatican's Relations with Napoleon, Mussolini, and Hitler* (Washington, DC: Catholic University of America Press, 1999); John Martin Robinson, *Cardinal Consalvi, 1757–1824* (London: The Bodley Head, 1987); Owen Chadwick, *A History of the Popes, 1830–1914* (Oxford: Oxford University Press, 1998); the article on Lamennais by Robrecht Boudens, OMI, in volume eight of *The New Catholic Encyclopedia* (New York: McGraw-Hill, 1967); Owen Chadwick, *The Secularization of the European Mind in the Nineteenth Century* (Cambridge: Cambridge University Press, 1975); Michael B. Gross, *The War Against Catholicism: Liberalism and the Anti-Catholic Imagination in Nineteenth-Century Germany* (Ann Arbor: University of Michigan Press, 2005); and John W. O'Malley, *Vatican I: The Council and the Making of the Ultramontane Church* (Cambridge, MA: The Belknap Press of Harvard University Press, 2018).

Entr'Acte: Bridge Builders

In sketching Johann Adam Möhler I drew on information from the Möhler entry in volume nine of *The New Catholic Encyclopedia* (*TNCE*), written by Raphael H. Nienaltowski, OFM; for Antonio Rosmini, on the eponymous article by Dennis Cleary, IC, in volume twelve of *TNCE*; and for Wilhelm Emmanuel von Ketteler, on Ludwig Lenhart's entry on the German social theorist in *TNCE*'s volume nine.

In summarizing the theology of another bridge builder, I relied on Cyril Vollert, SJ, "Matthias Joseph Scheeben and the Revival of Theology," *Theological Studies* (December 1945).

The gold standard of Newman biographies is Ian Ker, *John Henry Newman: A Biography* (Oxford: Oxford University Press, 1988). On Newman and Vatican I, see John R. Page,

What Will Dr. Newman Do? John Henry Newman and Papal Infallibility, 1865–1875 (Collegeville, MN: Liturgical Press, 1994). On Newman and Manning, see David Newsome's *The Convert Cardinals* (London: John Murray, 1993). In *Cardinal Manning: A Biography* (New York: St. Martin's Press, 1985), Robert Gray offers a revisionist view of the man slandered by Lytton Strachey in *Eminent Victorians*.

A serviceable survey of U.S. Catholic history in this period may be found in John Tracy Ellis, *American Catholicism*, second edition, revised (Chicago: University of Chicago Press, 1969).

Act Two:
Catholicism Explores Modernity, Gingerly

For an overview of this period, see Roger Aubert, Günter Bandmann, Jakob Baumgartner, Mario Bendiscioli, Jacques Gadille, Oskar Köhler, Rudolf Lill, Bernhard Stasiewski, and Erika Weinzierl, *The Church in the Industrial Age* (New York: Crossroad, 1981), volume nine of *History of the Church*, edited by Hubert Jedin and John Dolan.

For a brilliant analysis of Leo XIII, see Russell Hittinger, "Pope Leo XIII (1810–1903)," in John Witte Jr. and Frank S. Alexander, *The Teachings of Modern Roman Catholicism on Law, Politics, and Human Nature* (New York: Columbia University Press, 2007). See also Hittinger, "The Coherence of the Four Basic Principles of Catholic Social Doctrine: An Interpretation," in *Pursuing the Common Good: How Solidarity and Subsidiarity Can Work Together. Proceedings of the 14th Plenary Session of the Pontifical Academy of Social Sciences*, edited by Margaret S. Archer and Pierpaolo Donati, *Acta* 14 (Vatican City, 2008).

On Pius X and the Modernist controversy, see Russell Hittinger, "*Pascendi Dominici Gregis* at 100: Two Modernisms, Two Thomisms—Reflections on the Centenary of Pius

X's Letter Against the Modernists," in *Nova et Vetera* (English Edition) 5, no. 4 (2007). See also "Modernism" by John Joseph Heaney, SJ, in volume nine of *The New Catholic Encyclopedia* (New York: McGraw-Hill, 1967).

On Benedict XV, see John F. Pollard, *The Unknown Pope: Benedict XV (1914–1922) and the Pursuit of Peace* (London: Geoffrey Chapman, 1999).

On Pius XI, see Anthony Rhodes, *The Vatican in the Age of the Dictators (1922–1945)* (New York: Holt, Rinehart and Winston, 1973).

On Pius XII, see Robert A. Ventresca, *Soldier of Christ: The Life of Pope Pius XII* (Cambridge, MA: The Belknap Press of Harvard University Press, 2013); Ronald J. Rychlak, *Hitler, the War, and the Pope*, revised and expanded edition (Huntington, IN: Our Sunday Visitor, 2010); and Pierre Blet, SJ, *Pius XII and the Second World War: According to the Archives of the Vatican* (New York: Paulist Press, 1999).

Entr'Acte: Theological Renaissance

On Romano Guardini, see Heinz R. Kuehn, ed., *The Essential Guardini: An Anthology of the Writings of Romano Guardini* (Chicago: Liturgical Training Publications, 1997), and Romano Guardini, *The End of the Modern World* (Wilmington, DE: ISI Books, 1998).

On Blondel, see William L. Portier, "Twentieth-Century Catholic Theology and the Triumph of Maurice Blondel," *Communio* 38, no. 1 (May 2010).

I am also indebted to insights gleaned from Fergus Kerr, *Twentieth-Century Catholic Theologians: From Neoscholasticism to Nuptial Mysticism* (Oxford: Blackwell, 2007); Helen James John, SND, *The Thomist Spectrum* (New York: Fordham University Press, 1966); James Chappel, *Catholic Modern: The Challenge of Totalitarianism and the Remaking of the Church* (Cambridge, MA: Harvard University Press, 2018); Piotr Kosicki, *Catholics at the Barricades: Poland, France, and "Revolution," 1891–1956* (New Haven, CT: Yale University Press, 2018); and Dietrich von Hildebrand, *My Battle Against Hitler: Defiance in the Shadow of the Third Reich* (New York: Image, 2016).

Act Three:
Catholicism Embracing Modernity

On the necessity of Vatican II, see Bruce D. Marshall, "Reckoning with Modernity," *First Things* 258 (December 2015).

For insight into the Council's internal dynamics, see John W. O'Malley, SJ, *What Happened at Vatican II?* (Cambridge, MA: The Belknap Press of Harvard University Press, 2008); three important conciliar diaries (Yves Congar, OP, *My Journal of the Council* [Collegeville, MN: Liturgical Press, 2012]; Henri de Lubac, SJ, *Vatican Council Notebooks*, volume 1 [San Francisco: Ignatius Press, 2015], and Henri de Lubac, SJ, *Vatican Council Notebooks*, volume 2 [San Francisco: Ignatius Press, 2016]); and Louis Bouyer, *Memoirs* (San Francisco: Ignatius Press, 2015).

Thomas G. Guarino explores the creative tension between tradition and development that shaped both the debates at, and the documents of, the Council in *The Disputed Teachings of Vatican II: Continuity and Reversal in Catholic Doctrine* (Grand Rapids, MI: William B. Eerdmans, 2018).

The critique of the Pastoral Constitution on the Church in the Modern World is drawn from my essay "Rescuing *Gaudium et Spes*: The New Humanism of John Paul II," *Nova et Vetera* (English Edition) 8, no. 2 (2019).

Entr'Acte: The Council Reconsidered

On *Evangelii Nuntiandi*, see Lucas Moreira Neves, OP, *"Evangelii Nuntiandi:* Paul's VI's Pastoral Testament to the Church," Eternal Word Television Network (EWTN), https://www .ewtn.com/library/CURIA/CBISEVNU.HTM, reprinted from *L'Osservatore Romano*, January 17, 2001.

Karol Wojtyła's 1976 Lenten retreat conferences for Paul VI and the Roman Curia are collected in Wojtyła, *Sign of Contradiction* (New York: Seabury Press, 1979).

On the theological tensions within the reformist camp at Vatican II and the founding of *Communio*, see the de Lubac and Congar diaries and Bouyer's memoirs, noted above, and Joseph Ratzinger, "Communio: A Program," *Communio* 19 (Fall 1992).

Act Four:
Catholicism Critiques Modernity from Within

For the analysis of Benedict XVI's September Lectures, I am indebted to Father Raymond de Souza for his presentations at the annual Tertio Millennio Seminar on the Free Society in Kraków.

Entr'Acte: A Communion of Disciples in Mission

On the Synod of 1985, see Richard John Neuhaus, "What the Synod Wrought," *National Review* (February 14, 1986).

Act Five:
Catholicism Converting Modernity

On history being driven by narratives and the crisis of late modernity's self-understanding, see Robert W. Jenson, "How the World Lost Its Story," *First Things* 36 (October 1993).

Larry Seidentop enumerates several ways that Christianity shaped modernity in *Inventing the Individual: The Origins of Western Liberalism* (London: Penguin, 2015).

On the epidemiology of the sexual abuse crisis in the Catholic Church, see my *The Courage To Be Catholic: Crisis, Reform, and the Future of the Church* (New York: Basic Books, 2002).

Index

DANIEL SHEEHAN

GEORGE WEIGEL, Distinguished Senior Fellow of the Ethics and
Public Policy Center, is a Catholic theologian and one of America's
leading public intellectuals. He is perhaps best known for his widely
translated and internationally acclaimed two-volume biography of
Pope St. John Paul II: the *New York Times* best seller *Witness to
Hope* and its sequel, *The End and the Beginning*. His twenty-four
other books include *The Cube and the Cathedral: Europe, America,
and Politics Without God*; *Evangelical Catholicism: Deep Reform
in the 21st-Century Church*, and *Letters to a Young Catholic*. His
essays, op-ed columns, and reviews appear regularly in publications throughout the English-speaking world and, like his books,
are often translated into the major European languages. A frequent
guest on television and radio, he is also Senior Vatican Analyst for
NBC News. His weekly column, "The Catholic Difference," is syn-
dicated to eighty-five newspapers and magazines in seven countries.
He lives in North Bethesda, Maryland.